Making the Gospels

Making the Gospels

MYSTERY OR CONSPIRACY?

Paul W. Barnett

CASCADE *Books* • Eugene, Oregon

MAKING THE GOSPELS
Mystery or Conspiracy?

Copyright © 2019 Paul W. Barnett. All rights reserved. Except for brief quotations in critical publications or reviews, no part of this book may be reproduced in any manner without prior written permission from the publisher. Write: Permissions, Wipf and Stock Publishers, 199 W. 8th Ave., Suite 3, Eugene, OR 97401.

Cascade Books
An Imprint of Wipf and Stock Publishers
199 W. 8th Ave., Suite 3
Eugene, OR 97401

www.wipfandstock.com

PAPERBACK ISBN: 978-1-5326-5104-5
HARDCOVER ISBN: 978-1-5326-5105-2
EBOOK ISBN: 978-1-5326-5106-9

Cataloguing-in-Publication data:

Names: Barnett, Paul W., author.

Title: Making the gospels : mystery or conspiracy? / by Paul W. Barnett.

Description: Eugene, OR: Cascade Books, 2019 | Includes bibliographical references and index.

Identifiers: ISBN 978-1-5326-5104-5 (paperback) | ISBN 978-1-5326-5105-2 (hardcover) | ISBN 978-1-5326-5106-9 (ebook)

Subjects: LCSH: Bible. Gospels—Criticism, interpretation, etc.

Classification: BS2555 B15 2019 (print) | BS2555 (ebook)

Manufactured in the U.S.A.   APRIL 15, 2019

The English Standard Version is used with the permission of Good News Publishers

Dedicated to the father-in-law I never knew
Alexander Simpson (1911–50)
Missionary in Brazil

And on the day called Sunday,
all who live in cities or in the country gather together to one place,
and the memoirs of the apostles or the writings of the prophets are read,
as long as time permits.
  —Justin Martyr, *First Apology*, 67

Contents

Preface | ix

Introduction: Making the Gospel—Mystery or Conspiracy? | xii

1. The Amazing Discovery of Papyrus 45 | 1
2. The Disciples' Unexpected Role | 9
3. Jerusalem: The Peter Years (33–42) | 19
4. The Words of Jesus in the Letters of Paul | 31
5. Did Paul Reinvent Jesus? | 43
6. Jerusalem: the James Years (c. 42–62) | 50
7. The Anti-Pauline Counter Mission | 61
8. The Church in Antioch | 67
9. Rome: The Peter Years (c. 55–c. 64) | 69
10. The Sources: An Interim Report | 79
11. The Surprise: The Languages of Jesus | 87

    Excursus: Josephus and "The Language of Our Country" | 94

12. The Transmission of the Tradition | 96
13. Common Source "Q" and the Jesus Seminar | 104
14. Was Mark the Arch-Conspirator? | 116
15. Making the Written Gospel | 119
16. The Making of Mark | 126

    Excursus: Indications of Integrity | 142

17. Matthew's "M" Source | 151

18. Luke's "L" Source | 157
19. Luke's and Matthew's Use of Mark | 161
20. The Making of Matthew | 171
21. The Making of Luke | 182
22. The Making of John | 197

    EXCURSUS: Roman Involvement in the Arrest, Trial, and Execution of Jesus | 220

23. Why Are There Four Gospels? | 224
24. Making the Gospels | 233

    Bibliography | 237

    Author Index | 245

    Scripture Index | 248

Preface

THE FOUR GOSPELS ARE the world's most widely read books, but we do not know for certain how they came to be written. None of them has a title page so, strictly speaking, we do not know the names of their authors. However, as we will see, there are good reasons to identify them as Matthew, Mark, Luke, and John.

What then about the issue of provenance, the "where from" question? Again, there is a lack of certainty but I shall argue that Mark wrote his Gospel in Rome, Matthew in Galilee, John in Ephesus, and Luke somewhere in the Greek east.

As for the "when" question, we are on good grounds to date them relatively close to Jesus: Mark wrote his gospel about thirty years after Jesus, and the other three within a decade or so later. The chronological closeness of the Gospels to Jesus is highly significant.

It is right, therefore, to apply the word "mystery" to the origin of the Gospels. However, mystery does not imply mischief as if the writing of the Gospels occurred under a cloak of conspiracy. Rather, it simply means we do not know the certain answers to the "how," "who," and "where" questions.

Conspiracy is a word rarely applied to the messages about Jesus in the Gospels, but it is, nevertheless, to be inferred. The Gospels present him as a transcendent, other-worldly figure who effortlessly healed the sick, raised the dead, and was himself resurrected from the tomb. But the real Jesus of Nazareth, it is argued, was a lesser figure, a talented teacher and preacher to be sure, but not the Son of God who first heralded and then established the kingdom of God.

Who are the conspirators responsible for these portrayals of Jesus in the Gospels? In this study there are three in particular who are blamed for the repackaged Jesus: Paul, Mark, and the editor of the "Q" source.

According to William Wrede, who wrote early in the twentieth century, Paul as the earliest and most powerful advocate of Christianity, was its real inventor. It was he who established the essential framework of the message that Jesus was a crucified and resurrected redeemer. Wrede's views continue to be highly influential.

John Dominic Crossan and some others blame Mark for radically refashioning Jesus the peasant reformer as the Son of God and the Christ of God. Matthew and Luke uncritically copied Mark's confected Jesus into their Gospels.

Likewise, the Jesus Seminar theorizes that the source common to Matthew and Luke (called "Q") had multiple layers. The lowest articulated the teaching of the real Jesus, a teacher of wisdom. The upper strata, however, presented a distorted Jesus, one who spoke as a Messiah. Since Matthew and Luke used "Q" it means that their Gospels are consequently distorted.

The so-called "Third Quest" for the historical Jesus has identified other versions of Jesus, "as he really was." Ben Witherington III usefully reviewed these in *The Jesus Quest: The Third Quest for the Jew of Nazareth*.[1]

My approach where possible will be chronological. After an introductory chapter followed by a discussion about Papyrus 45, the earliest retrieved collection of the four Gospels, I will proceed sequentially through the thirty or so years between Jesus and the Gospel of Mark before eventually reaching the other completed Gospels written some years later.[2]

In the course of reflection on Matthew and Luke and their underlying sources, Mark, "Q," "L," and "M," I reached what was for me a radical conclusion, one that has profoundly changed my attitude to Jesus and the four gospels he inspired. I will defer until a later moment to share my radical new discovery.

I do not intend to burden the reader with exhaustive documentation for every aspect of this study. However I am grateful, first to Michael Bird for his encyclopedic yet concise contemporary study of the formation

---

1. Jesus the Talking Head (The Jesus Seminar), Jesus the Itinerant Cynic Philosopher (Crossan, Mack, Downing), Jesus Man of the Spirit (Borg, Vermes, Twelftree), Jesus the Prophet of Social Change (Theissen, Horsley, Kaylor), Jesus the Sage (Fiorenza, Witherington), Jesus the Marginal Jew (Meier, Stuhlmacher, Dunn, de Jonge, Bockmuehl, Wright).

2. For an interesting discussion of the social circumstances of history writers that are wider than an ecclesiastical context, see Last, "Social Relationships," 223–52.

of the Gospels, and second to the collection of essays, *The Writing of the Gospel*, edited by Marcus Bockmuehl and Donald A. Hagner.³ Then there are the renowned giants of New Testament scholarship to whom we owe so much—F. F. Bruce, C. K. Barrett, C. F. D. Moule, James Dunn, N. T. Wright, Richard Bauckham, Earle Ellis, Robert Yarbrough, and Martin Hengel (such an exceptional historian). I must acknowledge one other scholar, from another era, Thomas Manson, a meticulous source critic whose *The Sayings of Jesus* has been my constant companion.⁴

I gratefully acknowledge the advice of a long time friend, Allan Chapple, who is not responsible for the author's shortcomings.

---

3. Bird, *Gospel of the Lord*; Bockmuehl and Hagner, *Written Gospel*.

4. Manson, *Sayings of Jesus*, although older is detached from the current "Q" debates; cf. Robinson, Hoffman, and Kloppenborg, *Critical Edition of Q*.

Introduction: Making the Gospel— Mystery or Conspiracy?

THE GOSPELS ARE THE center and focus of the Bible. The Old Testament points forward to Jesus and the New Testament points back to him, bearing testimony to him. Catholic and Orthodox congregations stand for the reading of the Gospel and many Anglican congregations also stand, following the direction of the *Book of Common Prayer.* In the early centuries the copies of the Gospels far outstripped other manuscripts of the books of the New Testament. The Gospels are key to the message of the Bible.

Christian believers and their children love the Gospel story about Jesus and his stories and sayings. These have shaped the spiritual and ethical lives of millions throughout the two millennia of Christian history. The values taught by Jesus have powerfully influenced world civilization. The word "gospel" has become a synonym for truth even within modern secular culture.

It comes as a shock, therefore, to learn of attacks directed against the truthfulness of the Gospels. Major documentary television channels often run related programs during the major Christian festivals, Christmas and Easter. Almost invariably they put to air sensational claims for the authenticity of and new insights into the Apocryphal Gospels like the Gospel of Philip, or the Gospel of Judas, although these texts were written in later centuries, survive in only fragmentary form, and clearly promote a Gnostic (mystical) version of Christianity.[1] The message of these programs is clear: *these* "Gospels" present the "true" Jesus and the Gospels in the Christian Bible are spurious.

1. See Bock, *Missing Gospels.* For the Gospel of Judas see Wright, *Judas and the Gospel.* The extraneous "Gospel" that has greatest claim to authenticity is the (probably) second century Gospel of Thomas, on which see Gathercole, *Gospel of Thomas,* 178–79, who quotes Bruce: "We feel that we are no longer in touch even remotely with the evidence of eyewitnesses." Regarding the Gospel of Thomas see also Perrin, *Thomas.*

INTRODUCTION: MAKING THE GOSPEL—MYSTERY OR CONSPIRACY?   xiii

Revisions and Re-Portrayals

The years between Jesus and the writing of the Gospels were relatively few, about thirty for the Gospel of Mark, and about thirty-five to forty-five years for the other Gospels (see later, chapter 15). By comparison with other famous people from that era the lead-times between Jesus and the biographical texts about him is brief. Yet some have claimed that within those short periods the portrait of Jesus of Nazareth had been radically changed, re-portrayed unrecognizably, in contrast to Jesus as he really was, the teacher or prophet from Galilee.

One scholar notable for this was William Wrede who in 1908 wrote that Paul was the "second" and a more influential founder of Christianity than Jesus (see later, chapter 6). According to Wrede, Paul refashioned Jesus the teacher from Galilee into Christ the crucified and resurrected redeemer of all people. Wrede's view directly influenced Kazantzakis's novel *The Last Temptation of Christ* and the Martin Scorsese movie of the same name.

The real Jesus, it has been argued, had been a rabbi, a prophet, or a political subversive. According to Geza Vermes, Jesus was a charismatic rabbi (in the style of Hanina ben Dosa or Honi the Circle-Drawer from that era), and not the second person of the trinity, as in the Nicene Creed.[2] E. P. Sanders passed over Jesus' teachings and concentrating on his *actions* declared him to be an end-time prophet.[3] Samuel Brandon claimed that Jesus was a zealot sympathizer.[4]

One widely held view is that Greco-Hellenistic religion was the inspiration for the redefinition of Jesus. In the late nineteenth century and into the early twentieth century Sir James Frazer wrote at great length about ancient Egyptian religion and also about mystery cults devoted to dying and rising gods in the Greek East. It was a small step to see Jesus belonging to that religious world.

Frazer's *Golden Bough* and the arguments of the "history of religions" school were very influential in their day, and have been revived in more recent times by, for example, Burton Mack[5] and Robert Price.[6]

2. Vermes, *Jesus the Jew*.
3. Sanders, *Jesus and Judaism*.
4. Brandon, *Jesus and the Zealots*.
5. Mack, *Lost Gospel*, 216–17.
6. Price, *Deconstructing Jesus*.

The Greek Jesus

One line of argument is that the Gospels were written out of a polytheistic Greek culture, whereas Jesus himself had been a monotheistic Jew. It is claimed that the church re-shaped Jesus as a Greek "god." Maurice Casey's book title eloquently captures this theory: *From Jewish Prophet to Gentile God*.[7]

Other scholars corrected this simplistic Jew-Greek distinction. Martin Hengel, for example, established that Alexander's conquests three centuries earlier had introduced Greek culture into Palestine so that by Jesus' times Hellenism had significantly permeated Judaism.[8] Larry Hurtado and Richard Bauckham have shown that the Christians from earliest times in Christian history worshipped Jesus as "Lord."[9] They gave him the same name as the "Lord" of the Old Testament.

In other words, the racial and religious dichotomy between Jews and Greeks that would explain how Jesus the Jew became the Greek "Son of God" is not readily sustainable, and has fewer supporters today.

Likewise discarded is the view that the Gospel writers borrowed accounts of miracles in the Greek and Roman world and superimposed them upon Jesus. David Cartlidge and David Dungan in their book, *Documents for the Study of the Gospels*,[10] are able to list only eight known miracles from that era.

Asklepios a healing god	4th century BC
Pythagoras's miracles	AD 250–330
Vespasian's healing of a blind man	AD 69
A Syrian exorcist	2nd century AD
Rabbi Hanina ben Dosa	1st century AD
A Jewish boy calms the sea	AD 350
After the murder of Caesar	2nd century AD
The wine miracle of Dionysius	2nd century AD

Of these examples only two are more or less contemporary with the few decades between Jesus and the writing of the Gospels. One is the future emperor Vespasian's healings in AD 69 of a blind man and a man with a

---

7. Casey, *From Jewish Prophet*.
8. Hengel, *Hellenism and Judaism*.
9. Hurtado, *One God One Lord*; Bauckham, *God Crucified*.
10. Cartlidge and Dungan, *Documents for the Study*, 151–65.

crippled arm. The other relates to the Jewish Hanina ben Dosa, a pious rabbi from the era of the New Testament.[11]

Vespasian's two miracles are similar to and roughly contemporary with the miracles in the Gospels and, if accurate, are difficult to explain. Hanina ben Dosa, however, was not so much a miracle-worker as a devout man whose prayers were answered in dramatic fashion.

Another person of interest not mentioned in the above list was Apollonius of Tyana, a travelling philosopher who died in AD 100. Apollonius was less a miracle-worker than one who was said to have extra sensory perception. In Ephesus in AD 96, he claimed to have "witnessed" the death of the emperor Domitian in distant Rome, saying, "Take heart, the tyrant has been slain today."

When we turn to the Gospels, however, we are struck by the sheer number of Jesus' miracles.[12] There are thirty-eight *separate* miracles in all. Mark has nineteen, John has seven, there are two in "Q" (the source underlying Matthew and Luke), and there are three in "M" (Matthew's Special Source) and seven in "L" (Luke's Special Source).

The proposal that the church borrowed examples of local miracles and attributed these to Jesus is implausible. Jesus' miracles as recorded in the Gospels are distinctive and numerically overwhelming.

Nevertheless, the assumption remains that some person or group within the tight time frame between Jesus and the Gospels remade the teacher (or prophet) from Nazareth into Christ the crucified and resurrected redeemer in the manner of the mythology of dying and rising gods. They may not use the word "conspiracy" but that is what is to be inferred.

This book will seek to respond in general to the conspiracy mindset throughout but without laboriously engaging with too many specific examples. However, as we will see, those reconstructions are historically false. Jesus *was* a crucified and resurrected redeemer, but not in a mythical manner. The historical Jesus repeatedly saw himself as destined to die but be resurrected.[13] This was how his original disciples proclaimed him; and this was how Paul portrayed him. This is not a matter of dogma but of historical reality.

---

11. As discussed in Vermes, *Jesus the Jew*.
12. See Ashley, "Miracles of Jesus," 395–416.
13. Mark 8:31; 9:30–31; 10:32–34.

The Importance of 1 Cor 15:3-6, 11

This text has high claims to be among the most important in the New Testament:

> I delivered to you what I also received:
> that Christ died for our sins, according to the Scriptures;
> that he was buried;
> that he was raised on the third day, according to the Scriptures;
> that he appeared to Cephas . . . and all the apostles
> so we preach and so you believed.

"Christ died *for* our sins" is a redemptive statement that Paul did not create. It is a catechetical statement almost certainly formulated by the first Christians who "delivered" it intact to Paul. This probably happened when he made his first return visit to Jerusalem in *c.* 37. Since this was only three or four years after the lifespan of Jesus, it is overwhelmingly likely that it represented the beliefs of Jesus himself. We can be certain that Jesus' immediate disciples would not have misrepresented their master's teaching.

Another "tradition" Paul quotes in First Corinthians goes back to the Last Supper where Jesus stated that his death was "for" his people. This too is a *redemptive* statement (1 Cor 11:23–24).

Both traditions that Paul cites in First Corinthians are cast in the manner of the rabbis' judgments and must be treated as exact and honest statements. Paul received these traditions and delivered them to the churches. His model for this was that of a master rabbi delivering a judgment for a pupil rabbi to receive. The delivery and the receiving of a judgment was a matter of sacred trust.

So Jesus' original disciples followed by Paul were convinced that the One in whom they believed was the crucified and resurrected *redeemer*. The people of Galilee and Judea saw him as a rabbi and as a teacher, and these were true perceptions of the way he presented himself. But at heart Jesus knew his destiny was to die as a "ransom" for lost sinners (Mark 10:45) and be resurrected to bring them reconciled and forgiven to the Heavenly Father. This was the message he taught in private to his immediate followers who proclaimed that message after his resurrection.

The apostolic "tradition" that Paul delivered to the churches was not myth in the manner of the Greco-Roman cults. Christ's death was a real death occurring on the day after he was betrayed, after which he was buried in a tomb. His resurrection occurred on the third day following his death. He was seen alive by dozens of witnesses among whom were the apostles who bore witness to these events. The crucifixion and resurrection of Jesus actually happened and, according to the will of God, are the means of human redemption "Christ died *for* our sins . . . he was raised on the third day" (1 Cor 15:34).

William Wrede and those who follow him in asserting that Paul made Jesus into a mythical redeemer are wrong. On the contrary, the evidence is that Jesus was an actual, events-based redeemer. The conviction that Jesus had come to die and be raised alive can be traced back to Jesus himself, which is why his disciples and Paul insisted on proclaiming that message.

The Evil Influence of Paul

As we will see, Wrede blamed Paul for founding his—not Jesus'—brand of Christianity (chapter 6). If that were the case, we would expect the Gospels, as finished works, to betray many influences of Paul. In fact, however, it is the other way around. As we will see, Jesus and his words profoundly influence Paul's letters but only rarely do Paul's teachings figure in the narratives and teaching of the Gospels.

Mysteries

At the same time we must candidly acknowledge our lack of complete understanding about the processes by which the Gospels were written. As we will indicate, there are identifiable sources underlying Matthew and Luke. But were those sources dependent on oral or written sources? How is it that those sources were in Greek and not Aramaic? Were the sources compiled in Jerusalem or perhaps in another center of Christianity, Galilee, or Antioch?

While we will offer reasoned and reasonable responses to these questions, it has to be admitted that there are no rock solid answers, the absence of which tend to fuel notions of conspiracy. Yet these unanswered questions do not veil something sinister.

It is a matter of record that the first Christians publicly proclaimed the gospel and that only later their oral message came to be written as the Gospels as we now have them. First there was the spoken gospel and then the written Gospel. It is evident and obvious that we do not know the processes and means by which this happened. That we do not know about all the details of the formation of the written Gospels is readily acknowledged. Nevertheless, given our remoteness of time and culture from that era, it should be no surprise that we don't know for certain the "who," the "how," and the "where" of their creation.

So the use of the word "mystery" is appropriate. That is to say, we have to be content with not knowing everything, or at least many things. Yet, as we will see, there is enough firm data to be confident in the integrity of the Gospels, as we have received them.

Time Frame

When were the Gospels written? Let me anticipate later discussion of this critical question. I will propose that Mark completed his Gospel shortly before the death of Peter, which occurred in Rome in 64 or 65. Copies of this Gospel were then disseminated from the World Capital. Matthew and Luke, impressed that Mark's Gospel had been written under the authority of Peter, used that text as the narrative basis of their own Gospels. I believe that Matthew and Luke completed their Gospels by the year 80, probably sooner. John follows his own independent tradition and I think also completed his Gospel within the same overall time frame, 65–80, but possibly about the same time that Mark wrote.

When we consider that the ministry span of John the Baptist and Jesus was 29–33 it becomes clear that the lead time between Jesus and the Gospels was quite short, say 30 years for Mark and 35–45 years for Matthew and Luke.

29-33	64/65-80
Jesus	Gospels

The opinion I am advancing is that while there are many unanswered and unanswerable questions about these years, it is not true to the facts to see conspiracies here, whether explicit or implicit.

Sources of the Synoptic Gospels

Matthew, Mark, and Luke are called "synoptic" because their texts can be set out and viewed "alongside" one another. For the present we will not include the Gospel of John in our considerations.

It is now almost universally agreed that Mark's Gospel is the earliest of the three Synoptics and that Matthew and Luke based their narratives on Mark, following his order and often using his words. If we remove Mark from Matthew and Luke we discover three other sources for these gospels: a common source that Matthew and Luke both used (referred to as "Q"), a source that only Luke used (referred to as "L"), and a source that only Matthew used (referred to as "M").

> Matthew = Mark + "Q" + "M"
> Luke = Mark + "Q" + "L"

Synoptic Gospel relationships are a little more complex than this simple equation, but for the moment this analysis will suffice.

In the following pages we will focus on the time frame between Jesus (33) and the writing of Mark (64/65) and Matthew and Luke (70–80). The dates are approximate but close enough for our purposes.

The Letters

Here we must introduce a fact that may be new to some readers. The three sets of letters on which I focus in this study—by Paul, James, and Peter's First Letter—were written *before* the Gospels.[14]

So the question is: do these letter writers know anything about the sources that channel their way from Jesus into the finished Gospels? Upon investigation we find that the letters of Paul, James, and Peter echo, quote from, and refer to Mark (an earlier version), and to the sources "Q," "M," and "L."

Our logical course, therefore, will be to identify references to these synoptic sources in the letters of Paul, James, and Peter. This we will do in

---

14. Few scholars doubt the pre-Gospels dating of the letters of Paul and James. For 1 Peter, however, the authorship and the dating are more debated. The presence together in "Babylon" (Rome) of Mark and Silvanus with the apostle and presbyter Peter—who was martyred under Nero (AD 64/65)—are reasonable grounds for believing First Peter was written before the Gospel of Mark. For arguments pointing to an early date of 1 Peter see Bockmuehl, *Simon Peter in Scripture and Memory*, 126–31.

chronological sequence, beginning with the letters of Paul as most probably the earliest written. (However, it is possible that James wrote before Paul.) We will discuss these issues in more detail later. For now we merely seek to establish two things: (1) that the sources underlying the Synoptic Gospels were source-streams that made their way from Jesus into the finished, written Gospels, and (2) that three letter writers know of these sources and echo or quote them.

Now, however, we need to pause and widen our angle and consider the sensational discovery of a codex (primitive book) from the end of the next century. It is known as Papyrus 45, abbreviated as P^{45} and it is the earliest collection of the four Gospels (it also contains the Acts of the Apostles).

one

The Amazing Discovery of Papyrus 45

The Discovery

In 1931 there was a sensational archaeological discovery: a book. It was found in a graveyard at a place called Oxyrhynchus ("city of the sharp-nosed fish") in Middle Egypt. The book had been preserved for eighteen hundred years in the humidity-free sands, and in a part of the ancient town that the annually flooding Nile did not reach.

The book, which is partly mutilated, would have been substantial in its original form being 25 cm high (10 inches), 20 cm wide (8 inches), and 5–6 cm thick (2–2.5 inches). In all it was a book of 224 pages.

At that time most writing had been on scrolls, made up of sheets of papyrus reeds that had been flattened out and glued together in a line. The original "books" of the New Testament, including the Gospels, would have been written on scrolls that the church reader had to unwind—an awkward and difficult task.

So the next generation of Christians hit upon the idea of stitching pages together at the middle and creating what scholars call a "codex," a primitive book.[1] The reason these Christians of the second century did this was as a simple matter of practical convenience. Public reading of the gospels and letters was so much easier from a codex than from a scroll (bulky and heavy). The core activity of Christians when they gathered in church was to publicly read their sacred texts. This was the task of the lector, the public reader; very few people back then were literate.

1. See Hurtado, *Earliest Christian Artifacts*, 43–93.

All surviving Christian texts were written on codices. How do we know this? It is because our earliest manuscripts, including small fragments, are written on both sides of the "paper." Scrolls were written on only one side.

But what was this codex, discovered in 1931? Amazingly, it contained the four Gospels and the Acts of the Apostles. These had been put together as a "book" for reading and teaching in church meetings. Individuals did not own books back then (unless they were wealthy).

Because it would be fifteen hundred years before the invention of the printing press, all texts were copied by hand, a slow and laborious task that made books prohibitively expensive. In any case, only a minority of people could read. Thus a codex with four Gospels was the special possession of a church. Only the lector (official church reader) would take the codex and read from it at the church meetings.

The codex was acquired by Chester Beatty, a philanthropist, and called Papyrus 45 (or P^{45}). It is on display in Dublin. Other codices were discovered: P^{46} (containing the Letters of Paul and the Letter to the Hebrews) and P^{47} (containing the Revelation). These three codices—P^{45}, P^{46}, and P^{47}—contain almost the entire New Testament.

It is estimated that these three codices had been written and were in use by the AD 200.

There are at least three reasons to regard P^{45} as "sensational" and "amazing." First, this text is almost 150 years earlier than the previous earliest complete text, the famous *Codex Sinaiticus* (discovered in St Catherine's Monastery, Mt. Sinai, in 1844, and now on display in the British Library). The discovery of P^{45} provided scholars with the critical means of cross checking other manuscripts to recover the likely original text of the Gospels.

The second remarkable feature of P^{45} is that it confirms that there were four authentic Gospels. Why is this important? It is because some groups of Christians on the margins of the mainstream churches were disputing that there were "four" Gospels. Early in the second century a sectarian leader named Marcion claimed there was only one Gospel, Luke's. Soon afterward another leader, Valentinus, wrote his *Gospel of Truth* claiming in effect that there were *more* than four Gospels. The chance discovery of P^{45} confirmed the earlier indications that so far as mainstream Christians were concerned there were four Gospels.

Thirdly, the discovery of P^{45} containing the four gospels confirms the emphasis on the fourfold gospel mentioned in Irenaeus, Tatian, and the Muratorian Canon (see below). The P^{45} codex is indisputable, "hard copy" evidence of the fourfold gospel. It answers the modern conspiracy theories that said orthodox mainstream Christianity was actually marginal but that heretical and sectarian Christianity was central. P^{45} is a silent but eloquent witness that confirms the views of Irenaeus and other leading church fathers in the second century. Christian orthodoxy was based in the teachings of the four Gospels: Matthew, Mark, Luke, and John.

The Fourfold Gospel

The crisis created by Marcion and Valentinus forced the church leaders in the years following to make the fourfold gospel explicit. Previously it had probably been more or less assumed, possibly with a degree of toleration of other texts. The rival churches established by gifted leaders like Marcion and Valentinus forced the issue of canonical definition.

Irenaeus: The "Quadriform" Gospel

Irenaeus was a native of Roman Asia who later became missionary in southern Gaul. He knew that he was joined to the apostolic age through his mentor Polycarp, bishop of Smyrna, who had been a pupil of the apostles:

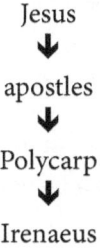

> Polycarp . . . *was* not only *instructed by apostles*, and conversed with many who had seen Christ . . . *whom I* [Irenaeus] *also saw* in my early youth.

> [Polycarp] . . . always taught the things he had learned from the apostles . . . a man who was of greater weight, and a man of more

steadfast witness of truth than Valentinus and Marcion and the rest of the heretics.[2]

In his work *Against Heresies* (written c. 180) Irenaeus insisted against the various alternative views that there could be only *four* authentic gospels: "It is not possible that the gospels can be either *more* or *fewer* in number than they are."[3] "For the living creatures [in Revelation] are quadriform, and the gospel is quadriform."[4]

The "gospel" was a single entity, but it was expressed in four Gospels. To underscore the gospel's fourfold expression Irenaeus even explained the origin of each:

> *Matthew* composed his gospel among the Hebrews in their language, when Peter and Paul were preaching the gospel in Rome and founding the church (there). After their death, *Mark*, the disciple of Peter, handed down to us the preaching of Peter in written form. *Luke*, the companion of Paul, set down the gospel preached by him in a book. Finally, *John* the disciple of the Lord, who also reclined on his breast, himself composed the gospel when he was living in Ephesus (in the province of Asia).[5]

Tatian: One Gospel "Through Four"

Tatian was a disciple of Justin in Rome, who returned to his native Assyria after his master Justin's martyrdom in 165. Tatian reassembled the four Gospels in chronological order as one entity, which became known as *The Diatessaron* [*dia tessarōn* = "through the four"]. Tatian used the Gospel of John as the broad framework for his harmonized gospel, into which he inserted Matthew, Mark, and Luke.

The earliest to refer to it was Eusebius (260–340): "Tatian *composed* in some way a combination and collection of the gospels, and *gave* this the name of *The Diatessaron*."[6]

---

2. Irenaeus, *Against Heresies* 3.3.4, in Roberts and Donaldson, *Ante-Nicene Fathers*.

3. Irenaeus, *Against Heresies* 3.11.6, in Roberts and Donaldson, *Ante-Nicene Fathers*.

4. Irenaeus, *Against Heresies* 3.11.8—euangelion tetramorphon, in Roberts and Donaldson, *Ante-Nicene Fathers*.

5. Irenaeus, *Against Heresies* 3.1.1, in Roberts and Donaldson, *Ante-Nicene Fathers*.

6. Eusebius, *History of the Church* 4.29.6, in Roberts and Donaldson, *Ante-Nicene Fathers*.

The creation of *The Diatessaron* strongly supports the idea of the fourfold expression of the one gospel.

Titles of the Gospels

Modern books have titles but ancient books like the Gospels did not have titles. At some point early in the second century the Christians gave titles to the four Gospels: "according to Matthew," "according to Mark," "according to Luke," and "according to John." Those titles, however, were incomplete. There is a word left out, the word "Gospel."

Do we see what this implies? There is one "gospel" but this one gospel has four expressions, one "according to Matthew," a second "according to Mark," a third "according to Luke," and a fourth "according to John."

We can see why the codex P^{45} contained the four Gospels in one "book," a "book" for the public reading and teaching of the gospel of the Lord Jesus Christ.

The form of the superscriptions—the one saving message of Jesus Christ—"according to" four writers implies that (in mind of the early church) these writings were not straight biographies of Jesus, but rather four expressions of the one saving message, the gospel.

The Muratorian Canon

This "one gospel through four Gospels" is confirmed by the Muratorian Canon, which originated in the last quarter of the second century. The opening line of the intact text begins: "The third book of the gospel, according to Luke," implying two prior books of the Gospel. Following the comments about Luke, the Canon continues, "The fourth gospel is by John, one of the disciples."

Again, the point to notice is that the gospel is a single entity of which there are four "books" or "Gospels," each written "according to" a named evangelist.

Manuscripts of Individual Gospels in the Second Century

The presence of a *codex* containing the four gospels in Oxyrhynchus was anticipated by the discovery of other manuscripts that were current during the second century.

p^{52}	Early 2nd C	a few verses of John 18
p^{67}	c. 125–150	a few verses from Matt 3 and 5
p^{64}	c. 125–150	A few verses from Matt 26
p^{4}	c. 125–150	Portions of Luke 1, 2, 3, 4
p^{75}	c. 175	Portions of Luke 3, 4, 5, 6, 7, 9, 17, 22. Much of John
p^{77}	c. 175–200	a few verses of Matt 23
p^{103}	c. 175–200	a few verses from Matt 13 and 14
p^{104}	c. 175–200	a few verses from Matt 21
p^{90}	c. 175–200	a portion of John 18–19
p^{1}	c. 200	portions of Matt 1
p^{66}	c. 200	most of John

The chance survival of fragile papyri in the sands of Egypt is evidence that the Gospels of John, Matthew, and Luke were in circulation and use by the beginning of the second century and that all four canonical gospels were in circulation and use by the end of the second century. These fragments were originally part of codices that were read in church meetings from the end of the apostolic age.

The absence of manuscript evidence for Mark is striking. Perhaps it reflects a lower opinion of this Gospel at that time compared to the more comprehensive Gospels of Matthew and Luke. It is only in modern times that the significance of Mark as historically the earliest Gospel has been appreciated.

References to Authors of Gospels: Papias (AD 110)

Papias, bishop of Hierapolis, writing in the first decades of the second century (c. 110), explained the origins of the Gospels of Mark and Matthew (see later, chapter 16).[7] Mark wrote his Gospel based on Peter's instruction. "Matthew compiled his oracles in the Hebrew language." Furthermore, by giving the name of six disciples in the order they appear in the Gospel of John it appears that Papias knows that gospel also.[8]

---

7. Reported in Eusebius, *History of Church* 3.39.3–16.
8. See Bauckham, *Jesus and the Eyewitnesses*, 417–20.

We conclude that Papias referred directly to the origins of the Gospels of Mark and Matthew and indirectly to the Gospels of Luke and John. Based on Papias's information it is reasonable to assert that these Gospels were in circulation and being used by the end of the first century at the latest.

Reading the Gospels at Church Meetings: Justin Martyr in Rome (c. AD 150)

We cannot overestimate the importance of this great teacher and writer. In his *First Apology* (65–67) Justin gives extensive detail about a typical church meeting.[9] After a baptism "where there is water," the baptized person is brought to "the place where the other Christians are assembled" and where they pray for the newly baptized. This was followed by the members' kiss of mutual greeting.

Then the lector read at length from the memoirs of the apostles or the writings of the prophets, upon which the president instructs and exhorts the people, based on these readings.[10] Next, "the president of the brethren" led the congregation (standing) in the prayer called Eucharist ("Thanksgiving") after which the people shared in the meal of bread and wine. Finally, the wealthy members were invited to make a contribution for the care of orphans, widows, the sick, the poor, those in prison, and foreigners.

The lector's public reading of "the memoirs of the apostles" would have included one or the other of the Gospels. In his hand would have been a codex, but whether it was one Gospel, or two, three, or four we do not know.

Quotations from the Gospels

The church "fathers" tend to quote extensively from the New Testament. Clement of Rome, Justin Martyr, and Irenaeus quote large tracts of New Testament texts. These are called "citations." It has been estimated that much of the New Testament can be reconstructed from the quotations in the major second century writers.

---

9. Justin Martyr, *First Apology,* 65–67.

10. See 1 Tim 4:13: "Until I come devote yourself to the *reading*, the *exhortation* and the *teaching*."

Conclusion

Christianity was initially a relatively small movement so it is understandable that there are only a few texts that have survived from the early years of the second century. In fact, the only texts to come down to us were preserved in the crisp, dry climate in Egypt, the earliest of which to have been discovered is P^{45}.

The fact that P^{45} contains the four Gospels strongly supports the fourfold nature of the Gospel and is confirmed by references in Irenaeus, Tatian, and the Muratorian Canon. The combined witness of that codex and the insistence of those leaders effectively ensure that the mainstream Christians believed in four Gospels, neither fewer nor more.

The existence of P^{45} and a dozen earlier parts of Matthew, Luke, and John, together with various references by name to the Gospels is strong evidence that the four Gospels were in existence and use at least by the end of the first century. Indeed, as we shall suggest, the four gospels were written within the narrow band 64/5–80.

It is of critical importance to note the brevity of the lead-time between Jesus's lifespan and the written Gospels. Those who assert conspiracies to remake Jesus by Paul or Mark usually imply that the lead-time was of vaguely indefinite length, thus allowing for redefinitions of Jesus. The three decades between Jesus and Mark scarcely provide the opportunity for such changes. This is especially so since throughout those few years we are well informed about the busy missionary activity and the activities of the churches occurring throughout the Mediterranean basin.

Those few years were not a dark tunnel for conspirators to refashion Jesus. There were many windows through which even from this distance we can see what was going on: missionaries were preaching the gospel; churches were being formed; texts were being read to the members for theological and ethical issues to be resolved. The written Gospels would grow out of these activities, and sooner rather than later.

two

The Disciples' Unexpected Role

Over-familiarity with the gospel story distracts us from recognizing the role the disciples of Jesus played in the making of the Gospels. To the popular mind these men were notable for their ordinariness. A majority were humble fishermen, one had been a customs tax collector, and the others we assume were farm workers.

Yet it is likely that they were literate, able to read if not to write. Jewish boys aged five were taught to read in the synagogue school. This was to enable them to read the Scriptures. The customs officer Levi (also known as Matthew) would have been literate as well as numerate. We should not think the disciples were unintelligent because of their lack of education and the physical nature of their work. Had different career paths opened before them they may have displayed considerable ability.

It should not be forgotten that Jesus the rabbi was a consummate educator. Steeped in the Jewish Scriptures, Jesus displayed remarkable capacity in understanding their meaning and intent. What is more, Jesus their teacher was *the* great storyteller and religious instructor in ancient Judaism. We would be right in thinking that Jesus' impact on these men over three years of intense daily contact would have been profound. We might even say that they graduated from Jesus' "school" as changed men.

At many points, however, they disappoint us by their obtuseness and their cowardice. Peter, their leader, was obstinate, impulsive, and morally weak. One of the twelve, Judas, was a traitor. On the one hand, however, these men do not impress us, while on the other they give us hope since we are like them.

The Importance of the Twelve

There are, however, several easy-to-miss aspects of these men that are very important for the formation of the Gospels.

The first is that their association with Jesus coincides exactly with the span of his public ministry that began with John's baptism of him in the Jordan, and ended with his resurrection in Jerusalem. Jesus' earlier years, from his birth to his baptism, are preludes to but not part of his God-given "public ministry" that began in 29 and ended in 33. Those are the key dates.[1]

The critical thing is that the years of these twelve men *prior* to Jesus' call of them are as irrelevant to the gospel story as *his* earlier years. Their four years of discipleship correspond *exactly* with his four years of public ministry.

The second is that Jesus knew that his public ministry was to be finite and short, and that these disciples were to have carriage of his deeds and teaching into the next generation following his passing. In particular, these men were to be the source of the information about him that would ultimately flow into the four Gospels. Indeed, we go so far as to say that the prime reason Jesus chose them and called them to be *with* him (Mark 3:14) was for the mission they were to pursue, the climax of which was the Gospels that were to be written.

Closely connected with this, thirdly, was that the gospel was a message about Jesus the *person*. Because the disciples had been with Jesus for the exact duration of his public ministry they were able to give eyewitness-based information about him that was both *historical* (setting Jesus in his historical context) and *biographical* (giving a sequentially-based record of his words and deeds).

Jesus was a rabbi, who lived in the era of the great rabbis, whose judgments fill the pages of the Mishnah (AD 200). The Mishnah quotes the *judgments* of these rabbis on the application of the law to daily life but it provides relatively little information about their historical contexts or the details of their lives. Jesus the rabbi does make judgments (in the Gospel of Mark—about association with sinners, fasting, the Sabbath, and purity[2]), but these are subsidiary to and encompassed within his overall *story*.

---

1. John the Baptist began preaching in AD 29 (Luke 3:1–2). According to the Gospel of John the ministry of Jesus extended over three to four years.

2. Mark 2:13—3:6; 7:1–13.

The Gospel Message as Biographical

The Acts of the Apostles gives summaries of the five speeches of Peter, each of which (especially the fifth—delivered to Cornelius in Caesarea: Acts 10:34–43) is biographical in character. We might have expected this Jewish man to cite references to Jesus relating to Jewish ritual or the law, but he does not. These messages focus exclusively on Jesus the Christ, his *person*, his atoning death, and his triumphant resurrection.

It is the same with the first sermon as quoted in Acts by Paul, delivered in a synagogue in Antioch in Pisidia (Acts 13:16–43). Although Paul quotes and amplifies Old Testament prophecy now fulfilled in Jesus, once again the emphasis is on Jesus the *person*, with no reference to the law or ritual.

The gospel as preached by Peter and Paul in Acts, or as written later by the four gospel-writers, is exactly opposite to the references to rabbis in the Mishnah. The Mishnah gives the judgments of the rabbis but virtually nothing about their life story.[3] The gospel, spoken and written, gives the biography of Jesus in his historical context, but relatively little of his judgments on the law.[4]

It should be clear, therefore that there is the closest of close connections between the disciples' time span following him corresponding exactly with Jesus' time span leading and teaching them. It was this that qualified them to be eyewitnesses. They were there *with* him. This means that the biography-based gospel of Jesus is eyewitness-based and, furthermore, one that locates Jesus credibly in his historical and cultural milieu.

John makes this very claim near the end of his Gospel:

> Now Jesus did many other signs in the presence of his disciples, which are not written in this book; but these are written so that you may believe that Jesus is the Christ, and that by believing you may have life in his name. (John 20:30–31)

---

3. Burridge (*What Are the Gospels?*, 248–49) observes, "Something similar emerges from a comparison of the gospels with Rabbinic material. Although the individual gospel units often find parallels with Rabbinic stories . . . there is no parallel to the overall gospel form in the Jewish material, probably because 'the center of Rabbinic Judaism was Torah; the center of Christianity was the person of Jesus'" (quoting P. S. Alexander).

4. This is less true in the Gospel of John where debates with the Pharisees relate to Jesus' identity (see e.g., John 7–10 *passim*).

The author and the other disciples were present when Jesus did the miracle signs that were written (we assume) by them in "this book." Readers of their eyewitness-based account were thereby enabled to "believe that Jesus is the Christ" and so were able to have "life in his name." Eyewitness-based testimony was inscribed in the disciples' "book."

The special role of these eyewitnesses is also clearly stated in the opening words of Luke-Acts:

> Inasmuch as many have undertaken to compile a narrative of the things that have been accomplished among us, just as those who *from the beginning were eyewitnesses* and ministers of the word have delivered them to us, it seemed good to me also, having followed all things closely for some time past, to write an orderly account for you, most excellent Theophilus, that you may have certainty concerning the things you have been taught. (Luke 1:1–4)

- "Many" wrote "narratives" about Jesus.
- The original "eyewitnesses" of Jesus who became "ministers of the word" in turn "delivered" these narratives to Luke.
- Luke wrote his Luke-Acts based on these eyewitness-authenticated narratives.

Jesus' Private Teaching to the Twelve

Jesus conducted his ministry to *two* audiences, one to the general public, and the other in private to the disciples. The insights these men derived from Jesus' private explanations informed them of the real significance of the words he had spoken in public, which were not generally understood by the public.

The Gospels portray Jesus the teacher in technical rabbinic terminology. The use of the word "disciple" for those who "followed" (Mark 1:16–20) him, "learned from him" and had taken his "yoke" upon them (Matt 11:28–30), implies that Jesus was a rabbinic teacher. Even a woman was "sitting at his feet" like the pupil of a rabbi (Luke 10:39).

Jesus, however, does not fit the usual pattern for the rabbis of that era. Rabbis typically had one or two disciples who followed the teacher. Jesus was followed by *twelve* men (a number evocative of the twelve tribes which, however, had long since been reduced to one, Judah). There were also women who traveled with him (Luke 8:1–3). This was a significant difference and marked Jesus out as a distinctive charismatic leader of a movement.

There was one other difference. Jesus spoke and debated in public, where his words were often not understood, despite their simplicity but which he then explained in private to the small group of disciples whom he had chosen and called to be with him.

Mark repeatedly narrates occasions where Jesus had given instruction in public, which he then explained to his immediate disciples in private.

1:29	And immediately he left the synagogue, and entered *the house* of Simon and Andrew.
4:10–11	those who were about him with the twelve asked him concerning the parables. And he said to them, "To you has been given the secret of the kingdom of God, but for those *outside* everything is in parables."
4:33–34	With many such parables he spoke the word to them, as they were able to hear it; he did not speak to them without a parable, but *privately* to his own disciples he explained everything.
7:17	And when he had entered *the house*, and left the people, his disciples asked him about the parable.
9:28	And when he had entered the house, his disciples asked him *privately*, "Why could we not cast it out?"

One of Jesus' sayings amplifies this distinction between his public teaching (often misunderstood) and his private explanation to his disciples and others:

> I thank thee, Father, Lord of heaven and earth, that thou hast *hidden* these things from the wise and understanding and *revealed* them to babes. (Luke 10:21/Matt 10:25)

The "wise and understanding" are the Pharisees and the wider community influenced by them, whereas the "babes" are the disciples, "sinners," and other humble-minded ones. This text supports the notion of what one scholar called Jesus' *esoteric* ministry.[5]

The thesis of this book is that the disciples *remembered* Jesus' teaching, both his public teaching and his private explanation of that teaching.

---

5. Meyer, *Aims of Jesus*, 111–13.

Furthermore, after his resurrection, when he was no longer with them, they began the task of assembling and recording his teaching and his deeds in such a way that these found their way into the four written Gospels thirty to forty-five years later.

Jesus the Teacher

During their time with him Jesus handed over to the disciples traditions that they duly received. That teaching was couched in memorable forms, in particular parables (brief and lengthy), poetic parallelism, to which must be added other poetical techniques, alliterations, assonance, rhythm, rhyme. Jesus' skills as a teacher mark him as superlative among the rabbis. His words were couched in such distinctive terms that they were remembered, enabling them to be preserved intact. It is likely that Jesus made particular use of pre-formulated aphorisms that condensed his theological teaching in an easily remembered form.

Written Texts

In addition, it is possible, even probable, that several disciples made notes of Jesus' teaching. Archaeology has revealed the existence of hand-sized, wax covered tablets for note taking and mathematical calculation. It is possible that one or more of the disciples took notes of their rabbi's teaching, which they then inscribed more permanently on a scroll.[6]

There is some evidence that Jews of that era engaged in note taking.[7] There is no reason in principle that literate members of Jesus' group might not have written down his teachings.

Attention is drawn to the Teacher of Righteousness, founder of the Qumran sect, whose teachings appear to have been written down during his lifetime, perhaps on waxed tablets.[8] According to S. Lieberman, it was "general rabbinic practice" for disciples to "write down the sayings of their master."[9] Even so emphatic an advocate of oral transmission as Birger Gerhardsson allows the possibility of the disciples making written

---

6. See further Bird, *Gospel of the Lord*, 45–48.

7. See Millard, *Reading and Writing*, 26, 27, 28, 63, 67.

8. Millard, *Reading and Writing*, 222–23; Talmon, "Oral and Written Tradition," 157–58.

9. Lieberman, *Hellenism in Jewish Palestine*, 203.

records (private notes) of Jesus' teaching.[10] This may explain the origin and transmission of the longer discourses in the Gospel of John whose format is dissimilar to the more pithy teachings in the Synoptic Gospels and less easy to memorize.

When did the practice of writing begin in the post-resurrection period? The teachings of the Lord were probably committed to writing earlier rather than later. Why was this done? Several overlapping reasons may be suggested. One is that the creation of congregations in Israel demanded *written* texts for public reading and instruction. Peter, the apostle to Judea, Samaria, and Galilee,[11] had been Jesus' prime disciple. The new churches created in Judea, Samaria, and Galilee were probably founded on the liturgical pattern of the synagogues, where the chief activity was the reading and hearing of sacred texts. Local churches lacked the ongoing presence of a Peter or a John. Texts were needed for the teachings of the Master, along with whatever summaries had been committed to memory at occasions like baptism (as was likely with Paul in Damascus). Someone who could read aloud was easier to find than an apostle!

Jesus' Teaching in Earliest Christianity: The Role of Peter

The disciples of Jesus were, in effect, a learning community. It may be thought that this ceased when Jesus was no longer with them. In fact, it did not. As we shall see, Jerusalem the earliest church continued to be a learning community, led by his senior disciple, Peter. The same Peter became the shepherd to believers throughout the Land of Israel (Acts 9:31–32).

The Jerusalem Church from Jesus to the Gospels (33–64)

I turn now to reflect on the church of Jerusalem from the time of Jesus (29–33) to the era when the Gospels were written (c. 64/5–80). I do so on the (reasonable) assumption that the raw material from which the Gospels were eventually written was initially shaped and developed in Jerusalem. I am referring to Mark, John, "Q," "L," and "M."

---

10. Gerhardsson, *Origin of the Gospel Traditions*, 68.
11. Gal 2:7–8; Acts 9:31–32.

16 MAKING THE GOSPELS

These five can be likened to separate channels through which passed "traditions" originating with Jesus that eventually became the five written sources, Mark, John, "Q," "L," and "M."

The Gospels: Mystery or Conspiracy?

The Gospels present Jesus in transcendental terms, as the unique Son of God, as the Lord and Savior of humanity. Many people cannot accept the genuineness of these claims and assert that the "real" Jesus must have been something less, a rabbi or prophet. In other words, some kind of conspiracy occurred between Jesus and the written Gospels that reshaped Jesus into a supernatural figure when the reality was that he was just a man, albeit an impressively charismatic teacher and leader.

The making of the primary sources Mark, John, "Q," "L," and "M," however, remain a mystery. We can imagine how Matthew and Luke wrote their finished Gospels. They possessed in Mark's Gospel a credible, completed basic biography of Jesus, as well as (between them) the completed sources, "Q," "L," and "M." There is no great mystery about how Matthew and Luke went about their tasks writing their Gospels. They were creative editors of raw materials that were already at hand.

The mystery is to explain *who* decided earlier to create these tradition streams, *when* and *where* they began, and which *courses* they followed. But this mystery is not necessarily explained as a conspiracy. What if Jesus of Nazareth in 29–33 was more or less as these sources and the completed Gospels presented him?

Chronology

The most logical approach is to study these sources *chronologically*. There are two phases of the Jerusalem Church that pretty well occupy the years between Jesus and the writing of Mark. The first was the initial decade-long period of Christian history when the leader of the Jerusalem Church was *Peter* (33–42). The second was the two-decade long era (42–62) when *James*, brother of the Lord, succeeded Peter as the leader of the Jerusalem Church.

As we will see, the Peter years (33–42) yield the critical knowledge of the centrality of his chronologically shaped gospel message about

Jesus. This evolved ultimately as the draft version of Mark, most probably before the death of Peter in 64 or 65.

During the James years (42–62) we have two external sets of sources that take us into the Christianity of Jerusalem. One such set was the letters of Paul (48–57) that allude to or quote from Mark (presumably an earlier version), as well as from non-Markan sayings of Jesus (from "Q," "L," and "M").

The other was the encyclical of James to Jewish-Christian congregations scattered throughout the eastern Mediterranean. The date of the Letter of James is disputed but the critical fact is that the letter reflects knowledge of as many as forty "words" of Jesus (at least in the opinion of some). These are mostly from the "Q" source.

Finally, there are the Peter years in Rome (c. 55–64). Here Peter's short First Letter cites five words of Jesus (mostly from "Q"), as well as numerous echoes from the letters of Paul and James, and perhaps also faint echoes from what would become the Gospel of John and the Acts of the Apostles.

We will "mine" these three letters in chronological order to see to what extent they quote from or echo the tradition sources that eventually find their way into the four Gospels.

Conclusion

The time span of Jesus' public ministry and the time span of the disciples' instruction by him coincided exactly (29–33). He knew that his ministry period was to be brief, so that his motive in calling them was to be *with* him, to learn from him while he was present with him, especially from his *private* teaching to them. They were to carry forward the message about him into the next generation and beyond into the written Gospels, which would be for the benefit of all succeeding generations.

That message was essentially about him as a *person*; his judgments on law and ritual were subsidiary, and in any case were always given in a biographical setting. Its content was narrative-based, setting Jesus in his historical and cultural context. Accordingly, the disciples' chief role after his passing was to provide eyewitness-based testimony about him, oral and written. It was not bare memory alone, however, but Holy Spirit-enabled recall and interpretation.[12]

---

12. John 16:12–14; also 2:22; 7:39; 12:16.

Jesus' contemporaries concluded that he was a rabbi or a prophet. These were understandable reactions. On the one hand, he taught and disputed in the manner of a rabbi, albeit a self-educated one (John 7:15—"The Jews therefore marvelled saying, 'How is it that this man has learning, when he has never studied?'"). On the other hand, however, his oracles were so potent that some of the people believed he was a prophet, like John the Baptist, or one of the prophets of old (Mark 8:28).

There was, however, this other "face" that Jesus showed in private to his immediate followers. To them he revealed himself as "the Son [of God]" and the Son of Man who was to initiate the kingdom of God, but who—paradoxically—was to be betrayed by the temple authorities to be killed by the Gentiles, after which he was to be raised from the dead.

Much of this "inner" revelation was not understood at the time by the twelve. But in the weeks and months that followed his ascension they began to grasp the enormity of his teaching about himself and his mission. These men, who were now called "apostles" ("authorized sent ones"), because they had been eyewitnesses from the time of John's baptism of him throughout his public ministry until his resurrection (Acts 1:21–22). They set about organizing their memories of Jesus' words and deeds into "traditions" that they proclaimed in Jerusalem. Quite soon, as we shall discuss later (ch. 16), they began to preserve these "traditions" in written form. A few decades later they were consolidated into the completed written Gospels.

The relationship between him and them was as a rabbi with his disciples, as the vocabulary of choosing, calling, teaching, and learning makes clear. Jesus, however, was the most exceptionally gifted rabbi of his era. Such was his genius as a teacher that his disciples were able later to recall his deeds and words.

Jesus explained to his disciples in private the message the public did not comprehend. It was this privately communicated teaching that passed into the earliest church that in turn was articulated in the Gospels a generation later. It was, however, teaching prompted and interpreted by the Holy Spirit after the Day of Pentecost.

three

Jerusalem: The Peter Years (33–42)

PETER WAS THE FIRST leader of the Jerusalem Church, a position he held from the ascension of the Lord (in 33) until Peter's flight from King Herod Agrippa 1 (in c. 42).[1]

In this chapter we shall be thinking about the development of the source material that eventually became incorporated in the four Gospels. Our reasonable assumption is that such developments occurred *within* the church community in the holy city.

Theoretically such developments may have occurred in other centers of earliest Christianity, for example, Damascus, Galilee (Capernaum), Caesarea, or Antioch. But these seem unlikely for the simple reason that the apostles appear to have remained in Jerusalem (Acts 8:1), even during the Saul-led persecution in c. 34. Furthermore, it appears that the apostles remained in Jerusalem until at least the early 50s. By default, our focus is on the Jerusalem community.

Unfortunately, the surviving evidence does not take us very far *inside* the Jerusalem Church. Our knowledge is limited. We know that there were 120 Galileans, including the mother and brothers of Jesus, led by twelve apostles. Their overall leader was Peter supported by John. These 120 were referred to as "Hebrews" who were Aramaic-speaking Jews from Galilee. Soon, however, this group was joined by Jerusalem-based "Hellenists" (Greek-speaking Jews) led by Stephen who were part of the overall community presided over by Peter. Members of both groups would have been bilingual.

We know of two forms of teaching that emanated from the Jerusalem Church during these years: the five sermons of Peter summarized in the

---

1. Acts 12:17.

book of Acts and the two pre-formatted liturgical statements quoted by Paul in First Corinthians. The sermons were directed to non-members, and the liturgical items to believers.

Besides these there were the remembered Aramaic words from the early church in Jerusalem, quoted by Paul:

1 Cor 16:22	*Maran atha*
Gal 4:6; Rom 8:15	*Abba*
2 Cor 1:20	*amēn*

What is surprising here is the infrequency of such Aramaic vocabulary. As we shall discuss later (chapter 11) this rare use of Aramaic bears on the question why the apostles seem to have preferred Greek as the linguistic vehicle of the new faith.

Peter's Public Proclamation

The early chapters of the book of Acts frequently refer to the apostles' "teaching."[2] The temple authorities complained that the apostles "filled Jerusalem with [their] teaching."[3] We assume that such "teaching" refers to the kind of material found in the sermons of Peter, recorded in summary form in Acts 2–10.

This means that very soon after Jesus' departure the apostles and members created teaching outlines that were both *from* Jesus (his teachings about himself) and *about* Jesus as the Christ (especially his miracles, death, resurrection, ascension, and ultimate return). Although we don't know the processes by which they established this "teaching" we are right to think that the one Jesus called "Rock" (*Cēphas/Petros*) would have presided over its formulation.[4]

From the outset, Peter and his associates asserted that the message of their movement was *Christ*-centered. This is surprising. Since Peter and the other apostles and members were all Jews we might have expected them to emphasize the rituals and rules of Judaism. On the contrary, from the beginning of Christian history their message was not centered

---

2. Acts 2:42; 4:2, 18; 5:21, 25, 28, 42.
3. Acts 5:28.
4. See Barnett, *Importance of Peter*, 47–57.

on interpretations of the law but on the *story* of Jesus the Christ, especially his death, resurrection, and ascension.

The five summaries of Peter's preaching about Jesus recorded in the Acts of the Apostles are each sequential and *biographical* in character. As noted, these provide a sharp contrast to the references to the great rabbis in the Mishnah (AD 200). The Mishnah records the judgments of the rabbis but supplies only sparse biography about them, whereas Peter provides biography about Jesus but is silent about his law-based judgments. Peter's account of Jesus said nothing about his judgments about the law of Moses or Jewish rituals. The Gospel of Mark records disputes over the Sabbath, fasting, and purity,[5] but Peter's sermons focused exclusively on Jesus as a *person*.

Peter's fifth sermon, which he delivered in Caesarea to the gentile God-fearer Cornelius and his family, illustrates the sequential-biographical character of his preaching (Acts 10:34–43).

- The baptism that John the Baptist proclaimed
- Jesus' ministry in Galilee
- Jesus' ministry in Judea and Jerusalem

In Jerusalem

- Jesus was put to death . . . on a "tree"
- God raised him on the third day
- Jesus appeared to chosen witnesses
- Jesus commanded them to testify about him

The four earlier sermons of Peter, which were delivered in Jerusalem, focused on the Christ's death, resurrection, and return but gave minimal information about the Galilee-to-Jerusalem narrative as in the fifth sermon. The probable reason is that the Jerusalem audiences already knew the main outlines of the Jesus story, whereas the God-fearer Cornelius based in gentile Caesarea may not have known these things.

Many have noticed a relationship between this fifth sermon and the Gospel of Mark. This Gospel closely follows the sequence of Peter's sermon to the God-fearer Cornelius in Caesarea. That Gospel is, in effect, an expanded version of Peter's spoken gospel. In other words, Peter's

---

5. Mark 2:13—3:6; 7:1–23.

narrative-based biography about Jesus became profoundly influential in the subsequent preaching of the gospel and ultimately in its *written* form.

Because we know so little about the inner life of that earliest Christian community we are unable to offer any confident suggestion about the origin of the traditions underlying the Gospel of John, or the sources "Q," or "L," or "M" that were incorporated in Matthew and Luke. But these sermons of Peter help us understand the early stages of the formation of the Mark tradition.

Fulfillment Texts and the Doctrinal Ethos of the Jerusalem Church

Peter's sermons in Jerusalem teach that the death, burial and resurrection of Jesus fulfilled many prophetic oracles. These fall into two categories, a text identified by Jesus and texts identified by the apostles.

(i) Jesus' Key Text

Peter and the other followers of Jesus knew that their teacher saw himself fulfilling great prophecies from the Old Testament, as in this example.
Psalm 110:1: The Lord at God's Right Hand
During that final week in the holy city Jesus quoted David's words:

> The Lord said to my Lord,
> "Sit at my right hand
> until I put your enemies under your feet." (Mark 12:36)

David was prophesying that his Lord (Jesus) would sit at God's (the Lord's) right hand while he was defeating the enemies of the Lord (Jesus).

This Old Testament text is often quoted in the New Testament, appearing in Paul's Letter to the Romans, the Letter to the Hebrews, and the three Synoptic Gospels.[6]

Psalm 110:1 is probably also the inspiration for the frequent references in the New Testament to the exalted Jesus now being at the "right

---

6. Acts 2:34; 1 Cor 15:25; Heb 1:13; 10:13; Mark 12:36; Matt 22:44; Luke 20:43.

hand" of God.⁷ It was probably the basis for the early Aramaic prayer, *Marana tha*, "Lord, come back [to us]."⁸

(ii) The Apostles' Texts

It seems that the apostles soon gathered texts from the Old Testament that explained who Jesus really was and the significance of what happened to him.

(a) Deut 21:23: Hung on a Tree

On two occasions in sermons in Acts Peter quotes from this text:⁹ "a hanged man is cursed by God."

According to Deut 21:23 a "hanged" man who was left unburied overnight was "cursed" by God. The consequence was the defilement of the land. The Apostle Peter, followed by Paul, understood this text as a prophecy of the crucified Jesus vicariously bearing the curse of God on sin. It was formulated in the earliest faith community in Jerusalem, presided over by Peter.¹⁰

Furthermore, it was Peter who referred more than once to Jesus as the "Servant of God," recalling Isaiah's songs of the Suffering Servant that set out strong vicarious themes.¹¹

In the text of the book of Acts it is only Peter who refers to the crucified Jesus as *ebed Yahweh*, "Servant of the Lord." The apostolic community in Jerusalem, almost certainly led by Peter, formulated the teaching tradition that "Christ died for our sins, according to the scriptures."¹²

---

7. E.g., Acts 5:31; Rom 8:34; Heb 1:3; 1 Pet 3:22; Rev 5:1.
8. 1 Cor 16:22.
9. Acts 5:30; 10:39.
10. Paul alludes to the same text in preaching in Antioch in Pisidia and both Paul and Peter cite this text in letters (Acts 5:30; 10:39; 13:29; Gal 3:13; 1 Pet 2:24).
11. Acts 3:13 (see Isa 52:13); 3:26; 4:27, 30.
12. 1 Cor 15:5.

(b) Ps 16:10: God's Holy One

In Jerusalem in the days immediately following the resurrection of Jesus Peter quoted from Psalm 16:10, which prophesied Jesus' resurrection. God did not leave his holy one decomposing in a tomb.

> You will not... let your holy one see corruption. (Acts 2:25–28)

David was the author of this Psalm, but it is not about him; it is prophetic of his descendant, the true "holy one" of God. Some years later Paul also quoted these words in the synagogue in Antioch of Pisidia.[13] Once more we are reminded of the prior influence of Peter.

(c) Joel 2:17: The Outpouring of God's Spirit

Peter saw the coming of the Spirit on the Day of Pentecost as the fulfillment of the prophecy of Joel 2:17. This was the evidence of the arrival of the last days.

> In the last days... I will pour out my Spirit. (Acts 2:17)

The Spirit gave the apostles a new power bravely to witness to the death and resurrection of Jesus to hostile audiences.

(iii) Summary

It is likely that the text identified by Jesus and then others by the apostles in Jerusalem were seen as prophetic of the key *sequence of events* relating to Jesus. It was not a coincidence that these prophecies, as noted in Peter's sermons in Acts 2–10, synchronize with events connected with Jesus.

Event (Acts)	*Prophecy*	*Fulfillment*
Rejection by Jewish leaders	Ps 118:22	Acts 4:11
Crucifixion	Deut 21:23; Isa 52:13; 3:13, 26; 4:27, 30	Acts 5:20; 10:39
Resurrection	Ps 16:10	Acts 2:25–28
Exaltation to God's right hand	Ps 110:1	Acts 2:34
Outpouring of God's Spirit	Joel 2:28–32	Acts 2:16–21

---

13. Acts 2:27; 13:35.

These texts became stock references throughout the New Testament, including in the Gospels, demonstrating that *events* centered on Jesus fulfilled the *promises* of the Sacred Scriptures. The gathering of these Old Testament texts around Jesus has been likened to him as a magnet attracting iron filings.

What stands out from Peter's sermons, and the fulfillment texts he quotes, is the degree to which these influenced later texts that were associated with Peter. As noted, the Gospel of Mark seems to have been an expanded written form of Peter's spoken gospel. It is also significant that a number of key texts that Peter appealed to in his Acts sermons are also key texts in Peter's First Letter.

OT text	Peter's preaching	First Letter of Peter
Ps 110:1	Acts 2:34	3:22
Deut 21:23	Acts 5:30; 10:39	2:24
Isa 52:13	Acts 3:13, 26; 4:27	2:24

According to Peter's teaching in Acts and in his First Letter, based on Old Testament prophecy, Jesus having "borne our sins in his body on the tree" is "at the right hand of God."

Peter's role as spokesman in earliest Christianity was established by his voice alone proclaiming the gospel in Jerusalem. Those five sermons reveal a message that was coherent and carefully crafted. Likewise, the fulfillment texts he quotes elucidate the key events associated with Jesus.

Reflection on Peter's message and his citation of fulfillment texts also point to the future and to his long-term influence in the documentation of Christianity. His spoken message developed into the *written* message of his disciple, Mark. As noted above, three of the key fulfillment texts in his Acts sermons reappear in Peter's First Letter.

The Jerusalem Teaching "Traditions"

Paul repeats two "traditions" that he "delivered" in Corinth that he had earlier "received" almost certainly in Jerusalem in c. 37 (when he stayed with Peter—Gal 1:18):

> For I received from the Lord what I also delivered to you, that the Lord Jesus on the night when he was betrayed took bread, and when he had given thanks, he broke it, and said, "This is my body which is for you. Do this in remembrance of me." In the

same way also he took the cup, after supper, saying, "This cup is the new covenant in my blood. Do this, as often as you drink it, in remembrance of me." (1 Cor 11:23-25)

I delivered to you as of first importance what I also received: that Christ died for our sins . . . that he was buried . . . that he was raised on the third day . . . that he appeared to Cephas to the twelve to more than 500 . . . to James to all the apostles. (1 Cor 15:3-7)

Peter's sermons referred to above were prepared for and delivered to outsiders. These two "traditions," however, were prepared and formatted for believers. The first is a liturgical text for the Lord's Supper, whereas the second is a form of catechism centered on the death, burial, resurrection, and appearances of the risen Christ. Both "traditions" have been carefully constructed for rote learning.

If we connect the two "traditions" they form a *continuous* narrative beginning from the fateful Thursday evening until the final appearance of the resurrected Jesus in Jerusalem about a month later.

Both Peter's preaching in Israel (Acts 2-10) and the liturgical and creedal outlines (1 Cor 11:23-25 and 15:3-7) are both *sequential* and *biographical* in character.

Sermons, Traditions, and Eyewitnesses

The apostles' preoccupation with *sequence* issued from Jesus' concern that his disciples were to be "with" him throughout his ministry years, from beginning to end (Mark 3:14). They were to be eyewitnesses, able to report at first hand the words and works of their teacher. So instilled in them was this principle of authentic reporting that they applied the same criterion for the election of the successor to Judas (Acts 1:21-22). Retrospective testimony to Jesus was to be *eyewitness* based.

The Beginning of Written Sources

Just as Jesus taught so as to be remembered, so too the disciples conveyed their teaching orally for the good memories of those who learned from them. We recall that Theophilus had been "catechized" (Luke 1:4, *katēchēthēs*) and that Paul delivered preformatted oral "traditions" to the Corinthian Christians, as already noted. Scholars make frequent reference to the role of oral instruction in an era when many were illiterate.

At the same time, however, we must take account of the synagogue culture of those times. Jews, proselytes, and God-fearers gathered on the Sabbath to *hear* the readings from the law and the prophets (Acts 13:16, 26, 43, 48). There is good reason to believe that the first Christians, who were Jews, would have expected to hear the *reading* of Christian texts. Mark directed the "reader" (i.e., the lector) to "understand" that is, to "explain" an obscurity in his text, for the benefit of the gathered *hearers* (Mark 13:14).

Luke's opening words in Luke-Acts refer to "many [who] have undertaken to compile a *narrative* of the things that have been accomplished among us" (Luke 1:1). It is clear that Luke is thinking of *written* texts. The careful work of source criticism identifies these "narratives" as derived from Mark and the so-called "Q" and "L" sources. It is likely that the "L" source was itself a collection of other sources. When source criticism is applied to Matthew we find the underlying sources Mark, "Q," and "M."

Peter's "Blocks" of Stories

It was probably after Peter's arrival in Rome in c. 55 that he and John Mark put together previously used sequences of stories about Jesus and shaped them into what would become the Gospel of Mark. It appears that beforehand Peter (and Mark?) had created various "blocks" of narratives about Jesus.[14] These sequences may have included the following:

1:21–34; also 1:35	Jesus' dramatic first "day" in Capernaum
2:1—3:6	The "conflict" stories in Capernaum
4:1–34	Jesus' "kingdom" parables
4:35—5:43	The lake-centered miracles
9:42–50	Various miscellaneous teachings
13:1–37	The Olivet Discourse
14:1—16:6	Jesus' last days in Jerusalem

This last mentioned passage is more intensely detailed than other Markan texts and it shows signs of having been written in c. 40 to address the crisis of Caligula's threatened desecration of the temple (Mark 13:14, "When you see the abomination of desolation standing where it ought

14. See Bird, *Gospel of the Lord*, 125, who directs attention to the Olivet Discourse (Mark 13) and the passion narrative (Mark 14–15) as possibly having been written before Mark wrote his Gospel. However, see later, chapter 16, "The Making of Mark."

28 MAKING THE GOSPELS

not to be ['Let the reader understand'], then let those who are in Judea flee to the mountains").

Each "block" is a complete, coherent entity. It is suggested that Peter initially narrated some of these as partially undigested versions of these passages, which were joined up by Peter and Mark for the completed Gospel.¹⁵

Blocks of teaching delivered orally by Peter

Written down (in Greek) for reading in the churches

Rewritten, joined together c. 55–64
(published posthumously by Mark after c. 65).

Since there is no discernible Aramaic original underlying Mark (apart from isolated words and phrases) we assume that these constituent blocks existed in Greek from the beginning.

Moreover, because (as seems likely) these blocks were created for teaching purposes in the early churches, they probably soon assumed written form to be publicly read in the church meetings. The first believers, who were Jews, would have sought to provide written texts for reading in the nascent congregations of Christians.

The book of Acts explains that Saul's persecution scattered the Jerusalem believers throughout Judea, Samaria, and Galilee. The author tells us that Peter traveled throughout those regions giving pastoral oversight to the churches.¹⁶ The many churches in these regions would have needed apostle-endorsed texts for reading in church meetings.

It is likely that the sources "Q," "L," and "M" fulfilled similar purposes. That is to say, they were to be read aloud and heard in the churches, but details are lacking.

The Importance of Peter

Since Peter was the unopposed leader of the Jerusalem community for its first decade, it is overwhelmingly likely that he played a significant role

---

15. See chapter 16, appendix, for the observation that the episodes that Mark narrates generally locate the place the incident occurred.

16. Acts 9:31–32; Gal 2:7–8.

in the formulation of the biographical outlines, the identification of key texts now fulfilled in Jesus the Christ, and in the formation of liturgical and catechetical outlines. The hands of the apostles, especially Peter's, point in just one direction, to Jesus.

Martin Hengel summarizes the importance of Peter at this very early stage in Christian history:

> Not only did [Peter] have the massive number of Jesus' traditions at his disposal but, as the first witness to the resurrection and by means of Spirit-prompted enthusiasm during the early times that followed Easter, he would have participated in giving decisive shape to *the development of the pre-Pauline beginnings of Christology and soteriology.*[17]

Peter's influence was no less great regarding the narrative shape of the *written* Gospel by Mark, which was to be followed closely by Matthew and Luke.

Peter was a highly significant leader in early Christianity. He had been the spokesman among the twelve who became the voice of the first Christians in Jerusalem and wider Israel. Later he became the senior presbyter in the Church of Rome. Peter was unmatched as leader of the two great centers of Christianity, Jerusalem, and Rome. Brilliant as he was, Paul was deeply indebted to Peter for his knowledge of Jesus.

Paul in Jerusalem

After his three years in Damascus and "Arabia" (i.e., c. 34–37) Paul returned to Jerusalem where he resided with Peter for "fifteen days." Furthermore, he also "saw" James the brother of the Lord.[18] It is likely that these meetings, as well as with other apostles, provided Paul with the opportunity to became acquainted with the "Jesus" traditions. As noted, this visit most probably represented the occasion when Paul learned the two "traditions" that he "delivered" to the church in Corinth and doubtless also to other churches he established.

---

17. Hengel, *Saint Paul*, 34; Cullmann, *Peter*, 65, concurs: "Peter was not far removed from Paul in theology. Indeed, I should go even further and definitely assert that within the circle of the twelve he is the one who in this respect *stands closest to Paul.*"

18. Gal 1:18-19.

It would not be feasible to limit these "traditions" to the two cited in First Corinthians. As we will see in the next chapter, Paul's letters to the Galatians, the Thessalonians, the Corinthians, and the Romans (written 48–57) contain numerous echoes of and references to Jesus' life and teaching.

We ask, where and from whom did Paul gather this other Jesus-based information? In the next chapter we will address this important question.

Conclusion

The earliest community of believers in Jerusalem was a learning and witnessing community, whose leader was Peter, the "Rock." The early chapters of Acts summarize no less than five of Peter's sermons, the core message of each was that Jesus was the Christ.

Frequent reference to the "teaching" of the apostles indicates that they had previously established specific patterns of "teaching." This "teaching" was focused on *events* related to Jesus, stated biographically and in chronological sequence, beginning with his baptism, but reaching their climax in his last days in Jerusalem. It is significant that references to law are absent; all attention is directed to *Jesus* in sequential, biographical terms.

Analysis of Mark's Gospel reveals first that it bears a close relationship with the public preaching of Peter, and also that there appear to have been a number of semi-independent blocks of narrative. These existed in Greek and were most probably in written form for public reading in the growing number of the churches.

four

The Words of Jesus in the Letters of Paul

THE LETTERS OF PAUL to churches in the four Roman provinces (Galatia, Macedonia, Achaia, and Asia) between 48–57, as amplified by the narrative of Acts, give us a unique and wide window into early Christianity. Paul's many references to and quotations from the words of Jesus point to the existence of sources that would in just a few years make their ways into the Synoptic Gospels.

Sources of Paul's Knowledge about Jesus[1]

This prompts the question: where and from whom did Paul have access to this critical information? There are two main possibilities.

One such source would have been through Paul's visits to the apostles in Jerusalem. We know of four visits to Jerusalem that would have provided him with access to the "Jesus" tradition.

- In c. 37 Paul "remained" with Cephas for fifteen days, when he also "saw" James, brother of the Lord, as well as former disciples of Jesus (Gal 1:18–19; Acts 9:27–28).

- In c. 47 Paul with Barnabas met with James, Peter, and John, and probably with others who had been the disciples of Jesus (Gal 2:1, 9; Acts 11:29–30).

---

1. There are two main sources of information for Paul about Jesus: (i) from God, by "revelation" near Damascus, and (ii) from fellow Christians by testimony ("traditions") and/or from early texts. See now Porter, *When Paul Met Jesus*, who raises the possibility that Paul had encountered Jesus (based on Acts 9:1–9; 1 Cor 9:1; and 2 Cor 5:16).

- In c. 49 Paul attended the council meeting in Jerusalem, presided over by James, when apostles were also present (Acts 15:8).
- In c. 52 Paul "went up and greeted the church [in Jerusalem]" (Acts 18:22).

These various visits allowed the possibility for Paul to gain an understanding of the teachings of Jesus that would have been cherished within the Jerusalem Church. In addition, Paul worked alongside various former members of the Jerusalem Church.

46–48	Paul with Barnabas in Antioch, Jerusalem, Cyprus, and Galatia.
47	Paul with John Mark in Antioch, Cyprus, Pamphylia, and Ephesus.[2]
49–52	Paul with Silvanus in Asia Minor, Macedonia, and Achaia.

We do not have details about transmission of the information, but Paul's extensive association with early members of the Jerusalem Church would have provided the opportunities for learning of Jesus' life and teaching. As we will see in this chapter, Paul gained a considerable body of information, which he must have received somehow, somewhere, from someone. Paul's four (known) visits to Jerusalem and his working connections with former Jerusalem Church members are promising possibilities for receiving the knowledge of Jesus' teaching that he displays in his letters.

Two of Paul's letters from the 50s in particular have numerous echoes of the source traditions. First Corinthians was written early in 55 and Romans in the winter of 57. It is likely that Paul had access to these sources either through his new colleague Silvanus (49–52) or also through Paul's visit to Jerusalem in 52 (Acts 18:22). Indeed, such is the extent of Paul's citations it is feasible to argue that such sources came to Paul in *written* form (a scroll) and in Greek.

The Letters of Paul

Paul's letters from the eastern provinces provide several advantages for the historian. One is that they can be located within a narrow time frame (48–57) and the second is that their references to the Jesus tradition are "gratuitous." Paul was not seeking to prove anything by his reference to

---

2. Col 4:10; Phlm 24; assuming these texts were written in and from Ephesus.

them. Rather, he was addressing current pastoral concerns within the churches for which he applied the words of the Lord.

So, let us work through some of Paul's use of Jesus' words in his letters, as far as possible chronologically.

Jesus' Words in Paul

(i) Galatians (*c.* 48)

Galatians is Paul's earliest surviving letter, written from Antioch in c. 48. Not all take this view, but it is an opinion that is capable of solid defense. The alternative date of authorship is only a few years later, so that precise dating is not critical.

(a)

3:1	O foolish Galatians! Who has bewitched you? It was before your eyes that Jesus Christ was publicly portrayed as crucified.
6:17	...I bear in my body the marks (stigmata) of Jesus.

Paul displays his awareness of the flagellation and crucifixion of Jesus, that is, of the *historical* Jesus. The most likely source of this information would have been a Jerusalem-based apostolic witness. Paul may have witnessed the crucifixion of Jesus but he doesn't say so. The prime candidate for this information would have been Peter, whom Paul met in c. 37 and again in c. 47. It is not known whether the flagellation-crucifixion tradition was yet secured in writing, but it may have been. If so it would have been an early part of the tradition that would be developed finally in the Gospel of Mark.

(b)

5:1	For freedom Christ has set us free; stand firm therefore, and do not submit again to a *yoke* of slavery.

Paul's words remind us of a saying of Jesus:

> Come to me, all who labor and are heavy laden, and I will give you rest. Take my *yoke* upon you, and learn from me, for I am

gentle and lowly in heart, and you will find rest for your souls. For my *yoke* is easy, and my burden is light. (Matt 11:28–30)

Contemporary Jewish texts leave no doubt that the "yoke" that is "heavy" and a "burden" is the law.[3] In its place Jesus' yoke (following *him*) is "easy," "light," and gives "rest" (Matt 11:28–30). Since the era of Hellenism following the Greek invasion of Palestine (332 BC) the Pharisees broke the law down into increasingly specific rules. For example, there were thirty-nine subsidiary rules for the single Sabbath commandment. These had become a heavy yoke (cf. also Acts 15:10—"a *yoke* . . . that neither our fathers nor we have been able to bear," quoted by Peter).

Paul's use of the language of "freedom" aptly captures Jesus' assertion of the blessings of *his* yoke. This text is found only in Matthew, which means we should think of it as belonging to the "M" source.

(c)

5:14	For the whole law is fulfilled in one word: "You shall love your neighbor as yourself."
6:2	Bear one another's burdens, and so fulfill the law of Christ.

Combining these references in Galatians implies that Paul was referring to and depending on the teaching of Jesus on the (second) key element in the law, the love of neighbor (as in Mark 12:31—"the second is this: you shall love your neighbor as yourself"; so Luke 10:28). The two great commandments that Jesus states occur separately in the Old Testament (Deut 6:5; Lev 19:18). It was Jesus, not the Old Testament, who connected the two commandments.

Summary: These three texts of Paul in Galatians indicate that he was aware of one text from the Matthew tradition ("M") and two from the Mark tradition.

(ii) 1 and 2 Thessalonians (*c.* 51)

Paul wrote these letters from Corinth to the Thessalonian Church in c. 51. He had established this church a short time before he wrote to its members.

---

3. Manson, *Sayings of Jesus*, 186–87.

Among their concerns were questions about the second coming of Jesus, to which Paul makes the following response.

(a)

> 1 Thess 4:15–17
>
> For this we declare to you by *a word from the Lord,* that we who are alive, who are left until the *coming* of the Lord, will not precede those who have fallen asleep. For the Lord himself will descend from *heaven* with a cry of command, with the voice of an archangel, and with the sound of the *trumpet* of God. And the dead in Christ will rise first. Then we who are alive, who are left, will be *caught up* together with them in the *clouds* to meet the Lord in the air, and so we will always be with the Lord.

Paul's words (italics) appear to adapt the words of the Lord Jesus:

> Then will appear in heaven the sign of the Son of Man, and then all the tribes of the earth will mourn, and they will see the Son of Man *coming* on the *clouds of heaven* with power and great glory. And he will send out his angels with a loud *trumpet* call, and they will *gather* his elect from the four winds, from one end of heaven to the other. (Matt 25:30–31)

Paul's "word from the Lord" and references to the coming of the Lord/Son of Man in/on the clouds from heaven heralded by the trumpet to gather/catch up the faithful combine to suggest that Paul knew the words of Jesus and adapted them pastorally for the Thessalonian church.

This text is found only in the Gospel of Matthew and we conclude it was therefore part of the "M" source.

(b)

1 Thess 5:2: "For you yourselves are fully aware that the day of the *Lord* will come like a *thief* in the *night*."

Paul's words appear to echo this end-time passage in Matthew:

> But know this that if the *master* of the house had known in what part of the *night* the *thief* was coming, he would have stayed awake and would not have let his house be broken into. (Matt 24:33/Luke 12:39)

The appearance of "thief" references in both Matthew and Luke points to dependence on the "Q" source.

1 Thess. 5:3: "While people are saying, 'There is peace and security,' then *sudden* destruction will come upon them as labor pains come upon a pregnant woman, and they will not *escape*."

Paul's warning appears to have been based on Jesus' warning:

> But watch yourselves lest your hearts be weighed down with dissipation and drunkenness and cares of this life, and that day come upon you *suddenly* like a trap. . . . But stay awake at all times, praying that you may have strength to *escape* all these things that are going to take place, and to stand before the Son of Man. (Luke 21:34–36)

These words are found only in Luke and therefore suggest the "L" source for Paul's words.

(iii) First Corinthians (*c.* 55)

Paul wrote First Corinthians from Ephesus in c. 55 in which he cites three teachings of Jesus.

(a)

1 Cor. 7:10–11: "To the married I give this charge (not I, but *the Lord*): the wife should not separate from her husband . . . and the husband should not *divorce* his wife."

Paul is loosely adapting several strands of Jesus' teaching:

> And he said to them, "Whoever *divorces* his wife and marries another commits adultery against her, and if she *divorces* her husband and marries another, she commits adultery." (Mark 10:11)

There is another point of contact. In 1 Cor 6:16 ("the two will become one flesh") Paul exactly reflects Jesus' words in Mark 10:8 ("the two shall become one flesh. So they are no longer two but one flesh").[4]

---

4. Unless both Jesus and Paul are depending on Gen 2:24.

The conclusion to be drawn is that Paul knew and understood Jesus' teaching on the permanence of marriage. Paul seems to have been depending on the Mark tradition.

(b)

1 Cor 9:14: "In the same way, the Lord commanded that those who proclaim the gospel should get their living by the gospel."

Paul is appealing to a teaching that "the Lord commanded." He is referring to Jesus' words quoted in nearly identical terms in Luke 10:7 and Matt 10:10.

| Luke 10:7 | the laborer deserves his wages |
| Matt 10:10 | the laborer deserves his food |

Both "words" of Jesus occur in his mission charges to disciples, which is also the context of 1 Cor 9:14. Paul may have known the traditions about the disciples' missions in Israel.

In sum, Paul's words in 1 Thessalonians and 1 Corinthians appear to point to "M," "Q," "L," and (early) Mark as their sources.

(c)

1 Cor 11:23–25	For I received from the Lord what I also delivered to you, that the Lord Jesus on the night when he was betrayed took bread, and when he had given thanks, he broke it, and said, "This is my body which is for you. Do this in remembrance of me."
	In the same way also he took the cup, after supper, saying,
	"This cup is the new covenant in my blood. Do this, as often as you drink it, in remembrance of me."
	For as often as you eat this bread and drink the cup, you proclaim the Lord's death until he comes.

This is a liturgical "tradition" that Paul (probably) received from Peter in Jerusalem in c. 37 (Gal 1:18), and which he delivered to the Corinthians in c. 50. It appears later in nearly identical terms in Luke 22:19–20:

And he took bread, and when he had given thanks,

he broke it and gave it to them, saying,

"This is my body, which is given for you. Do this in remembrance of me."

And likewise the cup after they had eaten, saying,
"This cup that is poured out for you is the new covenant in my blood."

Paul's "tradition" may have been limited to Jesus' precise Eucharistic *actions* and *words*. If so, it would mean that the words "on the night when he was betrayed" were not part of the tradition, but Paul's own creation. In other words, Paul somehow knew the narrative context of the Last Supper and the subsequent "betrayal" (or "handing over" of Jesus—by Judas to the chief priests, by the chief priests to Pilate, by Pilate to the soldiers[5]). It appears that Paul knew of the "Mark" tradition that had been developed under the aegis of Peter in Jerusalem.

Paul's concluding exhortation to the Corinthians (v. 26—"For as often as you eat this bread and drink the cup, you proclaim the Lord's death until he comes") implies his knowledge of Jesus' teaching about his second coming.

(iv) Romans (*c.* 57)

Paul wrote Romans in 57 during the three months (winter?) he spent in Corinth prior to his fateful return to Jerusalem (Acts 20:3). There are numerous references to, echoes from, and allusions to the teachings of Jesus in this letter.

(a) Rom 12

Rom 12:14	*Bless* those who persecute you; bless and do not *curse* them.
Luke 6:28a	*Bless* those who *curse* you, pray for those who abuse you.
Matt 5:44	*Love* your enemies, and pray for those who persecute you.

Paul is dependent on a "Q" source (loosely echoed).

Rom 12:17	Repay no one evil for evil, but give thought to do what is honorable in the sight of all.
Luke 6:29	To one who strikes you on the cheek, offer the other also, and from one who takes away your cloak do not withhold your tunic either.

---

5. The word *paradidōmi*, "I hand over" or "betray," appears repeatedly in Mark's narrative of Jesus' last day: 14:10–11, 42 (Judas to the chief priests); 15:1, 10 (the chief priests to Pilate); and 15:15 (Pilate to the soldiers).

Matt 5:39	But if anyone slaps you on the right cheek, turn to him the other also. And if anyone would sue you and take your tunic, let him have your cloak as well.

This is a "Q" source (loosely echoed).

Rom 12:18	live *peaceably* with all.
Mark 9:50	be at *peace* with one another.

This is an early Mark source.

Rom 12:20	if your enemy is hungry, feed him; if he is thirsty, give him something to drink. . . . Do not be overcome by evil, but overcome evil with *good*.
Luke 6:27	Love your enemies, do *good* to those who hate you.
Matt 5:44	Love your enemies and pray for those who persecute you.

This is a "Q" source.

(b) Rom 13:7

Rom 13:7	*Pay (apodote)* to all what is owed to them.
Mark 12:17	Jesus said to them, "*Render (apodote)* to Caesar the things that are Caesar's."

This is an early Mark source.

(c) Rom 14

Rom 14:14	I know and am persuaded in the Lord Jesus that nothing is *unclean* in itself.
Mark 7:15	There is nothing outside a person that by going into him can *defile* him.

This is an early Mark source.

Rom 14:20	Everything is indeed *clean*.
Mark 7:19	Thus [Jesus] declared all foods *clean*.

This is an early Mark source.

To summarize, in Rom 12–14 Paul makes extensive references to the sources "Q" and (early) Mark.

Dating of These Sources

We are fortunate in being able to date Paul's letter to the Galatians, his letters to the Thessalonians, to the Corinthians, and the letter to the Romans to the brief period 48–57. Our survey of the words of Jesus echoed by Paul in these letters thereby establishes the existence of the synoptic sources "Q," "L," "M," and an early version of Mark.

This observation bears on the dating of these sources. Of course, it would not be possible to claim that Paul used sources that were complete and finished. On the other hand, however, it is reasonable to suppose that they were sufficiently substantial to be employed by Paul in letters written 48–57. This points to the significant likelihood that the sources had begun to be formulated early, from the time of Jesus' ascension.

What is more, it is overwhelmingly likely that these sources had been *written* from the time they had begun to be assembled and, moreover, written in Greek. If so, it is possible that Paul had access to a scroll or scrolls on which the words of the Lord had been written.

Paul's Knowledge of Jesus the Man

Paul did not claim to have known the historical Jesus directly. True, he had "seen" the risen Lord (1 Cor 9:1) referring to the Damascus "revelation." His confession that he knew Christ "according to the flesh" (2 Cor 5:16) points back to his days as a persecutor when he had formed a "worldly" (*kata sarka*, "fleshly") misconception of Christ (which his recently arrived rivals in Corinth still have—2 Cor 11:1–4). Even if Paul had seen and heard the historical Jesus without the benefit of the indwelling Spirit it would have been with the same "worldly" misconception.

Nevertheless, Paul's information about Jesus is considerable.

---

6. See Wenham, *Paul*, 200–205.

7. See Wenham, *Paul*, 200–205.

8. The unusual verb *metamorphoō* occurs in NT only in these references. For argument that Paul knew about the transfiguration of Jesus see Wenham, *Paul*, 357–63.

1. Jesus was a descendant of Abraham the Patriarch (Gal 3:16).
2. Jesus was a direct descendant of King David. This is critical to the belief that he was the Christ, the Messiah of Israel (Rom 1:3; 9:5; 15:8; 1 Cor 15:3).
3. Jesus "born of a woman" (Gal 4:4–5) suggests that Paul knows of and confirms the virginal conception of Jesus. Paul's words are in agreement with Matthew's: "Mary, *of whom* Jesus was born, who is called Christ" (Matt 1:16). Jesus was born of the woman, Mary, not of her husband Joseph.
4. Jesus was born and lived in "poverty" (2 Cor 8:9).
5. Jesus was "born under" and lived under Jewish law (Gal 4:4).
6. Jesus had a brother named James and other brothers, unnamed (Gal 1:19; cf. 1 Cor 9:5).
7. Jesus had *twelve* disciples, to whom the risen Lord "appeared" (1 Cor 5:5; also Mark 3:14 pars).[6]
8. Peter was spokesman of the twelve (e.g., Mark 8:27–30 pars), a role that merged after the resurrection into his leadership of the apostolic mission to the circumcised in Israel (Gal 2:7–8).[7]
9. Jesus' manner was one of humility and meekness, agreeing with his words recorded in the Gospel, "I am gentle and lowly in heart" (2 Cor 10:1; Matt 11:29).
10. He was externally "transfigured" on a mountain (Mark 9:2; Matt 17:2), as Paul expects believers to be "transformed" inwardly (2 Cor 3:18; cf. Rom 12:2).[8]
11. Jesus called God "*abba*" (Gal 4:6; Rom 8:15; cf. Mark 14:36).
12. He ministered primarily to Israel/Jews (Rom 15:8).
13. He instituted the memorial meal on the night when he was betrayed (1 Cor 11:23–25).
14. He was cruelly treated at that time (Rom 15:3).
15. He was killed by the Jews of Judea (1 Thess 2:14–15).
16. He testified before Pontius Pilate (1 Tim 6:13).
17. His "death on a cross" (Phil 2:8) implies execution at *Roman* hands for treason (cf. Gal 3:1; 6:17).
18. He was buried (1 Cor 15:4).
19. He was raised on the "third" day and was seen alive on a number of occasions by numerous witnesses, most of whom are still alive, able to confirm this (1 Cor 15:5–7).

There is no item in the list that contradicts the Gospels. Nevertheless, the list is small in comparison with the details in the Gospels, and many of the items are liturgical.[9]

9. Rom 1:3/Luke 1:69; Gal 4:4–6/Luke 1:32; [3:23; 2:42; 1:68–70]; 2 Cor 8:9/Luke 10:58.

Martin Hengel responds to those who question the brevity of the list:

> It was simply impossible in the antiquities to proclaim a man crucified a few years ago, as *Kyrios*, Son of God and Redeemer, without saying something about who this man was, what he taught and did and why he died.[10]

Even so, there is a striking omission from this list. How can we explain the absence of reference to the miracles of Jesus, miracles that are so prominent in the Gospels? There are several possibilities. One is that Paul simply did not know that Jesus performed miracles. The other more likely possibility is that he did know and teach about the miracles but that the issue had not been raised in the churches so as to call for comment in his letters. His reference to the "signs and wonders" that Christ "wrought in [Paul]" is consistent with the likelihood that Paul knew of his master's "signs and wonders" (Rom 15:18).

Conclusion

Paul's letters to the Galatians, the Thessalonians, the Corinthians, and the Romans were written in a narrow time frame, between 48–57. References in these letters indicate that Paul echoed (early) Mark and the sources "Q," "M," and "L." We conclude, therefore, that (versions of) these sources were extant by the early 50s. Since they were in Greek, and not able to be translated into Aramaic, we conclude that they existed in Greek by the year 50, and arguably earlier.

Paul's details about Jesus' life, although extensive, are relatively unspecific. In fact, a number of these items are liturgical in character and thus most likely "received" from others before him. The omission of reference to miracles is an issue, but Paul's references to *his* miracles as wrought by Christ through him may indicate that Paul was aware of the miracles of the historical Jesus.

---

10. Hengel, *Acts*, 43–44.

five

Did Paul Reinvent Jesus?

THE GERMAN SCHOLAR WILLIAM Wrede is famous for saying (in 1908) that Paul was the "second founder of Christianity" who "compared with the first, exercised beyond all doubt the stronger—not the better—influence."[1] According to Wrede, Paul was an "extraordinary personality" who took "up the historical Jesus into the Pauline Christ," whose "Christ must . . . crush out the man Jesus." According to Wrede, this Paul "has thrust that greater person [Christ], whom he meant only to serve, utterly into the background."

Wrede claimed that Paul effectively removed Jesus the teacher and consequently replaced him with Christ the *crucified* and *resurrected* redeemer. Nevertheless, Wrede is careful not to assert that Paul was "the proper founder of Christianity" despite the fact that "the apostle laid the stress on thoughts that were not present in the original teaching of the Master."[2]

Wrede's view that Paul had "crushed" Jesus has proved remarkably influential, being followed by Rudolf Bultmann (New Testament scholar), Søren Kierkegaard (theologian), Friedrich Nietzsche (philosopher), Mahatma Gandhi (reformer), George Bernard Shaw (playwright), and Nikos Kazantzakis (novelist), to name just a few famous personalities.

So did Paul willfully recast Jesus of Nazareth according to his own preferred interpretation? We are right to associate the notion of conspiracy by Paul with William Wrede and those who share his views.

---

1. Wrede, *Paul*, 148, 151.
2. Wrede, *Origin of the New Testament*, 22–23.

Paul's Christology

Paul's Christology is marked by two characteristics. It is exalted and it is early. It is remarkable that such exalted views about Jesus should be as early as they are, for it is commonly but wrongly assumed that "high" views of Jesus *evolved* "upward" from "low" beginnings.

Jesus as "Son of God" appears and frequently in early and undisputed letters of Paul in, for example, Galatians, 1 Thessalonians, 1 Corinthians, 2 Corinthians, and Romans.[3] Very often Paul refers to Jesus in relationship to God the Father as "*his* Son," or "his *own* Son," or "*the* Son," indicating a uniquely filial relationship.[4]

It is clear that Paul thought of the Son of God as having preexisted his mortal life, a viewpoint that implies his incarnation.[5] Other early writers also believed that Jesus had existed prior to his birth, for example, the author of the Letter to the Hebrews, and Peter in his First Letter.[6] It is difficult historically to trace the origin of the belief of the preexistence of Jesus, except to observe that it was a doctrine that was held very early among the first Christians. Jesus himself was probably the source of this belief, which in turn came to be an article of faith.[7]

Paul applies the word "Lord" to Jesus in contexts that identify him (somehow) with the Lord God Almighty (Phil 2:9–11). How did Paul come to think of Jesus in such exalted terms? There are two interlocking responses to the question. First, it was the Lord from heaven who addressed Paul on the Damascus Road (Acts 9:5). We note that after his baptism in Damascus in c. 34 Paul immediately began to proclaim Jesus as "the Christ" and "the Son of God" (Acts 9:19–22). Secondly, Paul's meetings with the leaders of the Jerusalem Church on several occasions would have confirmed the scriptural (Old Testament) basis for regarding Jesus so highly.

From the beginning of his years as a Christian (*c*. 34) Paul refers almost interchangeably to Jesus as the Christ, the Son of God, and the Lord.

True, there are significant gaps in our knowledge about the sources of Paul's high Christology. Some details remain a mystery due to the

---

3. Gal 1:16; 2:20; 4:4, 6; 1 Thess 1:10; 1 Cor 1:9; 15:28; 2 Cor 1:19; Rom 1:3, 4, 9; 5:10; 8:3, 39.

4. Rom 8:3, 32; also Matt 11:25–27.

5. 2 Cor 8:9; Phil 2:6–7.

6. Heb 1:2–3; 1 Pet 1:20; see also John 1:1–3, 14.

7. So argued by Gathercole, *Preexistent Son*.

sheer absence of evidence. But that does not permit any notion of conspiracy. The inescapable facts are that Paul expresses a *high* view of Jesus and he does so at a point that is historically *early*. These two realities put to flight those views that claim Jesus was a mere prophet or rabbi who later evolved upward into a "god" and a "lord." All the evidence points in the opposite direction to Paul's early and exalted view of Jesus as the Christ, the Son of God, and the Lord.

This, however, does not mean that Paul was the "inventor" of a high Christology. As we have noted in a previous chapter (ch. 3), it was the Jerusalem Church under the leadership of Peter that, based on fulfilled prophecy, developed exalted views of Jesus that shaped the entire apostolic witness to Jesus. Paul was not the innovative inventor of this Christology but rather one who skillfully applied it to the needs of the churches. If we are looking for an inventor of a high Christology, then we need not look further than Peter, first (male) witness of the resurrected Jesus.

Jesus as Exemplar

A remarkable feature of Paul's letters is his references to Jesus as exemplar. On several occasions Paul interposes himself as one to be "imitated" since he has "imitated" Jesus. Through Paul's example, based on his imitation of Christ, the churches of Paul were being shaped by the memory of Christ's "way" of life and relationships.

Paul	Text	Gospel Parallel
1 Cor 10:33—11:1	Just as I try to please all in everything I do, not *seeking* my own advantage, but that of many, that they may be *saved*. Be *imitators* of me, as I am of Christ.	Luke 19:10 ("L") "The Son of Man came to *seek* and to *save* the lost."
2 Cor 10:1	I, Paul, myself you, by the *meekness* and *gentleness* of Christ, I who am *humble* when face to face with you	Matt 11:29 ("M") "I am meek and *lowly* in heart."
Rom 15:3	We who are strong ought to bear with the failings of the weak, and not to *please* ourselves; let each of us *please* his *neighbor* for his good, to *edify* him. For even the Christ did not *please* himself.	Luke 10:36-37 "Which of these three . . . proved to be a *neighbour* to the man who fell among robbers?" He said, "The one who showed him mercy."

Rom 15:7	Welcome one another, therefore, *as Christ has welcomed you*, for the glory of God.	Luke 15:2 ("L") The Pharisees and the scribes grumbled, "This man *receives* sinners, and eats with them."
Phil. 2:5-6	Have this mind among yourselves, which is yours in Christ Jesus, who, though he was in the form of God, he did not count equality with God a thing to be grasped, but he *emptied* himself, taking the form of a slave...he *humbled* himself...	Matt. 11:29 ("M") "I am gentle and *lowly* of heart and you shall find rest to your souls."

Paul's references to Christ's manner of life are unmistakable, but at the same time are allusive rather than precise. It appears that Paul had access to the "L" source and the "M" source.

Were these sources oral or written? While many (a majority?) argue for oral transmission, there is a stronger case for these texts to have been written down for teaching purposes in the churches.

The reason is that each of the texts quoted above appears to be part of a larger *narrative* matrix.

Luke 19:10	Jesus concludes his interchange with Zacchaeus.
Matt 11:29	(cited twice) is punch line of a longer episode.
Luke 10:36	Jesus concludes the Parable of the Good Samaritan?
Luke 15:2	It provides the setting for the three parables of "the Lost."

Each of Paul's "exemplar" texts seems to be part of a longer passage, most likely a *written* passage.

Once more we ask: how did Paul know about the manner of life of the historical Jesus? Once again, we offer the same answer: Paul had access to these written teachings through his four (known) visits to Jerusalem, and through mission associates who had been members of the Jerusalem Church (Barnabas, John Mark, and Silvanus).

Paul's Liturgical Texts

Of great significance are the two "traditions" embedded in First Corinthians:

11:23–25	"I *received* from the Lord what I *delivered* to you, that the Lord Jesus, on the night he was betrayed."
15:3–7	"I *delivered* to you … what I also *received* that Christ died for our sins … that he was raised on the third day."

Taken together these "traditions" teach that Christ died "for our sins" and that he was raised on the third day, sealing our salvation. William Wrede and others claim that *Paul* imposed these redemptive motifs on Jesus the teacher thereby eclipsing him and, as a consequence, redefining Christianity.

But Paul did not invent these words, but rather "delivered" to the Corinthians the pre-formatted "traditions" he had "received." From whom did he receive them if not from the apostles in Jerusalem? And when did the apostles formulate them? A matter of months after Jesus left them. The Lord's Supper tradition originated with "the Lord" at the Last Supper, "on *the night* he was betrayed." The point is: Paul did not create these redemptive traditions.

The two pre-formulated "traditions" embedded in Paul's letter, but which originated back-to-back with Jesus in Jerusalem, are the death knell to Wrede's view that Paul pushed Jesus the teacher to one side and replaced him with the crucified and resurrected redeemer.

Wrede's accusation that Paul recast his presentation of Jesus away from the "real" Jesus is not true to the facts. Such information that Paul gives us about Jesus is innocently consistent with Paul's life story and his genuine but incomplete knowledge about the One he called "Lord."

Wrede and those who follow him are wrong in asserting that Paul reinvented Christianity. On the contrary, he faithfully and effectively proclaimed the gospel in line with the proclamation of the other apostles:

> Whether it was I or *they* [the apostles] so *we* preach and so you [Corinthians] believed. (1 Cor 15:11)

Paul claimed that the "pillars" of the Jerusalem Church endorsed his preaching:

> I set before them [James, Peter, John] the gospel that I proclaim among the Gentiles, in order to make sure I was not running in vain, or had not run in vain. (Gal 2:3)

The John Tradition and Paul

The Patristic assertion is that John "issued" his Gospel in Ephesus.[8] Our problem is that we are not able to trace the development of the tradition that began with Jesus and developed into the Gospel of John (see chapter 22). I will argue that John created an earlier version of his Gospel during his years in Palestine before he moved to Asia (middle 50s?).

John's Gospel, more than any other, is filled with cultural, geographical, and political details that suggests the writer's closeness to the land in the time of Jesus (see later, chapter 22). Furthermore, John's name is often linked with the leader Peter in the earliest years of ministry in Israel[9] and in c. 47 he was named as one of the three "pillars" of the church in Jerusalem (Gal 2:9). However, there is little evidence from outside the Gospel to help us trace its journey from Jesus to its completion.

Paul and John each express a high Christology and speak extensively of the "kingdom of God" as present and active in the ministry of Jesus. The theme of servant-hood is common to both Paul and John.[10] Both authors make extensive use of the verb "believe."

However, their terminology differs at many points. For example, John frequently refers to Jesus as Son of Man, a term Paul does not use. Paul's Jesus is the heavenly Lord whereas John portrays Jesus as an earth-bound figure who was destined to go to the Father only after his passion.

There is the tantalizing possibility of a connection between Jesus' reference to "the temple" of his "body" (John 2:21) and Paul's many ecclesial references to "temple" and "body."[11] The physical temple is important in the narratives of the Synoptic Gospels but they do not speak about Jesus' body as the temple. Only the Gospel of John makes that connection, which may have influenced Paul. We know that Paul and John met in Jerusalem in c. 47 (Gal 2:9), and probably on other occasions as well.

---

8. In c. 180 Irenaeus wrote, "After them [Matthew, Mark, and Luke] John the disciple of the Lord, who reclined on his breast issued a Gospel while he was living at Ephesus in Asia" (*Against the Heresies* III.1.1). Irenaeus was well placed to make this statement. He had been the disciple of Polycarp who had been the disciple of John. Irenaeus's words, "issued a Gospel," make it possible to understand that John had written the Gospel (or a draft version) earlier (in Palestine).

9. Acts 3:1, 3, 4, 11; 4:13, 19; 8:14.

10. 2 Cor 4:5; John 13:16.

11. e.g., 1 Cor 3:16; 12:2.

Conclusion

The implied claim that Paul conspired to misrepresent Jesus, as proposed many years ago by William Wrede, a claim that continues in the popular media, is not sustainable. The very thing that Wrede accused Paul of doing, of making Jesus the teacher into Christ the crucified and risen redeemer, is exactly the message he "received" very early from the foundation apostles in Jerusalem, whose words are embedded as pre-formatted liturgy and catechesis in First Corinthians. These words were created in the shadow of the historical Jesus and "delivered" to Paul, most probably when he spent time with Cephas and James (Gal 1:18–19).

six

Jerusalem: The James Years (c. 42–62)

JAMES, THE BROTHER OF the Lord, became the leader of the Jerusalem Church in c. 42.[1] Peter fled from the hands of King Herod Agrippa 1 (probably in that year) making possible the elevation of James to the leadership, a position he held until his martyrdom in 62. In c. 44 Peter returned to Jerusalem following the death of the king,[2] but now as the second "pillar" after James (Gal 2:9). Soon after 48 Peter withdrew from Jerusalem for a brief period in Antioch (Gal 2:11) before moving west through Asia Minor and Corinth to Rome.

It is almost certain that James, head of the Jerusalem Church, was the author of the letter that bears the name of James. There were five men of that name in the New Testament, but there are positive reasons to identify the author as the brother of Jesus and long-time leader of the Jerusalem Church.[3]

The unadorned opening of the encyclical epistle from "James the servant of the Lord Jesus Christ" addressed to "the twelve tribes in the Dispersion" implies a sender of the considerable authority that James enjoyed.[4]

1. Acts 12:17; Gal 2:9.
2. Acts 12:20–23; Josephus, *Jewish Antiquities* 19:346.
3. Had the letter been pseudonymous, as many hold it to have been, we would have expected the writer overtly to claim to be "the brother of Jesus" or "First Pillar in Jerusalem."
4. Gal 2:9,12; Acts 15:19–21. Robinson (*Redating the New Testament*, 131–34) effectively responds to objections that James, brother of Jesus, was the author of this letter. Included among the objections is the linguistic consideration that James is written in "high *koine*" where Robinson appeals to the writings of Sevenster, Argyle, and Zahn in defense of Jacobean authorship.

Dating the Letter of James

The time frame of the epistle is defined by James's rise to power in c. 42 and his martyrdom in 62.[5] Did James write at the beginning of this two-decade period, at the middle, or at the end? Or, to be more radical, did he write sometime between his conversion in 33 and his elevation to the leadership in c. 42?

Much depends on James's qualified use of the words "faith," "saved," "justified," and "imputed," words that appear in Paul's letters.[6] But who was responding to whom? The more polemical tone in Jas 2:14-16 suggests that James was responding to Paul, not vice versa.

Was James responding to Romans written in 57 or to the Galatians written in 48? Since Paul's Galatians letter is quite polemical, James is more likely to be responding to it rather than to his more measured Letter to the Romans. In this case we would date James' letter to 49 or 50.

Another possibility, however, is that James was not responding to a letter but to *verbal* reports about Paul's keywords that had come to James's attention during Paul's decade long ministry in Syria-Cilicia. Paul informed the Galatians that the churches of Judea were hearing of his preaching in Syria-Cilicia (37-47).[7] If verbal reports of Paul's preaching were the explanation for James's response it would make his letter quite early, as early as the mid-to-late 40s, and therefore the earliest document of Christianity.

Whether James was responding to verbal reports of Paul's preaching, or to his Letter to the Galatians, we are able to say with reasonable confidence that James wrote his circular letter to a network of Jewish Christian churches by AD 50.

A Jewish Mission

Peter's initial ministry was to Jews in Jerusalem and then throughout the three regions of Israel: Judea, Samaria, and Galilee (Gal 2:7-8; Acts 9:31-32). At the same time, however, he took the gospel to Samaritans

---

5. James was executed under the High Priest Annas II during the interregnum between the death in office of the procurator Festus and the arrival of his successor Albinus (Josephus, *Jewish Antiquities* 20.200).

6. Jas 2:14-26; Gal 2:16; 3:6; Rom 4:1-6.

7. Gal 1:21-23.

and Gentiles.[8] Nevertheless, Peter's ministry (33–47) was directed primarily to Jews.

At the meeting in Jerusalem in c. 47 between leaders of the church of Jerusalem (James, Cephas, and John) and the leaders from the church in Antioch (Barnabas and Paul) it was agreed that the two missions were to continue, the Jerusalem-based mission to Jews and the Antioch-based mission to Gentiles (Gal 2:9). After 47, however, Peter was no longer in Jerusalem leaving James even more the center of power. This helps explain how the church in Jerusalem became more conservatively Jewish. In 57 James told Paul, "You see brother [Paul] how many thousands among the Jews of those who have believed. They are all *zealous for the law*" (Acts 21:20).

When Peter left Jerusalem for (a brief) ministry in Antioch-in-Syria (48–52?) it was most likely directed to Jews,[9] and we suppose also in his journeys westward, including at Corinth. Paul's reference in Corinth to "brothers of the Lord and Cephas" implies a Jewish mission, as distinct from Paul's gentile mission.[10]

A Jewish mission outside Israel is assumed by James's letter addressed to "twelve tribes of the Dispersion," that is, to Christian Jews living away from the holy land as part of the "diaspora" of Christian Jews. As to their location, its Greek language suggests countries to the east of Greece. Beyond that we cannot be sure.

We know that the high priest in Jerusalem exercised his authority in the Jewish diaspora as well as in the Land of Israel. James, as brother of the Lord, and head of the Jerusalem Church, was a kind of parallel leader to the high priest. James writes with complete authority over these scattered Jewish Christians, expecting his words to be heeded. James's dispatch of envoys to Antioch in c. 48 who gave his directions to Peter, Barnabas, and the Jewish members of the church implies the authority of the head of the church in Jerusalem beyond the borders of Israel (Gal 2:11–14).

There is an important point of contrast between Paul and James as sources for the words of Jesus. Paul was not part of the Jerusalem Church, but dependent for his knowledge on his four (known) visits to the city, and on his contact with those like Barnabas, Mark, and Silvanus who

---

8. Acts 8:14–25; 10:1—11:18.
9. Gal 2:11–16.
10. 1 Cor 9:5.

had been members of the church. James, however, was a member of the church in Jerusalem from its birth in 33 to his death in 62. James had direct access to the Gospel-tradition streams, whereas Paul's access was secondary and indirect.

Gospel Sources Underlying James's Letter

One striking feature of the Letter of James is its many allusions to Jesus' words as they would appear later in the Gospels in the Synoptic tradition. These belong to two categories. First, there are a number of "content links" between individual words in Matthew and James,[11] for example:

	James	Matthew
perfect	1:4	5:48; 19:21
righteousness	1:20; 3:18	3:15; 5:6, 10, 20; 6:1, 33
church	5:7	16:18; 18:17
"*parousia*	5:7	24:3, 27, 37, 39
oaths	5:12	5:33–37

This common vocabulary between James and the underlying sources behind the Gospel of Matthew points to commonality of thought.

Another and more remarkable feature is the frequency of phrases that appear also in the Gospels. John Painter has combined the lists of Ralph Martin and P. J. Hartin, making thirty-three in all.[12] Rather more conservatively, I have identified twenty-two possible textual links.[13]

---

11. For a complete list see Adamson, *Epistle of James*, 188.
12. Painter, *Just James*, 261–62.
13. I acknowledge the invaluable assistance of an older text, Manson, *Sayings of Jesus*. Manson addresses in turn the texts of "Q," "L," and "M" and engages in exegesis of those texts.

James	Matthew	Luke
1:2 Count it all *joy* . . . when you meet various trials. 1:12 *Blessed* is the man who endures trial.	5:10, 12 *Blessed* are those who are persecuted . . . *Rejoice* and be *glad*. [Sermon of the Mount] "Q"	6:22 *Blessed* are you when people hate you . . . on account of the Son of Man. Rejoice in that day, and leap for *joy*. "Q"
1:5 If any of you lacks wisdom, let him *ask* God, who gives to all generously.	7:7 *Ask* and it will be given you. [Sermon of the Mount]	11:9 *Ask*, and it will be given you. [Q source]
1:17 Every *good gift* . . . coming down the Father.	7:11 How much more will your Father . . . give *good gifts* to those who ask him. [Sermon of the Mount] "Q"	11:13 How much more will the heavenly Father give the Holy Spirit to those who *ask*. [Parable of The Friend at Midnight] "Q"
1:20 The *anger* of man does not work the righteousness of God.	5:22 Everyone who is *angry* with his brother shall be liable to judgment. [Sermon of the Mount] "M"	
1:22 Be *doers* of the word, not hearers only.	7:24 Everyone who hears these words . . . and *does* them. [Sermon of the Mount] "M" (?)	
2:5 Has not God chosen the *poor* to be . . . *heirs of the kingdom*.	5:3 Blessed are the *poor* in spirit, for theirs is the *kingdom* of heaven. [Sermon of the Mount] "Q"	6:20 Blessed are you *poor*, for yours is the *kingdom* of God. [Sermon on the Plain]
2:8 The royal law . . . "You shall love your neighbor as yourself."	Mark 12:31 The second is this, "You shall love your neighbor as yourself." Matt 22:39	10:27–28 You shall love . . . your neighbor as yourself. [Parable of Good Samaritan] "L"

JERUSALEM: THE JAMES YEARS (C. 42–62)

James	Matthew	Luke
2:10 Whoever keeps the whole law but fails in one point has become guilty of all of it.	5:19 Whoever relaxes one of the least of these commandments . . . shall be . . . least in the kingdom, but he who . . . does them . . . shall be called great in the kingdom. [Sermon of the Mount] "M"	
2:13 For judgment is without *mercy* to one who has shown no mercy, yet mercy triumphs over judgement.	5:7 Blessed are the *merciful*, for they shall obtain *mercy*. [Sermon of the Mount] "Q"	6:37 Forgive and you will be forgiven.
2:14 What does it profit . . . if a man says he has faith, but has no works?	7:21 Not everyone who says to me, "Lord, Lord" shall enter the kingdom of heaven, but he who does the will of my Father. [Sermon of the Mount] "Q"	6:46 Why do you call me "Lord, Lord" and not do what I tell you? [Sermon of the Plain]
3:12 Can a *fig* tree . . . yield olives or a grapevine figs?	7:17 Are *grapes* gathered from thorns, or *figs* from thistles? [Sermon of the Mount] "Q"	6:44 *Figs* are not gathered from *thorns*, nor grapes picked from a bramble bush. [Sermon on the Plain]
3:13 Who is wise and understanding among you? By his good life let him show his works in the *meekness* of wisdom.	5:5 Blessed are the *meek*. [Sermon of the Mount] "M" [?]	

James	Matthew	Luke
4:4 Do you not know that friendship with the world is enmity with God? Therefore whoever wishes to be a friend of the world makes himself and enemy of God.	6:24 No one can serve two masters; for either he will hate the one and love the other or he will devoted to the one and despise the other. You cannot serve God and mammon. [Sermon of the Mount] "Q"	16:13 No servant can serve two masters; for either he will hate the one and love the other, or he will be devoted to the one and despise the other. You cannot serve God and mammon. [Parable of Unjust Steward]
4:8 Cleanse your hands you sinners and *purify your hearts*, you men of double mind.	5:8 Blessed are *the pure in heart*, for they shall see God. [Sermon of the Mount] "M" [?]	
4:9 Be wretched and mourn and weep. Let your *laughter* be turned to mourning and your joy to dejection.		6:25 Woe to you that *laugh* now, for you shall mourn and weep. [Sermon on the Plain] "L" [?]
4:10 *Humble* yourselves before the Lord and he will *exalt* you.	23:12 Whoever *exalts* himself will be humbled and whoever humbles himself will be exalted. [Speech against Pharisees] "Q"	14:11 Everyone who exalts himself will be humbled and he who humbles himself will be exalted. [Parable of Wedding Feast]
4:11 Do not speak evil against one another, brothers. He that speaks evil against a brother or *judges* a brother, speaks evil against the law and judges the law.	5:22 Everyone who is angry with his brother shall be liable to *judgment*. [Sermon of the Mount] 7:1 *Judge* not that you be not judged. [Sermon of the Mount] "Q"	

James	Matthew	Luke
5:1 Come now, you *rich*, weep and howl for the miseries that are coming upon you.	19:23 It will be hard for a *rich* man to enter the kingdom of heaven. [Rich Young Man] "Q"	6:24–25 Woe to you that are *rich*, for you have received your consolation. Woe to you who are full now, for you shall hunger. [Sermon on the Plain]
5:2 Your *riches* have rotted and your garments are *moth* eaten.	6:20 Lay up for yourselves *treasures* in heaven, where neither *moth* nor rust consumes. [Sermon of the Mount] "M"	
5:12 *Do not swear*, either by *heaven* or by earth, or with any other oath, but let your yes be yes and your no be no, that you may not fall under condemnation.	5:34–35 *Do not swear* at all, either *by heaven* for it is the throne of God, *or by the earth* for it is his footstool. [Sermon of the Mount] "Q"	
5:19–20 My brothers, if any one among you *wanders from the truth* and some one *brings him back* let him know that whoever brings a sinner from the error of his way will save his own soul from death and will cover a multitude of sins.	18:15 If your brother *sins* against you, go tell him his fault, between you and him alone. If he *listens to* you have gained your brother. "Q"	17:3 If your brother sins, rebuke him, and if he repents, forgive him.

James and the Sermon on the Mount

Even in this relatively conservative list there are no exact or clear-cut quotations by James from the synoptic traditions. Sometimes they are little more than faint echoes.

Of the quoted texts from James that have echoes in the Gospels we note the following frequencies:

"Q"	12 from Sermon on the Mount
	5 from Sermon on the Plain
Mark	1 (?)
"M"	6 from Sermon on the Mount

The overwhelming impression is that James refers to (a version of) the Sermon on the Mount, which implies that it was already an embryonic *entity*, one that had already combined the underlying sources "Q" and "M."

While details are lacking, it seems that a group or groups in the Jerusalem Church had gathered texts to represent Jesus' teaching in the Sermon on the Mount. This observation would recognize the fact (historicity) of the Sermon on the Mount.

Jesus According to James: Teacher or Lord?

"Receive the word" (1:21) is an exhortation that sums up the message of the Letter of James. The many echoes of Jesus' words in this letter indicate that "the word" is the word that Jesus had spoken. This in turn strongly implies that in James' mind Jesus was first and foremost a *teacher*.

This observation has led some to assert that according to James Jesus was not also a Savior. After all, James does not refer even once to Jesus' death and therefore has nothing to say about the atonement, a doctrine that is so prominent in the letters of Paul, the Letter to the Hebrews, and the First Letter of Peter.

Some have bracketed the Letter of James with the "Q" source, which, it is claimed, is a teaching manual pure and simple lacking any narrative or doctrine about Jesus' death and resurrection.

Accordingly (some argue), there is something suspicious here. The Letter of James presents Jesus as a teacher, the Jesus as he really was, the authentic Jesus. Paul and Mark, however, have remade Jesus the teacher into someone he never was, a divine redeemer.

A careful reading of James, however, issues in a more nuanced picture. According to James's letter, "our Lord Jesus Christ" is "the Lord of glory," a Lord whose "coming" is to be the "judge," who will bring punishment to the wicked.[14] He is an eschatological figure, "the Lord," no less.

14.. Jas 2:1; 5:7–9.

Rather than look for a conspiracy by Paul and Mark, it is better to recognize that there were various schools of thought within the Jerusalem Church, of which the Letter of James represented one among others. While it is true that James is silent about the death of Jesus and therefore its saving effects, it does not therefore mean that James denied the truth of those doctrines. Silence does not necessarily imply a contrary view.

James quotes from the "Q" source, but also the "M" source. The "Jewishness" of the Letter of James is congruent with the recognized Jewishness of the "M" source (see chapter 17). Yet that source contains Jesus' famous invitation to those bowed down by the "yoke" of the law: "Come to *me*, all who labor and are heavy laden, and *I* will give you rest" (Matt 11:28). In other words, within the very Jewish "M" source there is the personal, *Jesus*-centered invitation to those burdened by law-keeping. We are not able to pigeonhole Jesus merely as a teacher of ethical behavior. His invitation was to come to *him*.

The Letter of James gives us a passing glimpse into a faction within the church in Jerusalem. There is much that we do not know because there is no way of knowing. Like our other reconstructions there is much that remains a mystery, and will remain a mystery. But that doesn't open the door to theories of conspiracy, for example, that Paul and Mark remade Jesus a mere teacher into something he never was, the Lord and the judge.

Conclusion

The reasonable assumption is that James the letter-writer was the brother of the Lord and long-time member, then leader of the church in Jerusalem (33–62). He wrote with authority to the Jewish Christian diaspora, although the precise dating is uncertain. His employment of the words of the Lord is striking, although the precise number is difficult to identify with confidence. That said, however, James's use of echoes of the Sermon on the Mount is significant.

Lack of evidence means that we do not know how James had access to the words and teachings of Jesus. Did they exist in oral form or in writing? Does his referencing of words from "Q" and "M" indicate the likely existence of those parallel sources within the faith community in Jerusalem? Did the existence of those and other sources imply factions or groups within the Jerusalem Church who identified themselves with those sources?

Once again we are forced to admit various mysteries underlying the writing of this letter, including its writing in high quality Greek. But the simplicity and moral "goodness" of the letter are silent witnesses against any notion of conspiracy.

seven

The Anti-Pauline Counter Mission[1]

ALMOST FROM THE BEGINNING of Christian history there was division within the church in Jerusalem over the terms by which a Gentile might be included in the covenant people of God.

Criticism of Peter

We first meet this problem in the late 30s. When Peter returned to Jerusalem after baptizing members of the household of the Gentile Cornelius in Caesarea those of "the circumcision party" made this serious accusation: "You went to uncircumcised men and ate with them" (Acts 11:3).[2]

---

1. The identity and mission(s) of the opponents of Paul have generated considerable interest and difference of opinion. For critical reviews see Ellis, "Paul and His Opponents," 264–98; or, more briefly Hafemann, "Paul and His Interpreters," 666–71, who concluded that the issue was "deadlocked." The position taken here is broadly in line with Ellis's viewpoint.

2. Acts 10:14–16, 28. We know from other sources that Jews would not eat with Gentiles. The much traveled Philostratus, biographer of the wonderworker Apollonius of Tyana, commented on the distinctiveness of the Jews:

> For the Jews have long been in revolt not only against the Romans but against humanity; and a race that has made its own a life apart and irreconcilable, that cannot share with the rest of mankind the pleasures of the table nor join in their libations or sacrifices. (*Life of Apollonius* 5.33)

The historian Tacitus a former senator and consul in Rome who became Proconsul of Asia early in the second century had extensive opportunities to observe their behavior in a province where there were large concentrations of Jews.

> The Jews . . . sit apart at meals, and they sleep apart. . . . They adopted circumcision and distinguish themselves from other people by this difference. Those who are converted to their ways follow the same practice. (*Histories* 5.5)

Luke introduces these complainants without further explanation. His description of them as "the circumcision party" (*hoi ek peritomēs*) identifies them as insisting on the circumcising of non-Jews as a prerequisite of belonging to God's covenant people.

The Titus Incident

Paul and Barnabas met similar hostility in c. 47 when they brought the uncircumcised Titus to Jerusalem (Gal 2:1, 3). Those whom Paul called "false brothers" attempted to have Titus circumcised, presumably as a condition of table fellowship. It is reasonable to believe that the "false brothers" held the same views as "the circumcision party" who confronted Peter a decade earlier.

The Galatians passage explains that James, Cephas, and John, leading "pillars" of the Jerusalem Church, joined Barnabas and Paul in resisting the circumcision of Titus. This critical incident in Jerusalem revealed at least two parties in the church in the holy city in c. 47:

The main church led by James, Cephas (Peter), and John	The "false brothers" faction
Free regarding the circumcision of the Gentile, Titus	Demanding the circumcision of the Gentile, Titus

"Agitators" in Galatia (Gal 1:7; 5:10)

In c. 48 Paul and Barnabas established churches in Pisidia and Lycaonia (southern Galatia) whereupon a counter-mission from Jerusalem sought to impose "works of the law" (male circumcision and observation of the Jewish Calendar) on the gentile converts.[3] Their message to the gentile believers was that unless they observed these "works" they could not be "children of Abraham" and not be members of the "Israel of God."[4]

Paul's intense scripture-based counter arguments[5] suggest that these "agitators" were proficient biblical scholars, almost certainly from the tradition of the Pharisees.

---

3. Gal 5:2; 4:10.
4. Gal 3:6–14; 6:16.
5. Gal 3:7–14; 4:21–31.

The Incident in Antioch

This critical incident is reported in both Paul's Letter to the Galatians (2:11–14) and in the Acts of the Apostles (15:1–2). Both texts indicate that members who had come from the Jerusalem Church were the source of the dissension and division that accompanied their visit. Paul states that the troublemakers were envoys from James,[6] whereas Luke more baldly describes them as "men" who had "come down from Judea."

The accounts emphasize different but related elements of the Jerusalem-based counter-mission. According to Galatians, the issue was the necessity for Jewish believers to discontinue eating with non-Jewish believers. Luke, however, said the issue was circumcision: "Unless you are circumcised according to the custom of Moses, you cannot be saved."

When we combine the data from Galatians and Acts (which is reasonable to do) it appears that the men from Jerusalem demanded, as a condition of covenantal membership, that male Gentiles submit to circumcision, and that all Gentiles commit to the adoption of Jewish dietary rules, and adherence to the Jewish calendar. In a word, the counter-mission was a proselytizing mission. These missionaries expected and demanded that baptized Gentiles adopt the tenets and practices of Judaism.

"Trouble" in the Gentile Churches in Syria and Cilicia

The "apostles and elders" in Jerusalem sent an important letter to "the brothers who are of the Gentiles in Antioch and Syria and Cilicia" (Acts 16:23). The letter referred to recent "trouble" created by the visit of a Jerusalem-based proselytizing mission to Paul's home province. Some time later Paul and Silas "went through Syria and Cilicia, strengthening the churches" by delivering the letter from Jerusalem (Acts 16:41).

Paul had spent about a decade in this province (AD 37–47), although our knowledge is limited to just a few matters. First, Paul's preaching of the gospel was so vigorous that it came to the attention of the distant churches in Judea (Gal 1:22–24). Second, Paul established a network of gentile churches in this province (Acts 15:23, 41). Third, (almost certainly) Paul received "the forty strokes less one" from the synagogue

---

6. We may only speculate why James changed his attitudes between 47 and 48. Was it in reaction to the new Procurator of Judea, Tiberius Alexander, who was an apostate Jew and a heavy-handed governor AD 46–48? See Josephus, *Jewish War* 2.220, 223.

authorities during these "hidden years" in Syria-Cilicia.[7] Fourth, Paul's "rapture" to "the third heaven"/"Paradise" (2 Cor 12:2–3) of which he writes in c. 56 would have occurred during the years he spent in his home province.[8] The onset of the mysterious "thorn" occurred at that time (2 Cor 12:7).

Paul claims that since Damascus he had consistently proclaimed the way of "faith" in Christ and not the "works of the law," and that the Jerusalem "pillar" apostles, James, Cephas, and John endorsed the rightness of this message (Gal 2:3), whereupon they extended the right hand of fellowship to him for a further "going" to the non-Jewish world (Gal 2:9).

Unfortunately the texts do not specify the teachings of those who "troubled" Paul's gentile churches in Syria-Cilicia. However, there is no reason to doubt that they were conservative Jewish Christians who insisted that non-Jewish believers adopt the "works of the law," that is, male circumcision, the adoption of dietary rules, and the observance of the Jewish feasts.

Second Corinthians (c. 56): Peddlers, Super Apostles, False Apostles

The argument that Paul's three epithets in the sub-heading apply to the same missionaries in Corinth depends on the unity of Second Corinthians.[9] Paul's accusation of "*peddling* the word of God" (2:17) implied

---

7. 2 Cor 11:24; Deut 25:1–3. The most likely explanation is that Paul preached in the synagogues of Syria-Cilicia AD 37–47 that Christ crucified, not law-keeping, was the pathway to "life" and for this heretical teaching he received this brutal flogging multiple times. A person condemned for heresy could choose to be expelled from Judaism, or be beaten. Paul repeatedly chose the beating in order to remain a Jew. See Barnett, *Paul in Syria*, 20–24.

8. Barnett, *Paul in Syria*, 24–24, 126.

9. For extended surveys of the literary integrity of 2 Corinthians see Harris, *Second Epistle to the Corinthians*, 8–51. In defense of its unity, see Vegge, *2 Corinthians*, 12–34; and for the contra view, see Welborn, *End to Enmity*, xix–xxii, for advocacy of a partition theory. Welborn goes so far as to say, "The composition of 2 Corinthians is so problematic that the unity of 2 Corinthians must be regarded as a hypothesis in need of demonstration" (xix). Welborn thinks that there were five original letters that were later combined as our 2 Corinthians. Dunn, *Beginning from Jerusalem*, 835, however, strikes a fatal blow against partition theories:

> My only problem is with envisaging the situation and motivation which caused some anonymous collector or editor to chop off the introductions and conclusions to each letter and simply to stick the torsos together in such

a pecuniary motive; his ironic depiction of them as "*super* apostles" was because they claimed *superiority* over Paul (11:5; 12:11); and his deadly ascription of them as "*false* apostles" was because they preached "*another* Jesus . . . a *different* gospel" (11:4). These descriptors are damning of those who had come to oust Paul from his leadership of the church in Corinth.

They came as an alternative mission, with an alternative message. They sought to match Paul so as to supersede him, and thus exclude him, installing themselves in his place.

Paul	*Counter-Mission*	*2 Corinthians*
Paul is a Jew	They are Jews	11:22
He calls himself a minister	They call themselves ministers	6:3 | 11:23
He calls himself apostle	They call themselves apostles	1:1 | 11:5, 13
He preaches the word of God	They preach the word of God	2:17; 4:2
He preaches the gospel	They preach the gospel	10:14 | 11:4
He preaches Jesus	They preach Jesus	4:5 | 11:4

They describe themselves and what they do along identical lines as Paul. In every sense they are an alternative but, according to them, a *superior* mission. C. K. Barrett identified them as "Jews, Jerusalem Jews, Judaizing Jews" who "constituted a rival apostolate to Paul's."[10]

Further qualifiers should be added. First, these newcomers were Pharisees, as indicated by Paul's mirror exegesis of his Midrash on Exod 34:29–35 (2 Cor 3:7–18). It was necessary for Paul to fight Scripture with Scripture. Second, they came as "ministers of Christ" who "preached . . . Jesus . . . the gospel" (11:23, 4). They were, in their eyes, but not in Paul's, a *Christian* mission.

Paul's engagement with the counter-missionaries throughout Second Corinthians provides an invaluable profile of their identity and objectives. It is reasonable to see that letter as complementing the data about them in Galatians, and in their proselytizing activities in Antioch and within the province of Syria-Cilicia.

---

an awkward way as to raise the questions which the various amalgamation hypotheses are designed to resolve. Why not retain them as complete letters?

10. Barrett, "Paul's Opponents," 251. We agree with this well-known definition, except that "Judaizing" does not mean "proselytizing Judaism," but rather "*living as* a Jew" (Gal 2:14). For a contra view to Barrett's see Watson, *Paul, Judaism*, who identified the false apostles with Apollos and his companions (in my opinion, implausibly).

There are two further dramatic observations that emerge from Second Corinthians. One is that they must have been fluent Greek speakers to win the support of the church in Greek-speaking Corinth, and the other is that they were accomplished orators (11:5).[11]

Conclusion: This Faction and the Gospel Sources

If these men came from Jerusalem, as Barrett rightly said, the profile of them we discover from this letter opens a remarkable window through which to see a major faction within the church in Jerusalem. It is quite unexpected to consider that there were Pharisaic Jews in the holy city who were Christians,[12] and who were accomplished Greek speakers whose rhetorical skills had impressed the Corinthians.

If this is correct it raises the question of this faction's influence on the developing traditions that would later be woven into the Gospels. It is, however, difficult to detect their signature doctrines—chiefly their focus on the law and "works of the law"—within the sources Mark, "Q," "L," and "M."

Perhaps, though, this law-based faction influenced "M," the most "Jewish" of the Synoptic sources? This is unlikely. The "M" source is firmly directed to the inclusion of the Gentiles, and without any suggestion of the necessity for Jewish practices ("works of the law"). Furthermore, negatively quoted in "M" is the burdensome "yoke" (of the law) that Jesus sets against his "easy" yoke.

---

11. Rabban Gamaliel II, from late first into second century, was said to have had one thousand students, five hundred of whom studied the Torah and five hundred who studied Greek wisdom (quoted in Feldman, *Jew and Gentile*, 37).

12. But see Acts 15:5; 21:20–21.

eight

The Church in Antioch

THE CHURCH IN ANTIOCH became the second center of Christianity, after Jerusalem (Antioch was the third city of the empire, after Rome and Alexandria). The big question is: did Antioch become one of the centers that produced texts that ultimately found their way into the Gospels? For example, did Antioch become the creator and custodian of the "Q" source?

The probable answer is in the negative, for the reason that an apostle, one who had been a disciple of the Lord, was not the founder of this church.

Christianity in Antioch

Christianity was introduced to the great metropolis of Antioch in the middle-late 30s by successive waves of Greek-speaking Jewish believers. Some had been displaced by Paul's persecutions in Jerusalem in c. 34 while others—for reasons not known—had traveled there from Cyprus and Cyrene (North Africa). The first wave confined their ministry to Jews, but the second spoke also to "Greeks" (i.e., Gentiles). At point the believers in Antioch were said to be a "church" (Acts 11:26).

Based on Acts 11:19–26 it appears that the foundation membership of the church was exclusively Jewish. We do not know the names of the first leaders.

In the early-to-mid 40s the church in Jerusalem sent Barnabas to supervise this new church. Barnabas in turn brought Paul from Tarsus to share the pastoral load, caring for this now expanding church. It is likely that Paul's presence was the catalyst for the inclusion of additional gentile believers, for example, Titus (Gal 2:1).

According to Acts 13:1 the leaders of the church were Barnabas, Simeon who was called Niger, Lucius of Cyrene, Manaen (former courtier of Herod the tetrarch), and Paul. Each named leader was Jewish, which probably reflected a dominant membership in the church in the year 47.

It was during the absence of Paul and Barnabas in their mission to Cyprus and Southern Galatia that Peter came to the church in Antioch (Gal 2:11). When the missionaries returned they faced a crisis. James had sent envoys to put pressure on Peter, Barnabas, and the Jewish believers (a majority?) to separate at meals from the non-Jewish members (Gal 2:11–13).

Paul strongly resisted this move and the matter was debated and resolved later in Jerusalem. It is likely that the liberalizing decisions of the Jerusalem Council in c. 49 as conveyed to Antioch by Judas called Barsabbas and Silas (Silvanus) settled the matter, making Jew-Gentile unity in this church a reality once more.

It seems that Peter continued as leader in Antioch, that is, from about 48 to 52. We do not know who led this church once Peter traveled on to the west.

Conclusion: Gospel Sources in Antioch

We are right to think that written ministry resources would have been formulated in the great centers of Christianity whose leaders were apostolic figures. Jerusalem, led by Peter then James, is a likely such a center, but so too is Rome as led by Peter. What, then, about Antioch?

Lack of apostolic foundation and subsequent leadership suggests that Antioch did not produce sources that would later belong to the Gospels.

nine

Rome: The Peter Years (c. 55–c. 64)

WE DO NOT KNOW how Christians first came to the imperial capital. According to the book of Acts there were Jews from Rome in Jerusalem for the Feast of Pentecost who heard Peter speak about Jesus the Christ (Acts 2:10). Perhaps some of these were baptized and took their new faith back to Rome. We may further suppose that these earliest believers in Rome, being Jews, continued as members of synagogues in Rome.

Our earliest knowledge of Christianity in Rome is dated to c. 49 when Claudius Caesar expelled the Jews from the city on account of "disturbances at the instigation of Chrestus."[1] It is widely accepted that "Chrestus" was a misspelling of "Christus" and that the Jewish Christians' adherence to Christ was the source of the "disturbances" that brought division to the synagogues and in turn prompted the Caesar to expel all the Jews from Rome.

Among the exiles were Priscilla and Aquila who may have been leaders of the followers of Christ in Rome, who were forced to emigrate to Corinth.[2]

Our next window into Christianity in Rome is in 57 through Paul's letter to a network of house churches that were part of his Gentile mission (Rom 16:3–16). Paul acknowledged the presence of a foundation layer in Rome, whom he does not name, but upon whose foundation he will not build. This assumes the existence of two Christian groups in Rome by the mid-50s, one led by Paul and the other by the unnamed foundation layer.

It appears that after his visit to Corinth Peter arrived in Rome, perhaps by the mid-50s. Almost certainly he was the unnamed

1. Suetonius, *Claudius* 5.4.
2. Acts 18:2.

apostolic foundation layer, upon whose structure Paul would not build (Rom 15:20–21).

Peter in Rome

We know that Peter left Jerusalem for Antioch in c. 48 and after several years traveled westward to Corinth (in 52 or 53). After some months in Corinth he traveled to Rome, probably via Sicily. There is a credible tradition that Peter founded Christianity in Syracuse, Sicily.[3] From there he traveled to Rome, either by road from Puteoli (Naples) via the Appian Way or by sea through Ostia ("mouth" of the Tiber), arriving in the mid-fifties.

References to "Babylon" (code for Rome; see below) in 1 Pet 5:13 establish that Peter did, in fact, come to Rome. He identified himself as "apostle" (1:1) and "presbyter" (or "elder"—5:1). There can be little doubt the Peter was the senior presbyter of the apostolic church in Rome[4] and the unnamed foundation layer Paul mentions in Romans (Rom 15:20).

There are strong hints that Peter was a casualty of Nero's attack on the Christians following the Great Fire in July 64. Hints in the Gospel of John suggest that Peter was crucified (cf. John 21:18–19: "Truly, truly, I say to you, when you were young, you used to dress yourself and walk wherever you wanted, but *when you are old*, you will stretch out your hands, and another will dress you and carry you *where you do not want to go*." This he said to show by what kind of death he was to glorify God. And after saying this he said to him, "Follow me").

Since the overwhelming opinion was that Peter was the influence and authority behind the Gospel of Mark (see later, chapter 16) a likely

---

3. The Catholic cathedral in Syracuse, Sicily, contains an inscription on both sides of the nave: *ecclesia syracusana prima divi Petri filia, et prima post Antiochenam Christo dicata*. Possible translations are: "The church of Syracuse is the first daughter of St. Peter and the second after the church of Antioch dedicated to Christ" or "The Church of Syracuse first daughter of the divine Peter and the first since that of Antioch dedicated to Christ." The inscription does not arise directly out of any text in the New Testament and for that reason may represent a very old tradition that arose from Peter's journey from Antioch through Corinth to Rome.

4. Paul's mission in Rome, as indicated by Rom 16, appears to have been a distinct and separate group. Peter's letters to and from Rome (Romans and Philippians) make no mention of Peter, except perhaps to an unnamed foundation layer (Rom 15:20).

scenario is that Mark joined Peter in Rome some time between c. 55–64 where both men collaborated in the completion of the Gospel of Mark.

Mark completed the Gospel and began disseminating it soon after Peter's death (in 64 or 65) at the hands of the tyrant, Nero Caesar.

The First Letter of Peter

Based on these considerations it is suggested that Peter wrote this letter some time between 55 and 64 (see chapter 9). References to "fiery trial" (1 Pet 4:12) may point to Peter having written the letter during Nero's attack on the Christians (but before the death of Peter). References to Silvanus and Mark suggest that these men assisted Peter in the writing of the Letter (1 Pet 5:12–13).

Words of Christ in the First letter of Peter[5]

In the First Letter of Peter the reference to "Babylon" (5:13) most likely locates the writing of the letter to Rome ("Babylon" was a code word for Rome).[6] Like James's letter, the First Letter of Peter is marked by high quality Greek writing that raises problems for direct authorship by the Galilean fisherman. Following Edward Selwyn's suggestions, however, the superior Greek is to be attributed to Peter's amanuensis, Silvanus.[7]

Did the Jesus "words" in this letter come to Peter from his own memory, or indirectly through other epistolary filters?[8] For example, Silvanus was previously a fellow-worker with Paul in his mission in Macedonia and Corinth (he is known as Silas in the Acts of the Apostles where, it appears, he was a Roman citizen—Acts 16:37). Thereafter, he disappears from view until he reappears in 1 Pet 5:12.

---

5. Some of this material appeared earlier in Barnett, *Birth of Christianity*, 133–35.
6.. Rev 14:8; 16:19; 17:5; 18:10.
7. Selwyn, *First Epistle of Peter*, 9–17.
8. See Gundry, "'Verba Christi,'" 336–59; Gundry, "Further *Verba*," 211–32. For a contra view see Best, *1 Peter*.

First Peter and the Jesus Tradition

Peter in First Peter	Jesus in the Gospels
2:12 seeing your good works they will *glorify* (*doxasosin*) God	Matt 5:16 Let your light so shine before men that they may see your good works and give *glory* (*doxasosin*) to your Father who is in heaven. "M" source
2:19 (context of non-vengeance): for this is *thankworthy* (*touto gar charis*)	Luke 6:32–34 / Matt 5:36 (context of non-vengeance) what *credit* is it to you (*poia charis estin humin*) x 3 "Q" source
3:9 Not returning (*apodidontes*) *evil* for evil	Luke 6:27/Matt. 5:44 Do good to those who *hate* you "Q" source
3:14 if you should *suffer* for *righteousness*, blessed.	Matt. 5:10/Luke 6:22 (?) Blessed are those who are *persecuted* for *righteousness* sake "M" (or "Q?")
4:14 if you are *reproached* (*oneidizesthe*) for the name of Christ, *blessed*..	Matt. 5:11 Blessed are you when men *revile* (*oneidisōsin*) you "M" (or "Q"?)

This list is fairly conservative. Robert Gundry, for example, finds more echoes of the words of Jesus, including from the Johannine traditions.[9] Whatever the precise extent of these "words" of Jesus, their fact is secure.

It is clear that the tradition underlying the Sermon on the Mount is prominent (from a pre-synoptic tradition later traceable in Matthew). Whether that tradition was written or oral cannot be determined with confidence from First Peter. Nevertheless, as with the Jesus traditions found in the Letters of Paul and James, it is more likely that Peter drew from traditions that were *written*, and moreover written in Greek most probably from early times.

The *verba Christi* in First Peter confirm the usage of these words by leaders in the apostolic age and imply that such material had been

---

9. Gundry, "'Verba Christi,'" 336–50.

assembled and was in circulation prior to their inclusion in the letters in which they appear.

Does the First Letter of Peter have any other echoes from gospel sources? There are possibly three from the Markan stream.

Gospel of Mark	The First Letter of Peter
For even the Son of Man came not to be served but to serve, and to give his life as a *ransom* (*lytron*) for many (10:45).	knowing that you were *ransomed* (*elytrōthēte*) . . . with the precious blood of Christ, like that of a lamb without blemish (1:18–19).
some began . . . to *strike* (*kolaphizein*) him (14:65).	if you do wrong and are *beaten* (*kolaphizomenoi*) for it you take it patiently? (2:20).
those who are supposed to rule over the Gentiles *lord* it (*katakyrieuousin*) over them (10:42).	not as *domineering* (*katakyrieuontes*) over those in your charge (5:3).

There are relatively few words common between First Peter and Mark. In the first, the noun (*lytron*) appears in Mark 10:45 (repeated in Matt 20:28) and the verb (*lytroomai*) only in Luke 24:21 and Titus 2:14. The second, to "strike" or "beat" (*kolaphizō*), appears in Mark 14:65 (repeated in Matt 26:67), and appears in 1 Cor 4:11 and 2 Cor 12:7. The third, "rule" or "lord it over" (*katakyrieuō*), is repeated from Mark 10:42 in Matt 20:25 and also it appears in Acts 19:16.

Each word is connected with Jesus: what he *said* about his death as a *ransom*, the *beatings* he received, and his contrast with *domineering* officials. Given the rarity of the words and their association with Jesus it is possible their presence in the Markan tradition triggered their repetition in Peter's letter.

There is also a possible (oblique) reference by Peter to the Gospel of John.

Gospel of John	The First Letter of Peter
Jesus said to Simon Peter: "Feed my lambs. . . . Tend my sheep. . . . Feed my sheep" (21:15–17).	So I exhort the elders . . . as a fellow elder and a witness to the sufferings of Christ . . . shepherd (*poimanate*) the flock (*poimnion*) of God that is among you . . . exercising oversight (*episkopountes*) (5:2)

Do we have here Peter's updated version of Jesus' original words to him by the lake side, words that Peter directed to the fellow presbyters (1 Pet 5:1–2)? It is possible that Peter's command to the Anatolian presbyters to "shepherd the flock" catches Jesus' intent in his lake side commands to Peter, to "feed," "tend," and "feed my sheep" (John 21:15–17).

A positive answer to this question might imply that the Gospel of John (or an earlier version) predated the writing of Peter's letter.

Other Sources in the First Letter of Peter[10]

First Peter is remarkable for its many echoes from other New Testament texts, apart from the sources of the Gospels.

(i) Rom 12 and 13

1 Pet 4	Rom 12 and 13
v7 the end . . . is *at hand* . . . keep . . . *sober* for your prayers	13:12 the day is *at hand* 12:3 think with *sober* judgment
v9 practise *hospitality*	12:13 practise *hospitality*
v10 as each has received a *gift* . . . *serving* one another	12:6 having *gifts* that differ
v11 whoever *speaks*	12:7 if service, in our *serving* . . . he who *teaches*, in his teaching

The repeating words in the two passages are not coincidental. What is the explanation? Is Peter depending on Paul's text, or vice versa? In other respects the texts are quite dissimilar. Therefore the most likely reason for the repetitions is that Paul and Peter were each depending on an independent and earlier written tradition directing congregational life in the early churches. On this account, each writer has adapted the tradition for the local needs of his respective readers.

---

10. See Ellis, *Making of the New Testament*, 133–38. Ellis estimates that pre-formed traditions represent 39 percent of the letter.

(ii) Acts 20:28

Jesus' command, "feed my sheep," became a fundamental instruction among the apostles. This is clear from Peter's own words in 1 Pet 5:2, but also in Paul's direction to the presbyters ("elders") of Ephesus in Acts 20:28.

1 Pet 5:2	Acts 20:28
Presbyters . . . *over-see* the *flock* of God . . . *shepherding* [them]	[Presbyters] . . . take heed . . . to all the *flock* . . . in which the Holy Spirit has made you *over-seers* . . . *shepherd* the church of God

The common elements ("presbyters," "over-see[r]," "shepherd," "flock of God"/"church of God") are striking. Did Peter copy these words from Acts, or vice versa? It is more likely that Peter and Paul were drawing from an early common tradition that had been formulated for guidance to local church leaders.

(iii) Jas 5:6–11

Even the casual reader will sense that there are words here in common with Jas 4:7–10. When the texts are set side-by-side the similarities become quite noticeable.

Jas 4:7–10	1 Pet 5:5–9
	5 for "God opposes the proud, but gives grace to the humble"
6 But he gives more grace; therefore it says, "God opposes the proud, but gives grace to the humble"	6 *Humble yourselves* . . . under . . . *God* . . . that in due time he may *exalt you.*
9 *Resist [the devil],* firm in your faith	9 *Resist [the devil],* firm in your faith

The similarities (the quotation from Prov 3:34; "humble yourselves" before/to the Lord/God) and the repeated "resist the devil" are such that we think that Peter and James were drawing upon the same early tradition. At the same time, however, these writers apply the tradition to their own individual situation.

(iv) 1 Thess 5:6, 23

1 Thess 5	1 Pet 5
6 be *watchful and sober*	8 Be *sober* and *watchful*
23 May the *God* of peace sanctify you completely, and may your whole spirit and soul and body be kept blameless at the coming of our Lord Jesus Christ.	10 The *God* of all grace who has *called* you to his eternal glory in Christ will restore, confirm, strengthen and establish you
24 He who *calls* you is faithful. And he will do it.	

Both passages come near the end of their respective letters. The injunctions to watchfulness and sobriety are identical (in reverse word order) and the final prayers to God are quite similar in intent if not in precise wording.

The passages that Peter quotes and adapts are evidence of the sharing of teachings within early Christianity. Peter is dependent on sources that will flow into the Gospel of Matthew (the Sermon on the Mount), but also of other sources that became part of other letters and the book of Acts.

The Church in Rome: A Collector of Sources

Analysis of the First Letter of Peter reveals its author to have been a collector of earlier sources. In addition to the "Q," "M," and Mark sources we hear (probable) echoes from the Gospel of John, the book of Acts, the Letter of James, and Paul's letters to the Romans and the Thessalonians. It is acknowledged that these are not necessarily direct citations, but possibly borne to Rome by other texts.

Either way, however, the many echoes of a wide array of texts points to the church in Rome as led by Peter to have been a significant collection point. This coheres well with the sense of the importance of the church in the world capital, whose senior presbyter was the revered apostle, Peter. The church in Rome had become a rich storehouse for apostolic teaching about Christ and the life of a disciple.

It was fitting that following the martyrdom of the great apostle that his disciple Mark should publish the definitive biography of the One whom Peter had so faithfully served.

Mystery Not Conspiracy

Peter's use of words from the gospel sources and other sources represent numerous mysteries. There is no way of knowing for certain how, when, and from whom Peter acquired this information. Was it written or oral, or a mixture of both? Did it exist in Greek, Aramaic, or in both? Our thesis is that Jesus' words quickly assumed a written form, expressed in Greek.

Are there grounds for suspecting apostolic sleight of hand? Were Peter and his authorities somehow seeking to present a reshaped Jesus, one that differed fundamentally from the so-called "real" Jesus, the historical rabbi from Nazareth? By no means is this plausible. Peter's letter is both eschatological and soteriological, but so too are the texts he introduces to buttress those teachings (e.g., 1 Pet 5:8, 10; and 1 Thess 5:6, 25). There is no hiatus, no inconsistency.

Conclusion

It appears that the Apostle Peter spent about a decade in Rome ("Babylon") as the senior presbyter in the church (55–64). For at least some of that time he had the company of Silvanus and Mark, both of whom would have contributed to the writing of Peter's First Letter. Peter's strong citations of and allusion to the Sermon on the Mount (as found in the "Q" source) point to that source being extant (in embryo) at and by the time Peter wrote.

This tends to confirm our earlier observation that the ethical teachings in the Letter of James were also quoted from (an early version of) the Sermon on the Mount ("Q" version). It is reasonable to conclude that the outlines and teaching of the Sermon on the Mount were established quite early in the period after Jesus.

It is possible, but beyond certainty, that Peter also referenced passages from as yet incomplete versions of the Gospel of Mark and the Gospel of John. It is significant that passages in Peter bear close similarity to passages from Romans, James, the book of Acts, and First Thessalonians.

It is remarkable that such a short epistle (103 verses) should reflect so much other source material to the degree that it does. We conclude that there was considerable scholarship busily engaged in ministry matters in

Rome, but the impenetrable nature of the text of Peter prevents us from peering into these labors. We must be content with viewing the fruits of those labors on the surface of this letter.

ten

The Sources: An Interim Report

It is time to take stock and reflect upon the words of Jesus from the Gospels' sources as they appear in the letters of Paul, James, and Peter.

It is almost universally agreed that Matthew and Luke employed Mark's text as the narrative "core" of their Gospels. They follow Mark's sequence and often repeat his exact words.

When we remove Mark from Matthew and Luke we find a body of text that is common to both. This is the so-called "Q" source. The presence of Mark and "Q" in Matthew and Luke is (rightly) called the "two document" hypothesis.

If, as our next step, we remove Mark and "Q" from Matthew, there remains a body of text that scholars refer to as "M." When we pursue the same process with Luke we find a remaining source known to scholars as "L."

Thus, by these surgical procedures we have laid bare three substantial bodies of text that were certainly extant by the 60s: (early Mark), "Q," "M," and "L," but which most probably began to be collected soon after the first Easter. They were in Greek at the end of their journey and most probably also at their respective beginnings.

Verses	
(early Mark)	?
"Q"	250
"M"	320
"L"	580

Broadly speaking the completed Matthew and Luke can be expressed as equations (the verse numbers in brackets are approximate):

Matthew (1068) = Mark (500) + "Q" (250) + "M" (320)
Luke (1149) = Mark (320) + "Q" (250) + "L" (580)

The existence of these sources is fundamental to the argument of this book, which is that the "traditions" that began with Jesus (29–33) traveled "stream-like" through the intervening years to "empty" (in the 70s) into three main source pools: "Q," "M," and "L." Matthew and Luke constructed their Gospels from these sources (based on the narrative of Mark).

Closely connected with this argument is to assert that in their letters Paul, James, and Peter reference words of Jesus from these "streams" that in an interim way, as it were, we can identify as belonging to our final source pools: "Q," "M," and "L."

The Sources in Paul's Letters

Paul's missions in the five Roman provinces of Syria-Cilicia, Galatia, Macedonia, Achaia, and Asia in the decade 48–57 provide the widest window through which we are able to view early Christianity. Historians have a debt of gratitude to Paul's ten letters written to or from churches in those provinces, and to the narrative of Acts 13–20.[1]

The following chronological sequence of Paul's letters have quotations of or echoes of Jesus' words, as we are able to identify them in the Gospel sources:

		Gospel	Source
Galatians	5:1	Matt 11:28	"M"
	5:14	Mark 12:31	Mark
1 Thessalonians	4:15–17	Matt 25:30–31	"M"
	5:3	Luke 12:39/Matt 24:33	"Q"
		Luke 21:34–36	"L"
1 Corinthians	7:11	Mark 10:11–12	Mark
	9:14	Luke 10:7/Matt 10:10	"Q"
	11:23–25	Luke 22:19–20	"L"

---

1. Paul provides little information about Paul's so-called "hidden years" in Syria-Cilicia, 37–47 (Acts 9:30—12:25 *passim*). See generally Barnett, *Paul in Syria*.

Romans	12:14	Luke 6:28a/Matt 5:44	"Q"
	12:17	Luke 6:29/Matt 5:39	"Q"
	12:18	Mark 9:50	Mark
	12:20	Luke 6:27/Matt 5:44	"Q"
	13:7	Mark 12:17	Mark
	14:14	Mark 7:15	Mark
	14:20	Mark 7:19	Mark

Conclusions

i. Paul makes reference in six verses to texts that will later appear in the finished version of Mark. This could refer to (a) "floating" Markan traditions; (b) to an early version of Mark (sometimes called "Ur-Markus"); or (c) to a finished version of Mark written some years before our estimated dating of Mark (after 64). Our tentatively held preference is for (a).

ii. There are five citations from the "Q" source, with a suggested connection to the Sermon on the Mount.

iii. Paul refers to two "M" source texts and one "L" source text.

We note that many of Paul's texts are inexact in their use of Jesus' words. This is possibly explained by their existence in oral form, or because the sources were themselves incomplete, or because Paul for some reason chose not to replicate Jesus' words exactly.

The Sources in the Letter of James

James was head of the Jerusalem Church c. 42–62 so that the authorship of his encyclical letter probably occurred somewhere within the church from 33, so that his collection of Jesus' words may have begun from that time. James and his brothers, who were the brothers of Jesus, met separately in Jerusalem from the group that Peter led (Acts 12:17).

As noted, almost all of James's texts are from the "Q" and "M" sources.

"Q"	12	from Sermon on the Mount
	5	from the Sermon on the Plain
"M"	6	from Sermon on the Mount

The seventeen from the "Q" source are either from the Sermon on the Mount or the Sermon on the Plain. The six from the "M" source are from the Sermon on the Mount.

James was applying the "word" of Jesus (from the Sermon on the Mount and the Sermon on the Plain) to the pastoral situation of his scattered Jewish-Christian readers. The quotes are recognizably from Jesus (as discernible later from the completed "Q" and "M") but are not exact quotations.

It is puzzling that James does not attribute these words directly to Jesus. We do not know why. Was it because these teachings only existed in oral form? Or did James quote the Lord inexactly, and in his own name, so that they came with his authority?

There are many mysteries. Yet the pastoral situation is imaginable and is no basis for finding sinister motives, for example, that this text refers back to Jesus merely as teacher, not as an eschatological figure. On the contrary, James presents "our Lord Jesus Christ" as the "Lord of glory" who is the returning "judge" (Jas 2:1; 5:18).

The Sources of the First Letter of Peter

Peter was in "Babylon" (Rome) from about 55 until his death after the second half of the year 64. The great fire that destroyed the greater part of the city erupted July 18, 64. Nero's assault on the Christians as described by Tacitus would have begun in the second half of the year and may have continued into the following year.

It was probably sometime after the outbreak of major persecution that Peter wrote to the Christians in Northern Anatolia. Peter's warning of the "fiery trial" coming to them (1 Pet 4:12) coincides with Tacitus's reference to the burning of crucified "Christians."[2] Peter's allusion to persecution in Rome anticipated a persecution that would bring suffering to the "brotherhood throughout the *world*."[3]

---

2. Tacitus, *Annals* 15.44—"they were fastened on crosses . . . and . . . were burned to serve as lamps by night."

3. 1 Pet 4:12; 5:9.

The Words of Jesus in First Peter and the Sermon on the Mount

We hear echoes of the Sermon on the Mount in the First Letter of Peter:

First Peter	Gospel Source
2:12 "good works"	Matt 5:16 ("M")
2:19 "thankworthy"	Luke 6:32–34/ Matt 5:36 ("Q")
3:9 "not returning evil"	Luke 6:27/Matt 5:44 ("Q")
3:14 "suffer for righteousness"	Matt 5:10/Luke 6:22 ("M" or "Q")
4:14 "reproached for the name"	Matt 5:11 ("M" or "Q")

Each of the "words" of Jesus appearing in First Peter seem to be connected with the (embryonic) Sermon on the Mount. Most, however, exhort the readers to respond to persecution as Christ had done in response to his sufferings, a key theme in this letter.

The Source of Peter's "Words"

Which source did Peter use for the words of Jesus that he echoes in his First Letter? Was Peter depending on his memory for particular teachings of Jesus? In that pre-literary era many people had encyclopedic memories with capacity to recall lengthy texts. Jesus had instructed Peter and the other disciples by aphorisms, parables, and poems. Perhaps Peter had merely dipped into his memory banks and reproduced these words.

On the other hand, however, five of the texts are so particular to the pastoral needs Peter was addressing (persecution) that it is difficult to explain his use of them based solely on general, orally based recall.

It is more likely that Peter had access to *written* texts, the written texts of "Q" and "M." I assume that these textual streams began flowing soon after the ministry period of Jesus (29–33). I can think of no reason why the finalizing of these sources would not have been completed before the time Peter arrived in Rome (*c.* 55).

Furthermore, since Rome was the political center of the world and the home of Peter, the preeminent apostle, it would be no surprise that these sources had made their way to that city. In other words, it can be plausibly argued that Peter was referring to written texts that had found their home there. We note, for example, that in Rom 16, written in 57,

Paul greets by name several dozen believers who were from the east, and who may have brought texts with them.

Peter in Rome was blessed to have the company of two accomplished scholars, Mark and Silvanus, who had been mission associates of Paul. These two men, with Peter, formed a kind of scholarly academy. From First Peter we know of their careful integration of Old Testament texts within the letter, as well as passages found also in Romans, Acts, James, and First Thessalonians. But that is true also of the words of Jesus that Peter and his colleagues effortlessly incorporated within the letter. It is reasonable to believe that they had access to written sources.

The Sources: Dates and Places

It is critically important to note that the dates of Paul's and Peter's citation of Jesus' words are more or less recoverable to within a few years, and of James's to a rather wider angle of possibilities. From which place or places did Paul, James, and Peter depend on for the Jesus traditions that they cite? It is probable that Paul and James depended on sources that were treasured in Jerusalem, and that Peter had such sources close at hand in Rome.

	Dates	Probable Origin of Sources
Peter	33–42	Jerusalem
Paul	48–57	Jerusalem
James	33–62	Jerusalem
Peter	55–64	Rome

We must be reminded, however, that while these dates are reasonably likely the places that were the homes of the sources, although plausible, remain uncertain.

Was Jesus a Merely Ethical Teacher?

In earlier chapters on the words of Jesus cited in the three sets of letters we were struck by their mainly *ethical* rather than theological character. Paul refers to Jesus' words touching a range of pastoral issues, including eschatology, marriage, payment of ministers, forgiveness of the persecutor, and respect for secular rulers. In James's letter the author appeals to the "word" for a range of social matters, including the excoriation of the wealthy and the needs of the poor. Jesus' words in First Peter are about patient suffering, which is the main pastoral theme of the letter.

Some have concluded that Jesus, therefore, was after all merely an inspired rabbi, and that eschatological, atonement, and divinity claims were superimposed later upon him. But the "real" Jesus, the Jesus of history, was no Son of God, no savior, and no returning lord. He was a teacher, pure and simple.

In fact, however, Jesus speaks (mainly) ethically out of these letters for a straightforward reason. The churches faced a battery of ethical challenges from their cultural setting to which the apostles must make pastoral responses. If there was a word from Jesus that could be applied, then that is what happened.

Furthermore, the attribution of a sinister motive to the apostles ignores the very christological emphases that are the central message of the letters. The suggestion that an apostolic letter could, at one moment, propose a high Christology and in the next appeal to a merely earthly human figure is self-contradictory.

Conclusion

Based on source criticism we are able to isolate the main sources that Matthew and Luke employed in constructing their Gospels—Mark, "Q," "L," and "M."

However, we are only able to identify these sources retroactively in the letters of Paul, James, and Peter from the completed Gospels of Matthew and Luke, which we suggest were written sometime in the 70s. We only know of the existence of these important sources through our analysis of the completed Gospels of Matthew and Luke.

If we didn't recognize these sources we would not know that various parts of the apostolic letters are actually the words of Jesus. It is only from (early) Mark, "Q," "L," and "M" that it is possible to see where Paul, James, and Peter were quoting from, or echoing a word of, the Lord Jesus.

Admittedly there are a number of mysteries and uncertainties in this study; for example, our suggestions for dates and places for the constituent sources. These are suggestions not certainties. By the time these letter writers quote them the sources were probably in *written*, rather than oral form.

So, yes, there are areas of uncertainty and mystery. But that in no way concedes some kind of conspiracy that would suggest that the Christians made the humble teacher Jesus into some kind of a god. Common sense historiography raises a high barrier against such a reconstruction.

eleven

The Surprise: The Languages of Jesus

An issue immediately to resolve is the length of the lead-time between Jesus of Nazareth and the earliest written Gospel. A span of many generations would weaken confidence about the accuracy of the record. Mark, however, wrote his Gospel about thirty years after Jesus,[1] the span of one generation.[2]

Chronology

A sense of chronology is of critical importance. The letters of Paul, James, and Peter are windows enabling us to see the development of Christianity within the period between Jesus and the first written Gospel.

29–33	Public ministry of Jesus
33–42	Peter's leadership of the church in Israel
33–62	James's membership of and leadership of the church in Israel
55–64	Peter's leadership of the church in Rome
64/65	Practical completion of the Gospel of Mark

The dates are secure to within a range of small variation.

From the apostles' letters and the book of Acts we know of constant gospel activity in the relatively few years between Jesus and the writing of the Gospels. By contrast it was more than eighty years after Tiberius Caesar's death that Suetonius wrote his *Life of Tiberius*. So far as we know,

---

1. See chapter 9.
2. Based on modern and western life expectancy a generation is between twenty-five and thirty years.

those eight decades were "dead" years with the absence of a cult following for the deceased emperor. Tiberius was not well remembered.

The relatively few years between Jesus and the earliest written Gospel text means an effective time constraint against the possibility of radically refashioning the traditions so as to obliterate Jesus as he was so as to replace him as, for example, a Greek miracle-working redeemer-god who died and rose again.

Two Mysteries

Two great questions concerning the thirty years between Jesus and the first Gospel are: first, were the source traditions recorded in Greek or Aramaic, and, second, was their mode of transmission oral or written?

My expectation was that the sources were chiefly oral and that they were expressed in Aramaic. Jesus was the great teacher of orally memorized parables and aphorisms, instructions that were delivered in the *lingua franca*, Aramaic, as I had supposed it to be.

This writer has to overcome his strong intuition and prejudice that Jesus' teachings were recalled by the memory in the language of the people, Aramaic. The weight of evidence, however, now points in another direction.

The Language of the Sources in the Letters

It was the examination of the sources (early) Mark, "Q," "L," and "M" as found in the letters of Paul, James, and Peter that attracted my attention. The dating of these letters is important. They were written between (approximately) 48–64, which means that the words they quote or echo must have been established beforehand.

The critical thing is that these sources are cited in the apostolic letters in Greek. Furthermore, the Greek citations in the letters cannot be back translated into Aramaic. Counterintuitive though it is, I think we must push back closer to Jesus and conclude that these text sources began to be written in Greek from or soon after the post-Easter period.

In support of this viewpoint I point once more to the relatively infrequent examples of surviving Aramaic in Paul's letters, the earliest texts in early Christianity. Surprisingly few words of Aramaic find their way into his letters:

Abba	Gal 4:6; Rom 8:15
Maran atha	1 Cor 16:22
Amēn	2 Cor 1:20

If the deposit of Jesus' teachings and the record of his deeds was transmitted in Aramaic we would expect considerable echoes of Aramaic in the letters of Paul, James, and Peter. But there are few such echoes.

By contrast, the two pre-formatted traditions Paul repeats in First Corinthians are in Greek (11:23–25; 15:3–7). Some scholars claim to have found traces of the original Aramaic in these texts, but the stubborn reality is that they survive in First Corinthians in Greek.

I have referred throughout to "mystery" about several aspects of the making of the Gospels. That the constituent sources are in Greek and appear to have been in Greek from the beginning of their journey is a significant mystery.

This raises the very important question about the languages Jesus spoke. The Aramaic words that appear (chiefly) in the Gospel of Mark are evidence that Jesus spoke Aramaic (see below). But did he also speak Greek? Jesus' conversations with the "Greek" woman of Syria-Phoenicia (Mark 7:26), his exchange with the centurion in Capernaum (Matt 8:5–13), and with Pontius Pilate in Jerusalem (Mark 15:2–5) support the probability that Jesus also spoke Greek.

The Languages of Palestine

Aramaic

Was Aramaic or Greek the common language of Palestine in New Testament times? Some say Aramaic, others Greek,[3] others again that Palestine was bilingual[4] or "multi-lingual."[5]

Aramaic had been the *lingua franca* of the Persian Empire, which included Palestine. Josephus's references cited in the appendix state that Aramaic was "our own tongue" and "the language of our country."

---

3. See Porter, *Criteria for Authenticity*, 126–41; Porter, "Use of Greek in First-Century Palestine," 203–28; Lukaszewski, "Issues Concerning the Aramaic"; Gleaves, *Did Jesus Speak Greek?*
4. Horsley, *New Documents* 5, 6–19.
5. Millard, *Reading and Writing*, 132–53.

Regarding Aramaic we note the occurrence of that language in the Gospels.[6] Embedded within these Greek texts are Aramaic place names (e.g., *Akeldama, Bethzatha, Gabbatha, Golgotha*), Aramaic surnames (e.g., *Cephas, Boanerges*), words in common usage (e.g., *korban, messias, cananaean, hosanna, pascha, rabbi, satanas*), words spoken by Jesus (e.g., *amēn, mammōn, raka, talitha cumi, ephthatha, abba, Eloi Eloi lama sabachthani*).

Greek

Eric Meyers and James Strange refer to the growing Greek usage in Israel: "Aramaic, at first the language of all the people, gradually suffered a decline that probably accelerated with each war against Rome. It appears that sometime during the first century BCE Aramaic and Greek changed places as Greek spread into the countryside and as Aramaic declined among the educated and among urban dwellers."[7] Judea as a now entrenched Roman colony attracted Greek-speaking bureaucrats and traders who promoted the spread of Greek.[8]

Greek was widely spoken in Judea and Jerusalem. Funerary remains in and around Jerusalem frequently bear the Greek language. Martin Hengel goes so far as to describe Jerusalem as a "Greek city."[9] He draws attention to the "Hellenists" (Greek-speaking Jewish émigrés) living in Jerusalem as well established in the book of Acts and indicating that one third of inscriptions in Jerusalem are in Greek.[10] As well, he argues that many Aramaic speaking indigenous Jews "had a good command" of Greek.

---

6. See Millard, *Reading and Writing*, 140–41; Jeremias, *New Testament Theology*, 1, 3–8.

7. Meyers and Strange, *Archaeology*, 90; Porter, "Jesus and the Use of Greek," 71–87. Historically, the majority of scholars (e.g., Wellhausen, Joüon, Bardy, Black, Wilcox, Feldman, Torrey, and Fitzmyer) supported Dalman's conclusion, that though Jesus might have known Hebrew, and probably spoke Greek, he certainly taught in Aramaic. See Buth and Notley, *Language Environment*, for articles debating the relative use of Aramaic and Hebrew in Palestine in the era of the New Testament.

8. Porter, "Jesus and the Use of Greek," 71–87.

9. Hengel, *Pre-Christian Paul*, 54–57.

10. Hengel, *Pre-Christian Paul*, 54–57, who goes so far as to assert that Jerusalem was a "Greek city" (54).

The rival missionaries from Jerusalem who came to Corinth to displace Paul (in c. 56) excelled in public speaking and rhetoric,[11] which would have been in Greek. The verbal skill of these "super apostles," as Paul calls them, provides indirect evidence for the currency of the Greek language and education in Jerusalem (see earlier, chapter 7).[12]

The evidence of Greek usage in the north is important. Jesus traveled extensively in hellenized regions to the north and east of Galilee where Greek was dominant. Galilee was ringed with Greek-speaking city-states—Tyre and Sidon to the northwest; Hippos and Gadara to the east; Scythopolis to the south. Sepphoris and Tiberias, the major cities of the tetrarchy of Galilee, were culturally Hellenistic.

Buying and selling in Galilee depended on capacity to understand Greek due to the travelers streaming along the Via Maris that passed through Galilee. Likewise the proximity of nearby city-states to Galilee implied travel to and from them to buy and sell. The degree to which Palestine had been Hellenized is evident in the inscriptions and papyri from that era, including even such intensely Jewish centers as Qumran, Masada, Muraba'at, and Jerusalem itself.[13]

Three of the disciples, Philip, Simon, and Andrew had Greek names and came from Bethsaida in Gaulanitis, a Greek-speaking principality. This was the obvious reason that Philip was sought out by some "Greeks" who wanted to meet Jesus—and why he quickly involved Andrew (John 12:20–22).[14]

Summary

Based on current research we are able to say that Aramaic and Greek were both spoken in the land of Israel in the era of Jesus. No doubt there were pockets where one language was more concentrated than the other. At the same time it is likely that many communities were fluent in spoken Aramaic and spoken Greek. To this day semi-educated vendors in Jerusalem speak Hebrew, Arabic, and English, and in Lebanon and Syria

---

11. 2 Cor 11:5–6; cf. 2:17. See earlier, chapter 7.

12. It was said that Rabban Gamaliel II (flourished late-first to second century) had one thousand students, five hundred of whom studied the Torah and five hundred who studied Greek wisdom (quoted in Feldman, *Jew and Gentile*, 37.

13. Millard, *Reading and Writing*, 102–17.

14. On the points made here, see Bockmuehl, *Remembered Peter*, 164–65, 167, 184–85.

fluency in Arabic and French is common. Overall, however, it appears that Greek usage had become more prominent than Aramaic.

The Languages of Jesus

To state the obvious: since Jesus is quoted in Greek and Aramaic in the Gospels it is reasonable to conclude that Jesus taught in both languages. Recent studies no longer limit probable conversations in Greek to Jesus meeting in private with the Syro-Phoenician woman, the centurion in Capernaum, and Pilate.[15] Many now accept that Jesus also taught *publicly* in Greek.

Large crowds from Greek-speaking regions—"all over Syria" (Matt 4:24); "the Decapolis" (Matt 4:25); "the coastal region around Tyre and Sidon" (Luke 6:17) came to hear Jesus teach. They would not have made that journey unless they knew Jesus would be speaking their language.

We can readily imagine that Jesus taught in both languages when attended by large crowds. Jesus would have ensured that both language groups understood his message. Those who understood in both languages would have the additional benefit of memory enhanced by repetition.

Accordingly the task of translating Jesus' words from Aramaic to Greek did not happen initially in the years after the first Easter—even as early as by the "Hellenists" in the Jerusalem Church[16]—Jesus himself had already done this in the course of his public teaching.

Recording the Words of Jesus

The popular view that Jesus' followers were illiterate artisans is rightly being questioned.[17] The four fishermen (Simon, Andrew, James, and John) ran a business cooperative. Several at least among his disciples were both literate and numerate, for example the customs collector, Matthew. Furthermore, archaeological discoveries have opened a window for our understanding of the creation of written records.[18] We are well able to

---

15. As argued, for example, by Porter, "Did Jesus Ever Teach in Greek?" 199–235.

16. So Hengel, "Eye-Witness Memory," 83.

17. So, for example, Fiensy, "Jesus' Socioeconomic Background" 224–55; Freyne, *Galilee, Jesus and the Gospels*, 241; Keener, *Historical Jesus*, 20–21, 182–84; Witherington, *Jesus Quest*, 82–86, 239–41.

18. See especially Millard, *Reading and Writing*, 154–84.

envisage the narratives of "the things that have been fulfilled among us" (Luke 1:1) being written post-Easter. This process may well have begun during the brief pre-Easter years.[19]

The Gospels were written in Greek; the sources underlying Matthew and Luke were written in Greek; echoes of these sources in the letters of Paul, James, and Peter were most probably written in Greek. The most logical conclusion is that the sources of the Gospels were also written in Greek *from their beginnings* based on the likelihood that Jesus taught often in Greek (as well as Aramaic). Jesus' words and deeds were committed to writing in Greek from earliest times. Our understanding is that this process began during those few years Jesus was active in his messianic ministry, accompanied as he was by the twelve disciples ("apprentices").

The consequence of this is significant and controversial: Aramaic-based oral transmission played only a temporary role in early Christianity. If this explanation is correct it means that the elaborate theories of oral transmission developed by Kenneth Bailey and followed by James Dunn,[20] for example, need to be reconsidered. Jesus delivered his message of the kingdom in both Aramaic and Greek and from the beginning may have written in both. However, the case is strong that the message was soon written in Greek.

A Brief Lead-Time

The brevity factor should be recognized. Because we are able to date the letters of Paul that echo many of Jesus' words (especially 1 Corinthians in 55 and Romans in 57) we are able to set the practical limits by which Paul had access to these source traditions.

We are able to plot the lead-time of thirty or so years between Jesus and the writing of Mark's Gospel. This is a brief and limited period, certainly not the time span in which a radical refashioning of Jesus would

---

19. Building on the 1961 essay of Hans Schürmann, a 1975 essay by E. Earle Ellis argued that such records were produced during Jesus' ministry ("New Directions in Form Criticism," published again in his *Prophecy and Hermeneutic in Early Christianity*, 237–53 (at 240–47). See also Bauckham, *Jesus and the Eyewitnesses*, 287–89; Ellis, *Making of the New Testament*, 22, 32; Gerhardsson, *Reliability of the Gospel*, 11–13, 85; Craig S. Keener, "Assumptions in Historical-Jesus Research," 45–48; Millard, *Reading and Writing*, 185–229.

20. Dunn, *Jesus Remembered*, 205–10, referring to Bailey, "Informal Controlled," 34–54.

have occurred. The deviating, Gnostic re-portrayals of Jesus occurred in the *second* century. Valentinus, for example, wrote his *Gospel of Truth* more than a century after Jesus.

What, then, about the question of mode of transmission of the words and deeds of Jesus? This important question will be addressed in the next chapter.

Conclusion

This chapter has offered suggestions about the languages of first century Palestine and the languages in which Jesus taught. Widely held are the twin views that the Aramaic was the principal language, that Jesus conversed in Aramaic, and that his teaching was remembered in Aramaic.

The evidence, however, points to the currency of *both* Aramaic and Greek but with the latter gaining the ascendancy. This, it is argued, is reflected in Jesus's use of both but with his greater use of Greek. From the beginning, therefore, Greek became the vehicle for the new faith, including in the creation of the sources that would evolve into the text of the four Gospels.

As to the mode of transmission, there is a better argument for transmission by individual eyewitnesses than for some form of community-based story telling. Oral transmission doubtless had a role, but it was secondary and diminished with the passing of the years. To this important subject we now turn.

Excursus: Josephus and "The Language of Our Country"

Josephus initially wrote the *Jewish War* "in the language of our country," Aramaic, and sent it to people of "Parthia, Babylonia, and Arabia and the Jewish Dispersion in Mesopotamia and the inhabitants of Adiabene."[21]

In Rome, Josephus determined to translate the *Jewish War* into the Greek tongue "for the sake of such as live under the government of the Romans."[22]

Josephus made these comments regarding Greek:

---

21. Josephus, *Jewish War* 1.6.
22. Josephus, *Jewish War* 1.3.

> I have also taken a great deal of pains to obtain the learning of the Greek, and understand the elements of the Greek language, although I have so long accustomed myself to speak *our own tongue*, that I cannot pronounce Greek with sufficient exactness. (*Jewish Antiquities* 20.11)

Note that Josephus refers to Aramaic as "our own tongue."

This is how Josephus worked on the rewritten Greek version of *Jewish War*.

> Then, in the leisure that Rome afforded me, with all my materials in readiness, and *with the aid of some assistants for the Greek*, at last I committed to writing my narrative of the events. (*Against Apion* 1.50)

Josephus may be understood to be saying that Greek was unknown to him and that Aramaic was "our own tongue" and "the language of our country."

Is it possible, however, that his background as an aristocrat and a Pharisee cloistered him in an Aramaic-speaking world so that he was not schooled in writing Greek?

Again, the vast expanses of Greek in *Antiquities*, *War*, *Apion*, and *Life* make it difficult to believe that Josephus had to learn to write Greek *de novo*. The quality of the Greek of these extensive texts does not reflect the labors of a late learner. It is more likely that Josephus had at least a rudimentary knowledge of spoken Greek before his "assistants" supported him through the writing of *Jewish War*.

It appears that *Jewish War* is thoroughly Greek and reflects no dependence on an Aramaic original, but is an independent, rewritten work.

twelve

The Transmission of the Tradition[1]

For decades there has been considerable interest in the processes by which Jesus' words and deeds were later recorded in the four Gospels. How were the teachings and actions of Jesus of Nazareth remembered and written down in these four texts?

In the first part of the twentieth century scholars like Rudolph Bultmann believed that the written Gospels reflected the circumstances of the churches decades *after* Jesus, that is, at the time the Gospels were *written*.[2] Accordingly, the Gospels were sources of information about the churches in the 70s and 80s rather than about Jesus of Nazareth in the 30s. Bultmann thought that the information about Jesus reached the evangelists by oral transmission, only to be radically reshaped by them.

The Scandinavian authorities Harald Riesenfeld and Birger Gerhardsson shifted the focus back on Jesus as a *rabbinic* teacher who carefully instructed his disciples to memorize his teaching who then "delivered" these "traditions" to the churches.[3] In time, the Gospels grew out of these carefully controlled formulated and formatted teachings. While Bultmann envisaged a Hellenistic setting for the final writing of the Gospels, for Gerhardsson the setting from start to finish was Jewish.

More recently, James Dunn has argued for a theory of "informal controlled tradition."[4] Dunn acknowledges the influence of Kenneth Bailey who lived for many years in Egypt where he observed the storytelling practices in this middle-eastern, Arabic setting. Dunn, follow-

---

1. See earlier [x-ref] (chapter 4)
2. Bultmann, *History of the Synoptic Tradition*.
3. Gerhardsson, *Gospel Tradition*.
4. Dunn, *Jesus Remembered*, 206.

ing Bailey, proposes that the written Gospels grew out of an anonymous "informal controlled tradition" that began with Jesus and ended with the writing of the Gospels some decades later.

Bultmann	informal, uncontrolled tradition
Gerhardsson	formal, controlled tradition
Dunn	informal, controlled tradition

Each of these theories has attracted criticism. Bultmann held that the Jewish tradition of Jesus became radically overlaid as a Hellenistic tradition. The process ended with a Jesus who was unrecognizable in terms of his Jewish character and milieu.

Gerhardsson's more rigid approach has been faulted as anachronistic, reflecting the ethos of the Mishnah from two centuries later. Moreover, the Scandinavian approach was unable to account satisfactorily for the variations between the accounts of the Gospels. While Gerhardsson's approach creates questions for the *writing* of the Gospels, his hypothesis makes sense when we consider the carriage of the *oral* traditions that originated with the apostles and which were mediated by Paul to the churches. As noted, Paul the trained rabbi transmitted these traditions carefully.

A flaw in Dunn's approach (following Bailey) is that it is based on a setting that is modern (not ancient), and Arabic (not Jewish). But there are other problems.[5] So far as we know the religious culture of the Jews of that era was synagogue-based where the congregants gathered to hear the *reading of texts*. Rabbis instructed student-rabbis by rote learning, not story-telling.

One issue is Dunn's rejection of the notion that the Gospels were literary works, as if written by scholars sitting at desks, poring over manuscripts. For Dunn, this is an impossibly modern concept not at all resembling the ethos of story telling from that era. The Gospels are merely the written versions of the various anonymous oral streams that reached their authors. It is claimed this hypothesis explains why the book of Acts has three accounts of Paul's conversion and why there are significant variations of the Gospels' accounts of the same incident.

Dunn combines his appreciation of anonymous orality with his relative disdain for written forms. It is important, however, to recognize the

---

5. See the sustained critique of Witherington, "Christianity in the Making," 197–226.

remarkable quality of the literature of the New Testament. Each Gospel is the product of significant skill, so much so that scholars and lay readers continue to find new and deeper insights within them. The same is true of the letters of the New Testament and the Apocalypse.

Not only are these gospel texts substantial pieces of literature, they also embody the principle of *eyewitness testimony*, whether direct or indirect. By contrast, Dunn makes the span between Jesus and the Gospels murky and uncertain so that we have reduced confidence in our capacity to see Jesus in those texts. Ben Witherington III offers this observation about Dunn's approach:

> We have the impact crater, not the meteor, that made the impact in the Gospels, not Jesus in all his fullness, but rather the remembered Jesus.[6]

However, in the Gospels we do not have the crater but the meteor. This is because the Gospels arose out of personal, identified testimony.

The Eyewitnesses to Luke

According to the Bailey-Dunn theory, the mode of transmission was anonymous and corporate. However, the evidence is that it was substantially borne by *identified, individual eyewitnesses*. After the resurrection the eleven disciples established the criterion for electing the twelfth disciple.

> one of the men who have *accompanied* us
>
> during all the time that the Lord Jesus went in and out among us, beginning from the baptism of John
>
> until the day when he was taken up from us
>
> —one of these men must become with us a witness
>
> to his resurrection. (Acts 1:21–22)

Jesus' ministry was circumscribed by his baptism by John at the earlier extremity and by the ascension at the other. Only one who fulfilled the criterion of being *present with Jesus throughout* this finite span was qualified to be with the others "a *witness* to his resurrection."

It is no accident that Luke begins his magnum opus like this:

---

6. Witherington, "Christianity in the Making," 202.

> Inasmuch as many have undertaken to compile a narrative of the things that have been accomplished among us, just as those who from the beginning were *eyewitnesses and ministers of the word* have delivered them to us. (Luke 1:1–2)

Grammatically speaking "eyewitnesses and ministers of the word" are the one group but who fulfilled consecutive roles.[7] During the span of Jesus' messianic vocation—from John's baptism of Jesus until his ascension—they fulfilled the role of "eyewitnesses from the beginning" (*ap' archēs autoptai*). The numerous references to "witness" in the Acts of the Apostles confirm the importance of this critical criterion for apostleship.[8]

After the resurrection until the time they delivered the narratives to Luke they had been "ministers of the word" (*hypēretai . . . tou logou*). In other words, it was those who fulfilled the "eyewitness" criterion of Acts 1:21–22 who delivered and thereby authenticated the narratives they gave to Luke for him to weave together as the text we know as Luke-Acts.

Of supreme importance is the fact that these eyewitnesses-ministers were *still alive* to deliver constituent texts to Luke. These men were the *living* bridge between Jesus of Nazareth and Luke's great two-volume history, Luke-Acts.

The Witness of the Disciple Whom Jesus Loved

The theme of eyewitness testimony also appears in the Gospel of John, first regarding the crucifixion and death of Jesus.

> But one of the soldiers pierced his side with a spear, and at once there came out blood and water. He who saw it has borne *witness*—his *testimony* is true, and he knows that he is telling the truth—that you also may believe. (John 19:34–35)

---

7. Thompson, *Luke*, 10–11.

8. Acts 2:32 ("This Jesus God raised up and of that we all are *witnesses*"); 3:15 ("You . . . killed the author of life whom God raised from the dead. To this we are *witnesses*"); 5:30–32 ("the God of our fathers raised Jesus . . . and we are *witnesses* of these things"); 10:39–43 ("They put him to death . . . but God raised him on the third day and made him manifest to . . . us who are chosen by God as *witnesses*"); 13:30–31 ("God raised him from the dead, and for many days he appeared to those who had come up with him from Galilee to Jerusalem, who are now his *witnesses* to the people").

The author was present at the crucifixion of Jesus and was writing about it to bear "witness" to what he had seen so that those who read his text "may believe."

In setting out his purpose in writing his Gospel, the author refers to the miracle "signs" of Jesus.

> Now Jesus did many other signs *in the presence* of the disciples, which are not written in this book; but these are written so that you may believe that Jesus is the Christ, the Son of God. (John 20:30)

The author was one of the disciples who was *present* when Jesus did the signs that he has written in his book. His witness to Jesus' *crucifixion* was so that readers "may believe" and his written witness to Jesus' miracle signs was also so that his readers "may believe." According to John, Christian belief is directed toward eyewitness-testified *facts*. Faith does not depend on emotions, feelings, or sentiment, but on verifiable data, and it is *this* his Gospel records.

In the final chapter the author of the Gospel identified himself.

> This is the disciple who is bearing *witness* about these things, and who has *written* these things, and we know that his *testimony* is true. (John 21:24)

This author is "the disciple whom Jesus loved" (21:20). He has written "these things" referring not only to the dramatic event by the lake (which presupposes Jesus' resurrection), but also about Jesus' crucifixion (19:34–35) and his miracle signs (20:30). Members of the author's faith community add their affidavit: they "know his *testimony* is true."

The author in these three passages refers to what he has *written* as his witness to key events that focused on Jesus. He was an apostolic eyewitness who had been with Jesus "from the beginning" (John 15:27— "And you also will bear witness, because you have been with me from the beginning").

The cumulative effect of these texts is to establish the connection between written eyewitness testimony in the Gospels of Luke and John as *the basis for faith commitment*. Faith responds to written, eyewitness-based evidence.

event ➔ eyewitness ➔ testimony ➔ faith

The Witness of Paul

Paul was not an "eyewitness" of Jesus but was dependent on those who were. We recall that the former persecutor on his first return visit to Jerusalem spent fifteen days in the home of Peter (Gal 1:18). We know of two other occasions when Paul met Peter in Jerusalem, as well as later in Antioch.[9] We are right to assume that Peter bore eyewitness testimony about Jesus (from his baptism to his resurrection) to Paul during those meetings, and therefore to think of Paul as a secondary, dependent witness.

There are good reasons for believing that Paul understood well the principle of eyewitness testimony. His citation of the Easter tradition supports this confidence.

> For I delivered to you as of first importance
> what I also received:
> > that Christ died for our sins . . .
> > that he was buried,
> > that he was raised on the third day . . .
> > that he appeared to Cephas . . . to the twelve . . . to more than five hundred brothers at one time . . . to James . . . to all the apostles. (1 Cor 15:3-7)

This carefully formatted tradition arose from the eyewitness testimony of Cephas, "the twelve," "the more than five hundred," James, and "all the apostles." This is an oral tradition but it is not anonymous. The witnesses to the risen Jesus are either precisely named (Cephas, James) or clearly identified ("the twelve," "the more than five hundred," "all the apostles").

Paul was not a primary eyewitness of Jesus, yet it is clear that he grasped the importance of relaying the testimony of those who were. Indeed, he brackets himself with them as custodians and transmitters of their message.

> Whether then it was I or they so we preach and so you believed.
> (1 Cor 15:11)

This text informs us that Paul took very seriously the eyewitness testimony to him by the apostles, which he then delivered to the churches.

---

9. Gal 2:1, 11; Acts 15:6.

The Witness of Peter in the Gospel of Mark

In chapter 16 I discuss Papias's information about Peter as the source of the Gospel that Mark wrote. This is confirmed by the remarkable *inclusio* created by references to Peter at the extremities of the Gospel as well as at its midpoint. Peter is also the disciple most frequently mentioned in the Gospel of Mark. Martin Hengel and Richard Bauckham have demonstrated the currency of the use of the *inclusio* in literature of that era, as a means of identifying the source and authority of a text.[10]

The Gospel of Mark depends on the testimony of his mentor, the eyewitness, Peter.

Again: The Importance of Chronology

It is helpful to keep in mind the issues of chronology in the making of the Gospels. There is no way of exactly dating the Gospel of Mark (see chapter 16). In my view, however, Mark wrote his Gospel shortly before the death of Peter in 64 or 65. The most likely scenario is that Peter and Mark in Rome collaborated in the writing of Mark's Gospel in the period 55–64. I believe Mark edited and disseminated his Gospel shortly after the death of Peter. This represents a span of about thirty years between the first Easter (in 33) and the completion of the Gospel (by 64 or 65).

The prologue to the Gospel of Luke indicates that the "eyewitnesses . . . of the word" were still alive to deliver various narratives to Luke. If these eyewitnesses were (say) thirty at the time of the first Easter it would mean that they were less than sixty when Luke was in Palestine during Paul's imprisonment in 57–59. This is the most likely occasion when Luke received the texts that he later employed in the writing of Luke-Acts (see chapter 21).

Obviously these calculations are speculative but perhaps not too far from reality. In that case it means that the period between Jesus of Nazareth and the writing of the Gospels was reasonably short. In my view, this is consistent with the argument that the Gospels arose out of sources that had not traveled far from Jesus their wellspring.

A longer lead-time would probably be consistent with the Bailey-Dunn theory of anonymous oral transmission. The preferred theory of

---

10. Hengel, *Four Gospels*, 82–83; Bauckham, *Jesus and the Eyewitnesses*, 124–27.

personalized and identified eyewitnesses is obviously more comfortable with the briefer span, which indeed seems to have been the case.

The Gospels Written for Oral Performance

The references to eyewitness testimony—verbal and written—points to a key element in the transmission of information about Jesus that came to be written in the pages of the Gospels. The theory of anonymous oral transmission as the explanation for the writing of the Gospels is less plausible, including the suggestion that it accounts for the variations between the Gospels.

Moreover, the elevation of the importance of oral transmission at the expense of written transmission is unconvincing. The high literary quality of the Gospels indicates that the writers were conscious of high expectations in their respective audiences. Besides, their literary efforts must not be seen through modern eyes as if directed to *individual* book readers. On the contrary, those authors wrote their texts to be read *aloud* to groups—the Jesus-synagogues—who came to the meetings to *listen*. In other words, the act of reading was an oral *performance*.

This goes some of the way to explain how the Gospels as we have them are so lively when read aloud in modern church gatherings.

thirteen

Common Source "Q" and the Jesus Seminar

"Q" as a source used by both Matthew and Luke has been hypothesized for several centuries by that dry as dust discipline known as source criticism.[1] In recent times, however, "Q" has become electrifyingly important to the study of Christian origins.

Members of the Jesus Seminar and others have proposed that "Q" represents the beliefs of the original post-Easter disciples of Jesus in Galilee that authentically reflect the mind of the pre-Easter Jesus. They argue that "Q," unlike the canonical gospels, has no passion narrative (so no atonement theology), no resurrection appearances, and no confession of Jesus as the Son of God. Accordingly, they contend that the agenda of the "real" Jesus was reformist and ethical and that the messianic and redemptive elements in the canonical gospels were distortions attributable to the influence of Paul and Mark.

This proposal assumes that the "Q" community were somehow walled off, quarantined from other currents of thought among the early Christians. According to N. T. Wright, "One of the attractions of Q in some quarters today is that it seems to say nothing about Jesus' death and resurrection, thus providing evidence of a flourishing type of early Christianity for which those . . . emphases, so strikingly evident in the canonical gospels, were unimportant."[2]

---

1. The existence of "Q" has always been doubted. See, e.g., Goodacre, "Monopoly on Markan Priority?" 583–62. See also Watson, *Gospel Writing*, who doubts the existence of "Q" and the theory that the Gospels were written consecutively.

2. Wright, "Resurrection in Q?" 87.

Despite the recent reconstructions of "Q" with attendant claims about its real but different Jesus, this view is not altogether new. Kloppenborg quotes Bultmann with approval for his assertion that "Q" was a "transitional stage between the unmessianic preaching of Jesus and the fully self-conscious *kerygma* [proclamation] of the Hellenistic churches."[3]

It may be agreed immediately that "Q" was indeed an early compilation that reflected the mind of Jesus of Nazareth. A matter of strong disagreement, however, is the contention that "Q" represents a merely ethical, reformist Jesus. On the contrary, I will argue that in "Q" Jesus is the Messiah, whose coming death and resurrection is presupposed.

In that case—and provided "Q" really did exist in a discrete form—the Jesus Seminar members and others who have elevated the importance of "Q" to redefine Jesus may have succeeded only in reinforcing the historical redemptive view of him as Messiah. Their "Q" strategy may prove to have been self-defeating, having an outcome opposite to their intentions.

But first, how good is the case for "Q"?

The Case for "Q"

First, a description of "Q" is in order. In broad terms, "Q" is the material found common to Matthew and Luke, but not found in Mark.[4] "Q" is the abbreviation of *Quelle*, German for "a source." It consists of about 250 verses that are mostly, but not entirely, sayings of Jesus. While some scholars use the term merely for a loose collection of sayings, others with greater probability are thinking of a body of teaching, a document. In this latter case, such a corpus is more likely to have existed in written than in oral form.

Many have argued in detail and at length for the existence of "Q."[5] Put simply, the case for a common source used by Matthew and Luke is called for because of the following considerations: (i) the significant number of critical texts that have identical or almost identical wording; (ii) "Q" follows the same sequence in both Matthew and Luke; (iii) "Q" as reconstructed has a historical and theological coherence.

---

3. Kloppenborg, *Formation of Q*, 21.

4. See the sharp critique by Akenson, *Saint Saul*, 324, of Koester and Kloppenborg who introduce into their "Q" material texts from Mark.

5. For example, Fitzmyer, "Priority of Mark," 3–39.

Due to the perceived superiority of Luke's version, Luke's reference is given before Matthew's, or alternatively cited as e.g., Q 11:3 (= Luke 11:3).

The "Q" hypothesis has always had critics not least since it depends on *both* a theory of Markan priority and the independence of Matthew from Luke.

Other hypotheses have been advanced. Some have argued that Matthew has incorporated Luke in his Gospel, thus explaining the "double tradition" (i.e., the common source, "Q").[6] Others follow the so-called Griesbach or "double-gospel" hypothesis that Luke made direct use of Matthew and that Mark then reduced both Matthew and Luke to his briefer, more or less bare narrative.[7]

Nevertheless, although the "Q" hypothesis and its close relative the Markan priority are not without issues most scholars remain unmoved by the criticisms or persuaded by the alternative explanations for the origin of and relationship between the Synoptic Gospels. The case for "Q" though beyond proof remains strong and, for this author at least, is the most plausible explanation of the relationship between the Synoptic Gospels.

The Content of "Q"

It seems wise to consult the cooler heads of the older source critics for their understanding of the contours and character of "Q" rather than the emotionally involved exponents and opponents of the Jesus Seminar. One such source critic from an earlier era was T. W. Manson who (based on the Lukan version) analyzed the contents of "Q" as follows:[8]

A. John the Baptist and Jesus	The preaching of John The temptations of Jesus The preaching of Jesus The Centurion of Capernaum John and Jesus
B. Jesus and his disciples	Candidates for discipleship The Mission Charge The privileges of discipleship

---

6. E.g., Hengel, *Four Gospels*, 169-207.
7. E.g., McNicol et al., *Beyond the Q Impasse*.
8. Manson, *Sayings of Jesus*, 39-148.

C. Jesus and his Opponents	The Beelzebul Controversy
	Flattery rebuked
	Against sign-seekers
	Against Pharisaism
	Disciples under Persecution
D. The Future	The time of Crisis
	The Fate of the Unrepentant Discipleship in a Time of Crisis
	The day of the Son of Man

Based on this arrangement of the contents, Manson comments:

> It is in fact possible on this order to establish a rough parallelism between Mark and Q—at least at the beginning and end of the documents.

This opinion, however, depends on the view that "Q," as we are able to reconstruct it, is the authentic original compilation. This is precisely the problem the members of the Jesus Seminar and others have with the "Q" source.

Is "Q" an Archaeological "Tell"?

The most prominent "Q" scholar among the Jesus Seminar is John Kloppenborg (now Kloppenborg Verbin). His first major text *The Formation of Q* was written in 1987.[9] His later text, *Excavating Q*, invites the pursuit of the archaeological metaphor.[10]

Kloppenborg Verbin assumes a degree of stratification in the present "Q" document whose "layers," he says, can be isolated and identified. Kloppenborg Verbin argues that "Q" began as a sapiential ("wisdom") document (cited as Q1), that was then revised with the addition of prophetic/judgement/apocalyptic passages (Q2), and that was finally revised by the addition of narrative passages (Q3).

By this method Kloppenborg Verbin effectively reduces the original "Q" Jesus to be a speaker of "wise" sayings and has removed any messianic, atonement, or resurrection associations from Jesus.

There are several problems with this approach.

First, the assumption that texts of that era were mono-cultural must be questioned. Contrary to various attempts to tease apart and analyze

9. Kloppenborg, *Formation of Q*.
10. Kloppenborg Verbin, *Excavating Q*.

separately language strands we observe that Second Temple texts routinely intermix wisdom, prophecy, eschatology, and apocalyptic vernacular, especially in passages that prophesy a coming messianic deliverer.

According to Edward Meadors,

> clearly defined "compartmentalized" stratification of "Q" classified as "sapiential," "prophetic," "apocalyptic," "polemical," "paraenetic," etc. accord poorly with the diversity of first century Palestinian life.[11]

Jesus' seamless use of these categories provides no basis for identifying earlier and later strands but is rather gratuitous evidence of his messianic consciousness in the context of those times.

Second, Kloppenborg Verbin's analytical "tools" are problematic. The first, "the determination of compositional principles" assumes at the outset that the sayings of "Q" were originally separate, the work of one or more editors. The second, that "compositional activity may be seen as insertions or glosses," is entirely subjective. In other words, these "tools" are arbitrary and will offer different verdicts on texts depending on the assumptions of the critics.[12]

The following criticism by Bart Ehrman is well made:

> Let me repeat: Q is a source that *we don't have*. To reconstruct what we think was in it is hypothetical enough. But at least in doing so we have some hard evidence, since we do have traditions that are verbatim the same in Matthew and Luke (but not found in Mark), and we do have to account for them in *some* way. But to go further and insist that we know what was *not* in the source, for example, a passion narrative, what its multiple editions were like, and which of these editions was the earliest, and so on goes beyond what we can know.[13]

N. T. Wright's comment, though briefer, is no less direct:

> I find it impossible to believe that we can now discern developmental layers within [documentary Q] which involve significant theological shifts and transformations.[14]

---

11. Kloppenborg, "'Messianic' Implications," 261.

12. For a critical assessment of Kloppenborg Verbin's judgements on specific texts see Ingolfsland, "Kloppenborg's Stratification," 227–31.

13. Ehrman, *Jesus*, 133; see also Baird, *History of New Testament*, 382.

14. Wright, "Resurrection in Q," 86. See also Witherington, *Jesus Quest*, 42–57.

The most prudent position to adopt is to take "Q" more or less at face value and analyze it for any signs of Messiahship and other critical indicators regarding Jesus of Nazareth. Our results as summarized below prove quite surprising and do not at all correspond with the Jesus whom the Jesus Seminar finds in "Q."

Conspiracy by Another Name?

Kloppenborg Verbin and others assert that the author of Q3 created a Messiah out of one whose actual role and vocation was as a Sage. Since "Q" became a basis for both the Gospels of Matthew and Luke it follows that their texts would have been likewise distorted. However, the stratification theories applied to "Q" are unconvincing. The source we call "Q" presents Jesus in messianic terms.

Christology in "Q"

Edward Meadors[15] has established a deep-rooted messianism in "Q," notwithstanding the absence of the word "Christ" and the lack of "organizing faith statements." Within Second Temple Judaism there was widespread conviction of a coming, anointed deliverer from the line of David who would reign within a kingdom blessed by God. The Jesus of "Q" fulfills this expectation.

(a) Jesus is implicitly this "Messiah"

(i) In his response to John the Baptist in Luke 7:22/Matt 11:4-6 Jesus declared the following:

> Go and tell John what you have seen and heard:
>
> The blind receive their sight, the lame walk, lepers are cleansed, and the deaf hear, the dead are raised up, the poor have good news preached to them. And blessed is he who takes no offense at me.

Here Jesus combines Isa 61:1-3 (the herald of the Lord) with Isa 29:18; 35:5-6; and 42:19 (the end-time Day of the Lord), a conflation already implicit in the Qumran fragment 4Q521 (7-14). Jesus concludes, "Blessed is he who takes no offense at *me*."

---

15. Kloppenborg, "'Messianic' Implications," 253-77.

Having established the significant role of John at the beginning of "Q," this exchange between the imprisoned prophet and Jesus' revelation that he is the "one who was to come" is critical.

(ii) A further connection between John the forerunner and "the one who was to come" is found in their respective references to the Spirit. John declared that the Coming One was to "baptize with the Holy Spirit and fire"[16] whereas Jesus declared that "if I by the finger/Spirit of God cast out demons then the kingdom of God has come upon you" (Luke 11:20/ Matt 12:28).

When the key texts from (i) and (ii) are considered together it is clear that the Jesus of "Q" regarded himself as the Spirit-anointed "One was to come," in short, the Messiah (regardless of the absence of the name).

(b) Jesus exercises "messianic'" authority.

This authority is seen in various sayings:

(i) His "I say to you" form of speech that occurs fourteen times in "Q" texts, and which implies a messianic status as opposed to the prophetic status of "thus says the Lord."

(ii) The various "woes" Jesus pronounces—against religious leaders[17] and the villages of Galilee[18]—indicate God's judgment against those who reject the messianic rule of Jesus that has now begun.

(c) Jesus promises a "messianic" banquet.

Jesus informs his followers,

> And you are those who have stood by *me* in my trials. And just as *my* Father has granted *me* a kingdom, I grant that you may eat and drink at *my* table in my Kingdom. And you will sit on thrones judging the twelve tribes of Israel.[19]

This is a powerful statement by Jesus where he refers to his (messianic) "trials," his "Father" (God), his (coming) "kingdom," and his (messianic) "table." In another "Q" passage he refers to "my banquet."[20] Given the background in Second Temple Judaism of the messianic banquet Jesus' claims to Messiahship are explicit.[21]

16. Luke 3:16–17/Matt 3:11–12.
17. Luke 11:43/Matt 23:6.
18. Luke 10:13–15/Matt 11:20–24.
19. Luke 22:28–30/Matt 19:28.
20. Luke 15:24/Matt 22:1–10.
21. See *1 Enoch* 62:12–16; *2 Apoc. Bar.* 29:1–8; *1QSa* 2:11–21.

(d) Jesus' "Messianic" names in "Q."

In "Q" Jesus identifies himself messianically:

(i) Jesus is "the Son" who calls God "my Father"[22] revealing a messiah-filial self-awareness that arises from 2 Sam 7:14; Ps 2:7 (also 4Qflor).

(ii) Throughout "Q" Jesus is "Son of Man," the Danielic title that is messianic.[23]

(iii) Jesus is the "Blessed one" who "comes in the name of the Lord."[24]

The Death and Resurrection of Jesus in "Q"

According to Kloppenborg Verbin, "Q seems curiously indifferent to both Jesus' death and a divine rescue of Jesus from death."[25]

(a) While "Q" has no narrative of Jesus' last days in Jerusalem and his death there (nor any associated theology of atonement) it does not follow that this source has no reference to the passion of Jesus.

In fact, numbers of texts only make sense in the light of the death of Jesus the Messiah:

(i) Jesus' word that one must "take up" one's "cross" and "follow" Jesus in order to be a disciple[26] presupposes awareness that Jesus himself carried his cross as in the Passion Accounts.[27]

(ii) In Jesus' lament over Jerusalem,[28] Ps 117:27 LXX is cited ("Blessed is he who comes in the name of the Lord"). In the Markan and Johannine traditions, however, this text is inextricably connected with the passion of Jesus.[29]

(iii) In the Parable of the Pounds/Talents[30] the central figure (the "Lord") departs to a far country and then returns to hold his servants

---

22. Luke 10:21–22/Matt 11:25–27.
23. Mark 14:61–62; Enoch 48:2–10.
24. Luke 13:34–35/Matt 23:37–39.
25. Quoted in Hultgren, *Rise of Normative Christianity*, 35
26. Luke 14:27/Matt 10:38
27. Also John 19:17; Mark 15:21.
28. Luke 13:34–35/Matt 23:37–39.
29. Mark 11:9; John 12:13.
30. Luke 19:12–27/Matt 25:14–20.

accountable. The telling of this Parable in the "Q" context would have necessitated some reference to the death and *parousia* of the Messiah.

(iv) Likewise, the narration of the sufferings of the messengers of God[31] and the homelessness of the Son of Man[32] would have demanded some mention of the fact and meaning of the death of that Son of Man.

(b) The notion of resurrection as a present fact in "Q" as, e.g., in the words "the dead are raised,"[33] referring to Jesus' resurrection of the widow's son at Nain and Jairus's daughter.

The theme of future resurrection in "Q" is found in both implicit and explicit references.[34]

(i) Jesus' words about the patriarchs and believers seated at table in the kingdom[35] while those watching gnashed their teeth implied the notion of a coming resurrection and final judgement. The "Q" saying by John the Baptist about Abraham makes sense only from a setting where the coming general resurrection was believed.[36] Again, Jesus' promise that his followers will sit upon thrones judging the twelve tribes[37] presupposes future resurrection and final judgement.

(ii) Jesus explicitly speaks of his own coming resurrection as the "sign" of the prophet Jonah. As Jonah was a "sign" to the men of Nineveh so one greater than Jonah, the Son of Man, will be in his generation. That "sign"—explicit in Matt 12:40, implicit in Luke 11:31–32—can only mean Jonah's "extraordinary escape from the sea monster"[38] that pointed to the resurrection of Jesus.

"Q"—Collection or Kērygma?

From the foregoing items it is evident that those who formulated "Q" believed that Jesus was the long-awaited Messiah of God, who had been rejected by the people of Israel and put to death only to be vindicated in

31. Luke 13:34/Matt 23:37.
32. Luke 9:58/Matt 8:20.
33. Luke 7:22/Matt 11:5.
34. See Wright, "Resurrection in Q," 85–97; Wright, *Resurrection of the Son of God*, 429–34.
35. Luke 13:28–29/Matt 8:11–12.
36. Luke 3:8/Matt 3:7–10.
37. Luke 22:30/Matt 19:28.
38. So Wright, "Resurrection in Q," 94.

resurrection by God. It is equally clear that they held the new, final era had come, blessed with the gift of the Spirit of God (Luke 12:10/Matt 12:32). The Messianic epoch had dawned and they were part of it.

If these were the convictions of the formulators of "Q" it does not follow, however, that they formulated this "collection" to be published as a "Gospel" in the way that Mark's book would be. It is better to regard "Q" as a "proto" gospel, an early draft, so to speak.

"Q" is a collection of texts for catechetical use, rather than a finalized and coherent document for winning the outsider's obedience to Christ. Such references found there to Jesus as Messiah, his death, resurrection, and *parousia* (Second Coming) strongly imply that such tenets undergirded the convictions of those who compiled these texts. Such was its evident value that within several decades Matthew and Luke embodied it as a major source within their own larger works.

The Origin of "Q"

As noted above, the texts of Matthew and Luke, written (we suppose) by AD 80 (or earlier), testify to the existence of "Q" by that time, that is, within half a century of the historical Jesus.

However, "Q" texts are cited or echoed in letters of Paul (written 48–57). We conclude, therefore, that "Q" had been (substantially) formulated in the decade and a half (33–49) between the historical Jesus and Paul's missions in Greece and Asia Minor. For the greater part of that time span the Jerusalem Church was led by Peter (33–42) who was more liberally minded than many in the holy city.

From c. 50, however, the church in Jerusalem became increasingly Pharisee-influenced. By 48, Pharisees who "believed" were engaged in law-based counter-missions against Paul in the church in Antioch,[39] and against the churches in Syria and Cilicia,[40] and in southern Galatia.[41] By the late 50s the church in Jerusalem was characterized by "many thousands . . . among the Jews of those who have believed, *all zealous for the law*" (Acts 21:21). Josephus notes that James's martyrdom was an offense to those who "were strict in their observance of the *law*" (Josephus, *Jewish Antiquities* 20.201).

---

39. Gal 2:11–14; Acts 15:1.
40. Acts 15:23.
41. Gal 1:6–9; 6:12–13.

However, the era of Peter's leadership in Jerusalem (33–42) was emphatically not law-dominated, and it would have been during those years that "Q" was formulated.

Luke refers to "narratives" that were "delivered" to him by "those who were from the beginning eyewitnesses and ministers of the word." Source criticism reveals that "Q" was among those "narratives." Thus, "Q" bears the exalted *imprimatur* of the original band of Jesus' disciples who were his "eyewitnesses and ministers." Although we don't know for certain when or where an apostle or apostles handed over this text to Luke, it doesn't diminish the sensational reality that the text of "Q" was endorsed by the highest authority, the original disciples of Jesus.

How did "Q" come to be written? One possibility is that the disciples of Jesus memorized his words as he spoke them, with one or more of their number copying them down.[42] In the post-Easter period when these disciples won converts for Jesus the Messiah the original disciples assembled the words and works of Jesus for catechetical purposes in the newly formed messianic synagogues ("churches").

In which language was "Q" originally written? For reasons mentioned previously (chapter 11) I believe that "Q" was written in *koine* Greek from the beginning. Attempts to revert the Greek "Q" into Aramaic fail.[43] As noted earlier, it seems first that more of Jesus' teaching was given in Greek than I had previously understood, and second that Greek was rather more widely used in the early church than I had thought.[44] It looks as though Peter and the early apostles saw Greek, the international language, as the vehicle for the teaching of Jesus.

"Q" is marked by an immediacy and freshness suggestive of closeness to the mind of the teacher of the disciple or disciples who compiled this text. It calls for a radical un-hypocritical attitude to the Torah as befitting the new age, a readiness to confess Jesus as the Son of Man, and an attitude of implicit trust in the goodness of the Father, free of anxiety. Those who follow Jesus are to be non-judgemental toward others, but rather, loving and generous toward them.

42. See earlier, chapter 12.

43. Casey, *Aramaic Approach to Q*, argues that there was no single source "Q" but rather sources used by Matthew and Luke and that these sources were written in Aramaic. Head and Williams, "Q Review," 131–44 have critically and negatively reviewed Casey's attempts to back translate various Greek "Q" passages into Aramaic.

44. Porter, "Jesus and the Use of Greek," 71–87, answering Casey, "In Which Language," 326–28.

Conclusion

More than one observer has identified an ideological agenda driving the Jesus Seminar. Its program implies a conspiracy by the original "Q" community who refashioned the reformist teacher into a messianic figure. The members appear determined to find an ethically motivated, non-redemptive, non-Pauline Jesus. To them "Q," with its absence of reference to "Messiah" or to Jesus' death (whether as an event or as an act of atonement) or to Jesus' resurrection, might easily have appeared an ideal place in which to find a non-messianic, reformist Jesus. Yet to find this Jesus it has been necessary to go to extraordinarily reductionist lengths in editorial deletions.

The members of the Jesus Seminar were probably right in identifying "Q" as a discrete document and possibly right in concluding that it always lacked a passion narrative and resurrection appearances. Yet, as it stands, "Q" testifies to Jesus, the Messiah, who fulfills law and prophets and who calls upon men and women to follow him in sacrificial discipleship. Indeed, "Q" may be the earliest document of Christianity, one that exhibits not a low Christology but one that is exalted and entirely consistent with the Christology set out in "the teaching of the apostles" or, as Paul calls it, "the faith."

"Q" witnesses to the same Jesus found in other traditions within the New Testament. If it had been "walled off" from other traditions, as some claim, that may only point to its earliness and that it had been the *source* of influence upon others, including upon the letter-writers Paul, James, and Peter, and the Gospel-writers Matthew and Luke.

The Jesus of "Q" is therefore probably the earliest Jesus we encounter, but he is not different in principle from the Jesus we meet elsewhere in the New Testament.

At the same time, however, it is freely admitted that mysteries and uncertainties abound respecting "Q." We can understand how such a manual came to be created in the first years of Christian history. However, we are surprised that the text was written in Greek from the beginning. Knowledge of the circumstances elude us, but the likely earliness of "Q" as written in Greek text is consistent with Paul's early citations and echoes of this text.

fourteen

Was Mark the Arch-Conspirator?

We come now to one of the alleged major conspirators, Mark, author of the first-written Gospel. Among those who have attacked the integrity of the Gospel of Mark, none have done so more powerfully than John Dominic Crossan and Burton Mack.[1]

According to Crossan, the Gospels are "neither histories nor biographies, even within the ancient tolerances of those genres."[2] He describes Mark's account of the trials of Jesus as "consummate historical fiction."[3]

Rather, the Gospel of Mark was directed at the church's pastoral situation at the time it was written, decades after Jesus. The Christian community was demoralized after the Roman destruction of Jerusalem (in the year 70). It was necessary to fabricate a new foundation for the tottering Christian movement. This, it is claimed, was Mark's motive in writing his Gospel.

Crossan assumed that the Gospels' accounts of miracles are legendary. For example, regarding the raising of Lazarus he wrote, "I do not think this event ever did or could happen. . . . I do not think that anyone, anywhere, at any time brings dead people back to life."[4] Crossan interprets

---

1. Crossan, *Historical Jesus*; Mack, *Myth of Innocence*. For a sustained critique of Crossan see Boyd, *Cynic, Sage or Son of God*, 203–27; also Witherington has usefully reviewed these in *Jesus Quest*, 58–92.

2. Crossan, *Historical Jesus*, xxx.

3. Crossan, *Historical Jesus*, 390.

4. Crossan, *Jesus*, 94–95, quoted in Eddy and Boyd, *Jesus Legend*, 47.

miracles in the Gospels as "not about Jesus' physical power, but about the apostles' spiritual power over the community."[5]

John Dominic Crossan is not alone in his views about the motives underlying the Gospel of Mark. Burton Mack, for example, observes regarding the passion of Jesus, "This story does not derive from history."[6] Mack describes Mark's trial narrative as "fabricated mockery" and "a very vicious fiction."[7]

Crossan and Mack speak for many in their absolute rejection of the historical integrity of the Gospel of Mark.

The implications are considerable, as Crossan and Mack understand well. Since Mark can't be trusted historically, it follows that neither can Matthew and Luke be trusted historically since they depend on Mark. This means that the three synoptic Gospels are of no value in connecting us with the Jesus of history who is also the Christ in whom we believe.

By destroying the transcendent figure we find in Mark, Matthew, and Luke it is necessary for authorities like Crossan, Mack, and others to redraw their version of an idealized Jesus. He is usually a wise peasant, a politically subversive activist rabbi, or a charismatic teacher who performs no miracle and who is no redeemer.

Responding to Crossan and Mack

The primary criticism of Crossan and Mack is that their rejection of Mark and re-portrayal of Jesus arises from their presuppositions. They reject Mark's historicity outright and on principle. Then they propose a scenario for the writing of the Gospel of Mark that is speculative. How do they know that the Christian community was demoralized after the fall of Jerusalem, and that Mark wrote his Gospel to raise the morale of the churches? These authors refer to Mark as "fiction" but their contrived, evidence-free scenario is the real fiction.

Their reconstruction depends on dating Mark after the fall of Jerusalem in 70. Several leading scholars, however, date this Gospel between the fire of Rome in 64 and the death of Nero in 68.[8] I believe the Gospel of Mark was completed a few years earlier (by 64) but a somewhat later

---

5. Crossan, *Jesus*, 82, quoted in Eddy and Boyd, *Jesus Legend*, 48.
6. Mack, *Myth of Innocence*, 23–24.
7. Mack, *Myth of Innocence*, 295, 339.
8. For example, Hengel, *Studies in the Gospel of Mark*, 13, 16.

date would be sustainable. The Crossan/Mack theory, however, depends absolutely on a post-70 date for this Gospel.

Furthermore, Crossan and Mack, in common with many scholars, do not sufficiently focus on the limited lead-time between Jesus and the writing of the first Gospel. If, as I believe, the first Easter was in 33 and the Gospel of Mark was published shortly after 64, we are considering a span of just over thirty years, equivalent to a single generation.

There are two implications of this brief time frame. One is that it is too brief a period in which to re-fashion Crossan's humble peasant figure into Mark's omnipotent Son of God. A second consideration is that elements of Mark's tradition appear in the mission letters of Paul written between 48–57, as noted earlier, chapter 4.

Crossan and Mack fail on two fronts. They ignore the evidence for Mark's integrity and in its place propose a contrived scenario to explain how Jesus the peasant became the miracle-working Son of God.

Mark: Mystery Not Conspiracy

Mark's integrity secures the integrity of the Gospels by Matthew and Luke who relied on Mark's text. Suggestions that Mark engaged in a conspiracy to present a work of fiction as if it were fact are implausible.

What then about the elements of mystery in this Gospel? It has to be acknowledged that there are many mysteries associated with the Gospel of Mark. The letters of Paul and Peter written 48–64 have echoes of Mark's text, suggesting that there was an earlier, as yet incomplete version of that Gospel. There is no way of knowing how extensive was this "early" Mark. It is likely that Peter and Mark finally worked out the argument and style of the Gospel of Mark in Rome during the 50s and 60s, a task that Mark had more or less completed by the time of Peter's death in 64.

The answer to these and related questions is that there is no answer. We simply do not know, nor in all probability, will ever know. We must be content not to know. At the same time, however, we can patiently live with the reality of not knowing with the assurance that conspiracy theories are untrue and that the main outlines of the narrative are true.

In a later chapter, "The Making of Mark's Gospel," I will discuss some of the elements of the Gospel that point to the integrity of the Gospel and add to the unlikelihood of deception by this writer.

fifteen

Making the Written Gospel

The earliest references to "the gospel" (Greek, *euangelion*) as a *verbal* statement occur in the letters of Paul to his churches, beginning in c. 48 in his encyclical to "the churches of Galatia." From that moment until the end of his letter writing in c. 65 (his Second Letter to Timothy), Paul will use the word *euangelion* sixty times, always with the sense of a *spoken* message. In his opening lines of his magisterial letter to the Romans he wrote:

> the gospel of God . . . concerning his Son . . .

"God" was owner and source of the gospel and its message was centered on "his Son."

The only other letter writers who use "gospel" in a verbal sense were Peter (once in his First Letter, 4:17) and John (once in Revelation, 14:6).[1] So we have another mystery. What prompted Paul to use this word?

We notice another word that is almost a synonym, *kērygma*. This word was used for important public proclamations, including imperial proclamations directed to the whole empire. Although Paul uses the noun only five times, the verb "proclaim" occurs often in his letters, for example:

> we proclaim (*kēryssomen*) Christ crucified . . . (1 Cor 1:23)

---

1. The book of Revelation is cast in letter-form: "John to the seven churches" (Rev 1:4).

The Origin of Paul's Vocabulary

There were two antecedents for Paul's use of the *euangelion* vocabulary. One was Semitic, the other Greco-Roman.

Paul was a biblical scholar whose theological universe was the Septuagint (abbreviated as the LXX), the Greek version of the Scriptures. One important example is:

> O thou that bringeth *glad tidings* to Zion go
> up to the high mountains; lift up thy voice with
> strength; thou that bringeth *glad tidings* to Jerusalem;
> lift it up, fear not; say unto the cities of Judah,
> "behold your God…"
> Isa 40:9 (LXX)[2]

There was a strong tradition of the prophet bearing the good news of God's expected saving actions.[3] The use of this "good news" language for temporal expectations and hopes also became part of mundane "daily life" in Judea and Galilee in the first century.[4]

The other usage of "good news" language as a background for Paul was its currency in the Greco-Roman world to which he belonged, especially once he engaged in ministry to Gentiles. This language appeared in official inscriptions, a famous example of which was the commemoration of Caesar Augustus's birthday, which led to the realignment of the calendar:

> the birthday of the god [Augustus] was for the
> world the beginning of *joyful tidings* which have been
> proclaimed on his account[5]

Greco-Roman literature also employed "gospel" language. Plutarch writes of the dispatch riders who rode toward Pompey bearing the "good news" (*euangelia*) that the enemy king Mithridates was dead. He wrote,

---

2. It may be of no consequence that this text uses the verbal form, *ho euaggelizomenos*. Nevertheless, it is curious that the LXX only has three references to *euaggelion* (2 Sam 4:10; 18:22, 25), but twenty-three references to the verb, *euaggelizomai*.

3. Horbury, "'Gospel,'" 7–30.

4. Horbury, "'Gospel,'" 13.

5. Quoted in Lane, *Gospel according to Mark*, 43. Also, Horbury, "'Gospel.'" The inscription is in the Berlin Museum.

"Such messengers are known at once by the tips of their spears, which are wreathed with laurel."[6]

Paul certainly knew of "gospel" language from the Septuagint, but he and his Gentile readers would have known this vocabulary from the political and literary culture of the Greco-Roman world.

Why the Written Gospel?

It is almost self-evident that the written Gospel secures the Jesus story in perpetuity. Even the best oral tradition is subject to slippage, sooner or later. Countries are subject to wars, invasions, immigration, re-settlement and natural disaster. The era of Jesus was no stranger to these. Consider, for example, the fire that destroyed three quarters of Rome in AD 64 and the Roman demolition of the holy city and its temple in AD 70. Awareness of this was reason enough for Mark to complete and publish his Gospel after the fire of Rome and Nero's assault on the scapegoated Christians.

Justin Marc Smith proposes a further (and complementary) reason. It was the Gospel writers' choice of the *bios* (biography) as the genre most suited to the publication of the Jesus tradition.

> *The genre of ancient biography was the genre best suited to imparting the words and deeds of Jesus to the widest possible audience. . . . The benefit of the biography was that its focus was on its subject. The narrative structure of the gospels as biographies allowed for an incredible amount of diversity in the arrangement of the and presentation of Jesus materials. . . . Biography . . . allowed the evangelists to present the Jesus traditions in a historical narrative, as opposed to a fictional or novelistic portrayal of Jesus.*[7]

In a later chapter that discusses the reason for *four* Gospels I will suggest that these four texts were written for the distinctive networks of mission churches of the leaders James, Peter, John, and Paul. Inevitably these bear the marks of the authors and their communities. Nevertheless, they reveal to a greater degree their authors' concerns for the churches for

---

6. Plutarch, *Life of Pompey*, 41 (Loeb Classical Library).

7. Smith, *Why Bios*, 212 (italics original). Earlier, Burridge, *What Are the Gospels?*, 248–49 observed, "If genre is the key to a work's interpretation, and the genre of the gospels is *Bios* [biography], then the key to their interpretation must be the person of their subject, Jesus of Nazareth."

whom they were written. In that sense they are to be bracketed with the authors' pastoral directions in their encyclical letters to those networks.

"Gospel" as a Book

This brings us to another mystery. How and when did *euangelion* as a verbal proclamation become *euangelion* as a written text?

During the first quarter of the next century four texts were given the superscription, "the gospel according to . . ." Curiously, however, it is only Mark that identifies itself as gospel: "The beginning of the gospel of Jesus Christ, the Son of God" (Mark 1:1)

The other three texts do not identify their genre. We can only guess the reason. Matthew is organized around five blocks of teaching, especially the Sermon on the Mount. Perhaps the Gospel of Matthew is Jesus the Christ's *discipleship manual*.

Because Luke's biography of Jesus is complemented by his chronicle of the spread of Christianity, the author is encouraging us to think of Luke-Acts as a *history* of the origin and growth of Christianity.

The Fourth Gospel does not employ the noun *euangelion* or its verb *euaggelizomai*. It is the testimony of the disciple whom Jesus loved "bearing witness (*martyrōn*)" to the miracle signs of the Son of God and his crucifixion to inspire belief in him.

Several reasons may explain why Mark entitled his book, "The Gospel of Jesus Christ." First, Paul may have so popularized the word *euangelion* for *verbal* proclamation that it was a small step for Mark to make that word his book title. Mark had traveled with Paul in Cyprus and had been with him in Ephesus (Acts 13:5; Col 4:10). He would have heard Paul often speak of the "gospel."

Second, since Rome was the world-center of Caesar worship and the source of Caesar's proclaimed "gospels" throughout the empire it was appropriate but exceedingly daring for Mark to publish the "Gospel" of the *crucified* Son of God from the same world capital. Mark's Gospel, written from Rome, was for "all the nations" and "the whole world" (13:10; 14:9).

Third, Peter and Mark may have been concerned to bequeath a written and permanent record of Jesus. James, original member of the Jerusalem Church from 33 and its leader from c. 42, was stoned in the year 62. The oral gospel had served a great purpose, but the written record preserved the message permanently.

The Making of Mark

There are credible early-second century witnesses who state that Mark wrote his Gospel under the authority of Peter, and based on his teaching (see chapter 16). Peter had been the leading disciple of Jesus (29–33), the leader of the church in the land of Israel (33–42), the second most senior "pillar" of that church (43–47), a member (leader?) of the church in Antioch (48–52), missionary traveler in southern Asia Minor and Corinth (53–54), before finally reaching Rome in c. 55 where he became the senior presbyter.

Throughout those years Peter had presided over the formulation and proclamation of the gospel of Jesus the Christ, including the formatting of the message and its fulfillment of prophecy. It is overwhelmingly likely that he had created shorter verbal presentations of the gospel and secured some of them textually for reading to the new Jewish Christian congregations who, as Jews, were familiar with the *literary* culture of the synagogues.

Now in Rome, Peter the apostle, as leader of the church, and with gifted colleagues Mark and Silvanus at hand (1 Pet 1:1; 5:1, 12–13), could begin supplying the information for Mark his "son" to set down what would be the first *written* Gospel.

Published after Peter's death under Nero's assault on the Christians, this short text quickly became the narrative core of the texts that Matthew and Luke would write.

What Is the Gospel of Mark?

Mark's opening words, which serve as his title, identify his book as a *proclamation*, for that is what a Gospel is. "The Gospel *of* Jesus Christ" is grammatically *from* him and *about* him. It is, therefore, his proclamation of himself. It is directed to its hearers, challenging them to recognize and affirm *his* sovereignty while at the same time demoting and relegating the Roman Caesar.

Mark's method is biographical and historical in character but it is not a "straight" biography or a history. Contemporary readers in the Greco-Roman world would have found it confronting and difficult to classify. This may have been the reason Matthew and Luke, while respecting it because of Peter, nevertheless found it necessary to create earlier chapters to give the appearance of a biography.

Papias's verdict on Mark is rather qualified (see later, chapter 16). Mark did not "write in order," i.e., sequentially (an implied reference to Luke who did) and he did not "compile the oracles" of Jesus (as Matthew did). According to Papias, Mark did the best he could, based on memory, and "he did no wrong" (literally, "did not sin"!). This is not high praise.

Dating Mark

There are several reasons for dating the writing of Mark to the mid-sixties. First, the early authorities Papias (*c.* 110) and Justin Martyr (*c.* 150) identify Peter as Mark's source.[8] By ancient convention, the prominence of Peter within Mark's text confirms him as the authority for this Gospel (see chapter 16). Second, Clement of Rome (writing in the 90s) locates the death of Peter in the recent past, almost certainly in the aftermath of the fire in Rome (in 64) and the accompanying assault on the Christians, graphically described by Tacitus.[9] Third, Peter's First Letter, written in the presence of Mark in "Babylon" (Rome, 1 Pet 5:12–13), and the Gospel of Mark are both conscious of being written from the center of the "world" (1 Pet 5:9; Mark 14:9). These circumstantial details make likely the completion of Mark by the mid-sixties.

It may be objected that Jesus' prophecies of destruction of the temple (Mark 13:1–2) were written after the event (i.e., September, AD 70). However, a careful reading of Mark 13 does not point in that direction. Rather, Mark interpreted the focus of Jesus' prophecies on Caligula's threatened defilement of the temple (in AD 40), which did not eventuate. There is nothing in Mark 13 that demands a post-70 writing of this Gospel.

Surviving Manuscripts of Mark?

It is significant that there are surviving manuscripts or partial manuscripts of Matthew, Luke, and John from the second century, but none

---

8. Eusebius, *History of the Church* 3.39. See also Justin Martyr, *Dialogue with Trypho* 106.3, where Justin refers to the "memoirs" of Peter, citing Mark 3:16–17, the only text that refers to the renaming of the sons of Zebedee. Identifying the "memoirs" of Peter with the apocryphal Gospel of Peter is not possible since the latter makes no reference to the renaming of these men. Clearly Justin's "memoirs of Peter" is his way of referring to the Gospel of Mark.

9. 1 Clement 5:1–5; Tacitus, *Annals of Imperial Rome* 15.44.

of Mark. Yet, Matthew and Luke depended entirely on Mark's narrative for the writing of their own texts. Clearly there was an existing Gospel of Mark.

Throughout the intervening years, Mark has been more or less neglected. Matthew had the Sermon on the Mount, Luke the great parables, and John the miracle signs. Compared with these riches Mark had little to offer, so it was thought. It was more or less tolerated as part of the fourfold Gospels.

With the rise of biblical criticism, however, Mark's unique worth has been recognized, especially that it is the earliest written Gospel, and therefore the closest in time to the historical Jesus. Scholars have also increasingly realized its literary and spiritual power.

sixteen

The Making of Mark

We are now ready to reflect on the writing of the four Gospels. Since by widespread agreement Mark is the earliest Gospel, it is appropriate to discuss it first of all.

Earlier we rejected the theories of Mark's origin that declared its text to be fundamentally untrue to the real historical figure of Jesus. In this chapter we will approach the Gospel of Mark more positively.

The Title: The Gospel according to Mark

The title, "The Gospel according to Mark," was not part of the author's original text, but was attached early in the second century. (The titles of the four Gospels are called "superscriptions"). Nevertheless, the Christian leaders of the second century were unanimous in ascribing to the four gospels the titles that would later appear in our Bibles.[1] As early as c. 110 Papias, bishop of Hierapolis not only referred to what would be called the Gospel of Mark, but also explained its origin.

While there are no surviving manuscripts of the Gospel of Mark from the second century there are (part) manuscripts of Matthew and Luke, which secure the prior existence of Mark. Those Gospels embodied and depended on Mark. Papyrus 45, dated to the late-second century, does contain the Gospel of Mark along with the other three Gospels and the Acts of the Apostles.

---

1. See Hengel, *Studies in the Gospel of Mark*, 64–85.

Peter, the Source and Authority for the Gospel of Mark

Early and widespread tradition identified Peter as the authority underlying the Gospel that Mark wrote. Papias wrote:

> And the Elder was saying this:
> On the one hand, Mark, becoming Peter's interpreter
> wrote accurately as many things as he remembered.
> On the other, [he did] not [write] in order the things said and done by the Lord.
> For he neither heard the Lord, nor followed him,
> but later, as I said, [he followed] Peter.
>
> [Peter] who was teaching in accord with the
> anecdotes yet not as it were arranging the Lord's
> oracles, so that Mark did nothing wrong
> in writing some things as he related [them] from memory.
> For he was thinking beforehand of one thing,
> (i.e.,) to omit not a single word of the things he had heard or to falsify anything in them.[2]

This "elder" had heard the words of the original disciples about the origin of the Gospel of Mark (in the 70s), which he was now passing on to Papias (in c. 110). In short, the information about the authorship of this Gospel went back to the apostles of Jesus. In other words, Papias's written words cite an early oral tradition about the Gospel of Mark from within the lifetime of the disciples of the Lord.

As noted in the previous chapter Justin Martyr, writing from Rome c. 150, confirms Papias's explanation, calling the Gospel of Mark the "memoirs of Peter."[3] Justin was probably depending on the memories of the fellow-Christians in Rome. Irenaeus was another leader who had extensive knowledge of the church in Rome. More expansively, he wrote "after their deaths [Peter's and Paul's], Mark the disciple and interpreter of Peter also handed down to us in writing the things preached by Peter."[4]

---

2. Eusebius, *History of the Church* 3.39.15, quoting Irenaeus, *Against Heresies* V. 33.4. Translation in Gundry, *Mark*, 1027.

3. Justin Martyr, *Dialogue with Trypho* 106.

4. Irenaeus, *Against Heresies* 3.1.1, in Roberts and Donaldson, *Ante-Nicene Fathers*.

Late in the second century notable church leaders Clement of Alexandria and Tertullian made similar comments. These, however, may have merely repeated the earlier traditions from Asia (Papias) and Rome (Justin and Irenaeus).

An Oblique Reference?

There is a curious reference in the Second Letter of Peter that may refer to the writing of the Gospel of Mark. Peter writes:

> I think it right, as long as I am in this body, to stir
> you up by way of reminder, since I know that the putting off
> of my body will be soon, as our Lord Jesus Christ made
> clear to me. And I will make every effort so that after my
> departure you may be able at any time to recall these things.
> (2 Pet 1:13–14)

As noted (chapter 9), Peter probably wrote his First Letter between the outbreak of the Great Fire of Rome (July 18, 64) and the beginning of Nero's assault on the Christians some weeks (or months) later. It would follow that Peter wrote his Second Letter soon afterward (the Second Letter refers to the earlier letter—2 Pet 3:1).

Since Peter knew that his end would be "soon" his thoughts probably turned to Jesus' prophetic word spoken on the Galilean beach thirty years earlier: "you will stretch out your hands . . . another will dress you . . . carry you where you do not want to go" (John 21:18). John, the author, explains: "This he said to show by what kind of death he was to glorify God" (John 21:19). Jesus' prophecy and John's explanation are consistent with Tacitus's record of Nero's crucifixion of Christians after the Great Fire.[5]

So what did Peter mean in saying, "After my departure you may be able at any time to recall these things"? He was not referring to the letter he is now writing since it is obvious that the letter will not fulfill that role. It is more likely that Peter was referring to the Gospel that Mark will complete, publish, and circulate *after* Peter's death. That text will make it possible for Peter's readers to "recall at any time" the fundamentals of the Christian message.

---

5. Tacitus, *Annals of Imperial Rome* xv.14—"they were fastened on *crosses*."

When did Peter and Mark write this Gospel? As discussed below, there is evidence of a version of Mark being read and explained as early as the 40s (Mark 13:14—"let the lector understand," i.e., *explain* to the congregation). Also, Paul's Letter to the Romans that he wrote in the year 57 echoes Mark at several points (chapter 4).

As discussed earlier (chapter 9) I argue that Mark completed the Gospel before the death of Peter (in 64 or 65) and disseminated it soon afterward. Peter was in Rome from the mid-50s until his death in the mid-60s. Mark was also in "Babylon" (Rome) by the mid-60s (1 Pet 5:13) and probably for some time before that. The presence of Peter and Mark in Rome for perhaps a decade from the mid-50s makes it possible that together they made considerable progress toward the writing of the Gospel of Mark that the author edited and published after the death of Peter.

The Authority of Peter

A feature of the Gospel of Mark is the frequency of references to Peter. The reader of Mark meets Peter first and last, and at the mid-point. By ancient convention this signals that Peter was the authority underlying this Gospel.

Based on extensive research in ancient literature, Richard Bauckham observed:

> according to literary convention of the time the
> most authoritative eyewitness is the one who was present
> at the events from their beginning to their end and who
> can therefore vouch for the overall shape of the story as well as for specific key events.[6]

Martin Hengel is equally emphatic. He refers to these first and last references to Peter as

> a signature, by means of which Mark indicates the one who for him is the most important guarantor of the tradition, an individual who at the same time was the most authoritative disciple of Jesus.[7]

Peter's name occurs no less than thirty-six times in the Gospel of Mark, which is relatively more frequent in this short gospel than in the

---

6. Bauckham, *Jesus ad the Eyewitnesses*, 146.
7. Hengel, *Saint Peter*, 42.

other two Synoptic Gospels.[8] After Peter the Zebedee brothers James and John appear next most frequently, nine times in all. But in all but two cases they are mentioned *with* Peter.

This observation supports the testimony of John the Elder to Papias that Peter was the eyewitness source for the Gospel that Mark wrote.

Mark as "Interpreter" of Peter

Papias stated that Mark "followed" Peter acting as his "interpreter." This is consistent with the relative linguistic abilities of both men. Peter's birthplace Bethsaida was Greek-speaking but his vocation as fisherman means that his speech was probably limited to "street Greek." On the other hand, the text of Mark's Gospel reveals a writer of grammatically correct *Koine* Greek, but also one who accurately translated the various Aramaic words like *talitha koum* (5:41), *Corban* (7:11), *ephphatha* (7:34), and *eloi eloi lama sabachthani* (15:34) that appear in the Gospel.

According to Papias, Mark "followed" Peter and acted as his "interpreter." The linguistically accomplished Mark was well able to translate Peter's Aramaic and limited Greek into acceptable Greek or Latin, according to the audience.

The Movements of Mark

Papias states that Mark "followed" Peter, but when? For Papias's testimony to be credible, we need to be able to demonstrate at the very least that there were opportunities for Mark to have been in the company of Peter.

In c. 42 Peter the fugitive from Herod Agrippa 1 went to the house of Mary, mother of John Mark, in Jerusalem, before fleeing further afield.[9] This implies that Peter, leader of the church in Jerusalem, was a long-term associate of Mary, and of her son. His bi-name is Jewish ("John") and Roman ("Mark"), which suggests social and economic prominence. His tri-lingual competence (Greek, Aramaic, Latin—see later regarding Latinisms) implies a superior level of education.

In c. 48 John Mark accompanied his cousin Barnabas with Paul on a missionary journey to Cyprus and then to Pamphylia, a coastal province

---

8. Bauckham, *Jesus and the Eyewitnesses*, 126, supplies the following statistics. The name Peter or Simon or Simon Peter occurs once in Matthew for every 654 words, once in Luke for every 670 words and once in Mark for every 432 words.

9. Acts 12:12, 17.

in Asia Minor. Luke refers to him as their "assistant."[10] On arrival in Perga, however, John Mark returned to Jerusalem.

In Antioch in c. 49 Paul proposed to Barnabas that they should revisit the Galatian churches. Paul rejected Barnabas' request for his cousin John Mark to accompany them. Barnabas and John Mark went instead to Cyprus.[11]

We next meet John Mark in c. 55 in the pages of Paul's letters to the Colossians and to Philemon, both of which were (probably) written from prison in Ephesus (not Rome, as widely believed). Paul strongly endorsed Mark as among his fellow-workers and urged the Colossians to "welcome him."[12] Another key fellow-worker present with them in Ephesus was Luke, the "beloved physician." Whatever differences there had been between Paul and John Mark they seem to have been put behind them.

Mark was in "Babylon" (Rome) in 64 where Peter refers to him as "my son."[13] Mark's relationship with Peter as a surrogate "son" went back to the first decade of the Jerusalem Church. When did Mark come to Rome? It is possible that Mark had been in Rome for some years, perhaps that he traveled with Peter from Corinth to Rome in the middle 50s.[14]

So, the question prompted by Papias's assertion that Mark "followed" Peter is: when did Mark follow Peter? There were two main opportunities. The first was between 33–42 in Judea (and possibly also in Samaria and Galilee) and the other was between c. 55–64 in Rome.

33–42	Mark with Peter in Israel
55–64	Mark with Peter in Rome
64	In Rome Peter writes 1 and 2 Peter
64/65	The death of Peter
65+	Mark edits and disseminates his Gospel

10. Acts 13:5.
11. Acts 15:35–41.
12. Col 4:10.
13. 1 Pet 5:13.
14. According to Paul's final letter, written c. 65, Mark was in Ephesus. Paul requested Timothy to "get Mark and bring him with you, for he is very useful to me for ministry" (2 Tim 4:11). Paul does not explain how Mark was to be "useful to me for ministry" since he knew that death was near. Perhaps the following words casts light on this: "When you (Timothy) come bring . . . the books (*ta biblia*), and above all the parchments (*tas membranas*)." Scholars puzzle as to the meaning of these, but the clue may be Paul's reference to Luke's presence with him. Were these blank scrolls on which Luke would write his Luke-Acts text?

Mark's Languages

Greek

It appears that the Gospel of Mark had always existed in Greek since it does not back translate as an Aramaic original. This calls for explanation, since the long-accepted view has been that Jesus taught primarily in Aramaic.

The thesis of this book rests on two assertions: first that Jesus taught in both Greek and Aramaic, but predominantly in Greek because it had become the dominant Palestinian language; and second, that Jesus' words and deeds were recorded in *writing* and in *Greek* from the beginning.

Accordingly, we both agree and disagree with the observation of Martin Hengel.[15]

> Since non-literary, simple Greek knowledge or competency in multiple languages was relatively widespread in Jewish Palestine including Galilee, and a Greek-speaking community had already developed in Jerusalem shortly after Easter, one can assume that this linguistic transformation [from "the Aramaic native language of Jesus" to "the Greek Gospels"] began very early.

Hengel is correct to assert the widespread currency of Greek in Jewish Palestine, but not in his assumption that this linguistic transformation [from "the Aramaic native language of Jesus" to "the Greek Gospels"] began very early. It is more likely that we should push the Greek of the Gospels and their constituent sources back to Jesus himself even before the birth of the church. Evidences of the use of Aramaic in the early church and early Christianity are negligible. Jesus spoke mainly Greek and his disciples recorded what they heard and witnessed in Greek from the beginning.

The Composition of the Gospel of Mark

It would not be correct to assume that Mark wrote his Gospel *de novo* during the time he and Peter were together in Rome (55–64?). On the contrary, as we have contended, it is more likely that the basic material of the Gospel had been formulated in earlier years, going back to the time of Jesus himself.

---

15. Hengel, "Eye-Witness Memory," 89.

(i) The Outline of the Gospel

A consistent pattern may be discerned in the sermons in the book of Acts, in particular Peter's fifth (Acts 10:34–43) and Paul's first (Acts 13:16–41). Each of the sermons is focused on Jesus the Christ and is *biographical*.

Peter, a "layman," delivered his sermon to a God-fearer based family, whereas Paul, a trained rabbi, delivered his to a synagogue congregation. There are distinct stylistic differences between the two sermons, yet both have a commonly held chronological sequence, a sequence that depended on the eyewitness testimony of the disciples who had been with Jesus from his baptism by John through to his resurrection in Jerusalem.[16]

Acts 10 Peter	Acts 13 Paul
John's preaching of baptism	*John preached a baptism* of repentance
	Jesus, *"seed" of David* (i.e., Messiah)
Jesus the *Christ*, who is Lord of all	
who preached and healed in Galilee	
Peter a witness in Galilee and Judea	*Jerusalemites* and rulers secure death at hands of Pilate [on a tree]
Jews in *Jerusalem* put him to death hanging him on a tree	
	They buried him in a tomb God *raised* him from the dead
God *raised* him on the third day	He *appeared* to those who came up from Galilee for many days
God made him *manifest* to chosen witnesses	These are now witnesses to the people
These he commanded to preach	through this man *forgiveness of sins* is proclaimed to you and by him everyone who believes is freed from
To him all the prophets bear witness that everyone who believes in him receives *forgiveness of sins* through his name."	everything from which you could not be freed by the law of Moses

The finished Gospel of Mark follows the same outline as these sermons, broadly speaking:

---

16. Luke 1:2; Acts 1:21–22.

1:1–11	John's Baptism of Jesus
1:12–10:52	Jesus in Galilee, calling disciples, healing, teaching
11:1–16:8	Jesus in Judea, his disputes, arrest, trial, crucifixion, and empty tomb

C. H. Dodd is noted for seeing the connection between the Gospel of Mark and Peter's teaching in Caesarea and Paul's in Antioch in Pisidia.

> We can trace in the Gospel according to Mark a connecting thread running through much of the narrative, which has some similarity to the brief summary of the story of Jesus in Acts x and xiii, and may be regarded as an expanded form of what we may call the historical section of the *kerygma*.[17]

R. A. Guelich commented along similar lines:

> [The] tradition underlying Acts 10:34-43 anticipates the literary genre of gospel, since Mark's Gospel directly corresponds formally and materially with this tradition.[18]

In brief, then, textual analysis shows a close connection between the summarized teaching of Peter in Acts 10 and Paul in Acts 13 and the written Gospel according to Mark. The apostolic verbal gospel evolved into the written Gospel.

We can say with confidence that the gospel format was established soon after the resurrection and was repeatedly declared as the basis of evangelism throughout the apostolic age.

(ii) Markan Blocks

Various chronologically connected blocks are discernible in this Gospel.

In Capernaum (1:21–32)

1:21	And they went into Capernaum; and immediately on the Sabbath he entered the synagogue.
1:29	And *immediately* he left the synagogue, and entered the house of Simon and Andrew.

---

17. Dodd, *Apostolic Preaching*, 46–52 *passim*.
18. Guelich, "Gospel Genre," 201.

| 1:32 | *That evening*, at sundown, they brought to him all who were sick or possessed with demons. |
| 1:35 | And *in the morning*, a great while before day, he rose and went out to a lonely place. |

The activities of this *day* in Capernaum were followed later by a cluster of events around the lake.

Crossing the lake (4:1–5:1)

4:1	Again he began to teach beside the sea.
4:35	*On that day*, when evening had come, he said to them, "Let us go across to the other side."
5:1	*They came* to the other side of the sea.

Mark intends us to see these events as occurring during the one *day*.

Another lake crossing (6:30–53)

6:31	And he said to them, "Come away by yourselves to a lonely place, and rest a while."
6:45	*Immediately* he made his disciples get into the boat and go before him to the other side.
6:53	And *when they had crossed over*, they came to land at Gennesaret.

Once again, the events of a particular *day* are on view.

In the north (8:27–9:2)

| 8:27 | And Jesus went on with his disciples, to the villages of Caesarea Philippi.[9] |
| 9:2 | And *after six days* Jesus took with him Peter and James and John, and led them up a high mountain. |

Unlike the other connected passages Mark 8:27 and 9:2 describe the longer period of *six days*.

It could be argued that Mark has engaged in contrived verisimilitude. But why would Mark do this in these few instances rather than cast the whole narrative like this? It is more likely that Mark has specifically remembered these sequences from Peter's narration of them.

Since there is no discernible Aramaic original underlying Mark (apart from isolated words) we assume that earlier constituent parts existed in Greek from their beginnings. Furthermore, because these blocks

---

19. After c. 54 Caesarea Philippi was renamed Neronias (Josephus, *Jewish Antiquities* 20.211). Mark's retention of the earlier name that was current during Jesus' ministry supports the general historicity of this Gospel.

were created for teaching purposes in the early churches, they had probably always existed in *written* form. The primary purpose for a synagogue meeting was the reading of sacred texts. The first evangelists, who were Jews, would have sought to provide written texts for *reading* in the original congregations of Christians.

Jesus' words, "when you see the desolating sacrilege set up where *he*[20] ought not to be (let the reader understand), then let those in Judea flee to the mountains" (Mark 13:14) points its *writing* soon after the event described (most probably Caligula's attempt to desecrate the temple in AD 40).

Paul's Letter to the Romans, written 57, also bears on the dating of possible "blocks" of teaching in Mark's Gospel. Paul exhorts the Romans (1) to "render" to authorities what is their due (Rom 13:7 echoing Mark 12:17); (2) not to cause others to "stumble" (Rom 14:13 echoing Mark 9:42); and (3) that all foods are "clean" (Rom 14:14 echoing Mark 7:19).

These echoes probably point to Markan teaching blocks circulating by the 50s, which like those mentioned above found their way into the final version of the Gospel of Mark.

Following Papias our hypothesis is that Mark wrote his Gospel based on source material Peter had provided. However, the outline of the Gospel and significant blocks of teaching had begun to be established in writing almost from the time of Jesus. This explains why Paul was able to cite the teachings from this tradition in his letters even though they would not reach their finished form until the mid-60s.

The Anti-Imperial Character of Mark

There are a number of key themes that make Mark the most "Roman" of the four Gospels. It is only Mark's Gospel that calls itself a "gospel." For two reasons his opening words ("The beginning of the gospel of Jesus Christ, the Son of God") were provocative.

First, the word "gospel" had been used for "good news" about the birthday of the god Caesar Augustus, as in the famous inscription in Priene (western Asia Minor) in 9 BC already mentioned. Mark's choice of the word "gospel" appears to have been calculated and provocative.

---

20. Because the antecedent of the pronoun is neuter gender we must assume Mark has deliberately violated the grammar to make a point that the lector must explain to the assembled believers. The "desolating sacrilege" is a man!

Secondly, "son of a god" was a title for the Caesar (Latin: *divi filius*). Mark's opening sentence (effectively the title of his book) was saying that not Caesar, but Jesus Christ, is the true "Son of God." The climax of this Gospel was the statement of the *Roman centurion* regarding the crucified Jesus: "*This* man was the Son of God" (Mark 15:39). The centurion was saying, in effect, "this man and not the Caesar is the Son of God." It is no exaggeration to say that the Gospel of Mark was politically subversive.

Thirdly, Mark pointedly narrates Jesus' authority over the unclean spirits in the man called "Legion" (Mark 5:1–20). The country of the Gerasenes to which Jesus had come was a place of evil—the suffering, shackled man living in the *tombs*, his own subjugation to the *forces* of uncleanness, and the presence of *pigs*. Jesus' deliverance of the man, *Legion*, and his destruction of the host pigs, points to his power and authority over Roman values.

Fourthly, it is unlikely to be accidental that, according to Mark, Peter and the disciples acknowledge Jesus as the Messiah at *Caesarea* Philippi, a cult center for Caesar Augustus. While its name was changed to Neronias during the rule of Nero,[21] the Gospel of Mark anachronistically but provocatively retains the earlier name. Readers [hearers] of Mark would not have missed the significance of the disciples' recognition of Jesus as Messiah in a city named *Caesarea* Philippi. There were also temples in Judea dedicated to Augustus in Caesarea and Sebaste, as well as thousands of statues and portraits of Augustus throughout the Roman Empire.

Fifthly, Mark reports Jesus' scathing words, "those who are *supposed* to rule over the Gentiles lord it over them."[22] God is the true ruler of the nations whereas the Caesars only *appear* to rule them.[23] They are pseudo rulers and also tyrants.

A Gospel for All the World

Mark was present with Peter when the First Letter of Peter was sent from Rome to the "brotherhood throughout the *world*."[24] Peter, Silvanus, and Mark would have been conscious that they lived in the center of the world, and that the nations revolved around that city.

21. Josephus, *Jewish Antiquities* 20.211.
22. Mark 10:42.
23. See further Price, *Rituals and Power*; Peppard, *Son of God*.
24. 1 Pet 2:17; 5:9.

As they planned the writing of the Gospel the two men would have been conscious that their text was being issued from the *world capital*.

Mark implies that this Gospel is for the *world*:

13:10	"the gospel must first be proclaimed to *all nations*"
14:9	"wherever this gospel is proclaimed in *the whole world*"

Years earlier Peter and Mark would have seen Jerusalem as the center of the world. But by the 60s the Jews in Palestine were closing their hearts to Jesus the Messiah. The belief that Jesus was the true Son of God was increasingly the credo of the Gentiles whose world capital was Rome. The Gospel of Mark is *Rome*-centric.

Mark's Gospel to "the whole world" of the crucified Lord who was "truly the Son of God" powerfully and pointedly displays Mark's reverse imperialism.

Paradoxically, however, both the First Letter of Peter and the Gospel of Mark urge civil obedience to the Caesar. Peter exhorts his readers in distant Anatolia to "honor the emperor" (1 Pet 2:17) and Mark records Jesus' admonition in Jerusalem, "Render to Caesar the things that are Caesar's" (Mark 12:17). Mark wrote his Gospel from Rome and soon afterward Peter wrote his encyclical to the international Christian "brotherhood" from Rome.

Jesus Binds the Strong Man (Mark 3:22–27)

Mark establishes at the outset that Jesus' signature action was the expulsion of unclean spirits. The Pharisees in Jerusalem came to Galilee accusing Jesus that "by the prince of demons he casts out the demons." After ridiculing the illogicality of this accusation Jesus gives this allegorical parable to explain his exorcisms:

> No one can enter a strong man's house and plunder his goods, unless he first binds the strong man. Then indeed he may plunder his house.

Jesus portrays himself as a violent intruder who enters the house of "a strong man" to "first" overpower him, and "then" steal his possessions.

Jesus' parable serves two purposes. It answers the scribes' accusation, but even more fundamentally explains Jesus' total mission. Jesus' crucifixion, Mark's dominant theme, will be the occasion that Jesus binds Satan to liberate his prisoners. What Jesus is doing in Galilee (delivering the spiritually oppressed) he will do once and for all in Jerusalem (deliver the captives of Satan). This he will do—potentially—for the "whole world."

The Paradox of Mark's Gospel

Paradox lies deep in the heart of the Gospel of Mark. First we meet Jesus the Christ, the Son of God and the Lord. The voice from heaven confirmed his identity as the "beloved Son" as the Spirit of power was poured out upon him. He was irresistible in his conflict with the unclean spirits, disease, and death. The men he confronted immediately followed him. His preaching and healing attracted vast crowds who converged on Galilee including from outside its borders. At no point was this Transcendent Figure defeated or thwarted.

On the other hand, however, from an early moment in his ministry an unlikely alliance of Pharisees and Herodians entered into a conspiracy to kill him. Jesus knew he was the "bridegroom" to be "taken away" from his people. Once publicly acknowledged to be the Christ he set out for Jerusalem where he must suffer, be rejected by the temple hierarchy and be killed; but he would rise from the dead after three days. In his journey to Jerusalem he twice repeated this prediction of death and resurrection. He was the shepherd-leader, who was destined to be struck down.

On his arrival in Jerusalem one of his disciples betrayed him; his appointed leader denied him; all abandoned him. The supreme council in the holy city convicted him, accusing him of claiming to destroy the temple and to be the Christ. The high priest handed him over to the Roman Military Prefect who found him guilty of treasonably saying he was "king of the Jews." The Roman execution squad immediately crucified him, but the centurion, observing the manner of his death, declared, "Truly this man was the Son of God" (Mark 15:39).

This paradox provokes a serious question. How do we explain the death by crucifixion of the all-powerful Son of God? What is Mark seeking to teach his readers by the seemingly irreconcilable realities of Jesus' omnipotence on the one hand and his degradation on the other?

Strikingly, this Gospel highlights the crucifixion of Jesus and downplays his resurrection. The immediate prelude to the crucifixion and its description occupies the greater part of two long chapters, whereas there is no account of resurrection appearances, only a few verses about the empty tomb. The *crucifixion* dominates this Gospel, both in anticipation and in description.[25] Mark, who employs so many Latinisms, would have known that the Romans reserved crucifixion for slaves and non-citizens. From the imperial perspective Jesus would have been viewed as the lowest of the low, effectively as a non-person.

It is a characteristic of the Gospel of Mark, as well as the other three, that they do not state their theological aims in bald, abstract terms. Mark's "message" is embedded within his narrative. The reader must go looking for it, prayerfully and thoughtfully.

Mark is saying that Jesus the son of David and not the Caesar is the true Lord and divine Son and that he demonstrates this by his servant's care of the needy and in his redemption of many through his passion. Jesus' power displayed in healing and exorcism is not different in principle from his absolute liberation of Satan's prisoners through the crucifixion. His deliverance of the imprisoned is the explanation of the seemingly opposite aspects of his character, his power, and his debility.

The Caesar who lived in a palace in Rome ruled the world through raw, terrifying power. Jesus' throne was the cross, a place of humiliation and suffering, from which he set free the prisoners of Satan.

If this was Mark's message on one side of the coin, his message on the other was that those who follow Jesus would face rejection and suffering, as he had. This is because their lives will bear loyal witness to the One who challenged the all-powerful Caesar.

It is astonishing that Mark would create a message about all-powerful Caesar from (probably) a modest dwelling in Rome. However, soon after Mark wrote his Gospel the devastating fire in 64 reduced the Eternal City to a charred wreck.

The paradox in Mark, as well as many other quite profound features, identifies the author as one of great literary ability. Peter was the source of the Gospel and the unique authority behind it. Yet Mark is no mere scribe who has merely recorded his teacher's messages. The text of this Gospel runs deep and raises profound existential and moral challenges.

Jesus the Redeemer

Although separated by many years, William Wrede and John Dominic Crossan have it in common that they both reject the idea that Jesus was

---

25. See Gundry, *Mark*, 1–15.

a redeemer. Wrede blamed Paul for reinventing his version of Christianity to say that Jesus was a redeemer. Crossan said that Mark radically introduced that notion years after the historical Jesus to address pastoral issues that were current after the fall of Jerusalem.

The stubborn reality, however, is that Jesus saw himself as *redeemer*.

> Whoever would be great among you must be your servant, and whoever would be first among you must be slave of all. For even the Son of Man came not to be served but to serve, and to give his life as a *ransom* for many." (Mark 10:42–45)

Jesus said that in the anticipated Christian community leaders were to be servants, based on his example. Even so exalted a figure as the Son of Man (Dan 7:13–14) came "to serve" others by giving "his life a ransom for many."

In support of the genuineness of Jesus' utterance is the reappearance of "ransom" vocabulary in several apostolic letters.

Titus 2:14	our great God and savior [who] gave himself to *redeem* us
1 Pet 1:18–19	You were *ransomed* from the futile ways inherited from your forefathers, not with perishable things such as silver or gold, but with the precious blood of Christ.

The critical detail here is the use of common language. In Mark 10:45 Jesus used the noun *lytron*; Paul and Peter use the verb *lytroomai*. The noun and the verb are obviously closely related. The most obvious explanation for Paul and Peter using that verb is that they had come to know that Jesus used its close verbal relative. In short, the vocabulary of "redemption" was well established in early Christianity, the explanation for which is that Jesus had first used the keyword "ransom."

For different reasons, Wrede and Crossan baulk at the doctrine that Jesus was a redeemer. References in the letters, as quoted, establish their conviction that Jesus *was* the redeemer he said he was. Jesus as redeemer is the central message of the Gospel of Mark.

Conclusion

The unanimous opinion of authorities in the early second century was that Peter was the source and authority for the Gospel that Mark wrote. References to Peter at the beginning, the end, and the mid-point of this text represent a convention that points to Peter as the authority for this Gospel.

Mark was no mere amanuensis, however, but a gifted narrator whose text, despite its seeming naiveté, is spiritually profound.

At the same time Mark's Gospel has many plausible geographical, political, and cultural details that inspire confidence in its historical integrity (see Appendix following this chapter).

Mark wrote his Gospel to be *read* throughout the whole world by the people of all the nations. He is deeply aware that he is writing in the shadow of the mighty Caesar, yet he fearlessly proclaims that the crucified Jesus, and not the Caesar, is the God-appointed Son of God.

This Gospel is deeply paradoxical. On the one hand, the Son of God is omnipotent and irresistible, while on the other he is subject to evil men who crucify him. Yet that death was not unplanned, but the outworking of the will of God for the redemption of the spiritual captives.

The credible external validation of this gospel and its powerful internal character defy suggestions of corrupt motivation and conspiracy. It appears to be unsophisticated, but on closer examination proves to be existentially challenging.

True, there are many mysteries surrounding the Gospel of Mark, for example, *how* did the spoken gospel come to be written, and *when*? Granted that Mark effectively completed his text shortly before or after the death of Peter, when did the writing process commence? The text as we have it is in Greek, but was it always in Greek, as it seems to have been? Mystery, however, does not demand conspiracy. Upon examination, the conspiracy theories prove to be contrived and unconvincing.

Excursus: Indications of Integrity

A. The numerous Latinisms in the Gospel of Mark are consistent with Rome as its Provenance.[26]

There is an extensive list of Latinisms embedded within the Gospel of Mark. These are consistent with the possibility that John Mark had Italian Jewish forbears, but also point to the likelihood that he wrote his Gospel in Latin-speaking Rome.

These Latinisms include individual words:

---

26. For these lists see Lane, *Gospel according to Mark*, 24; and Gundry, *Mark*, 1044.

Hrōdianoi	= *Herodiani*	3:6; 12:13
modion	= *modius*	4:21
chortos	= *herba*	4:28
legiō	= *legion*	5:9,15
aita	= *causa*	5:33
spekoulatōr	= *speculator*	6:27
dēnarion	= *denarius*	6:37
xestēs	= *sextarius*	7:4
kodrantēs	= *quadrans*	12:4
phragellōsas	= *flagellare*	15:15
praitōtion	= *praetorium*	15:16
kenturiō	= *centurion*	15:39

There are also phrases, for example: *symbyoliom edidoun* = *consilium dederunt* 3:6.

According to Robert Gundry, "The Marcan Latinisms consisting of individual words are military, judicial, and economic, such as would naturally travel wherever Rome extended her rule."[27] Furthermore, Mark's extensive use of Latin words points to his Latin-speaking ability.

The Latinisms in Mark are consistent with a Gospel that was to be proclaimed "to all nations," "in the whole world" (Mark 13:10; 14:9). Mark's Gospel to the whole world of the crucified Lord who was "truly the Son of God" powerfully and pointedly displays Mark's reverse imperialism.

Mark was present with Peter when the First Letter of Peter was dispatched from Rome to the "brotherhood throughout the *world*" (1 Pet 5:9, 13). Peter, Silvanus, and Mark would have been conscious that they lived in the center of the world, and that the nations revolved around that city.

B. The many vivid details are consistent with an eyewitness basis of the Gospel of Mark.[28]

(i) There are numbers of examples of vivid detail in the Gospel of Mark. Where do they come from? If they were present in all the stories in Galilee we might be inclined to view them as contrived.

---

27. Gundry, *Mark*, 1044.

28. For discussion of archaeological details relevant to the Gospel of Mark see Eddy and Boyd, *Jesus Legend*, 412-47.

Their haphazard occurrences, however, in which they are confined to small details, tend to support their authenticity.

1:32–33:

> That evening, at sundown, they were bringing to him all who were sick or possessed with demons. And the whole city was gathered together about (Greek: *pros*, "at," "facing") the door.

The Sabbath was now passed and the incapacitated can now be brought to him; the whole city (Capernaum) was, as it were, gathered expectantly facing the door of the house. This dramatic scene is vivid and unlikely to be a literary invention.

4:35–38:

> And leaving the crowd, they took him with them in the boat, just as he was. And other boats were with him. And a great storm of wind arose, and the waves beat into the boat, so that the boat was already filling. But he was in the stern, asleep on the cushion.

The details "just as he was," the "other boats," and Jesus "asleep on a cushion" are at the same time so vivid and gratuitous as not to be a fiction-based imagination.

5:2–5:

> There met him out of the tombs a man with an unclean spirit, who lived among the tombs; and no one could bind him any more, even with a chains for he had often been bound with fetters and chains, but the chains he wrenched apart, and the fetters he broke in pieces; and no one had the strength to subdue him. Night and day among the tombs and on the mountains he was always crying out, and bruising himself with stones.

Mark's images of this disturbed man who was prodigiously strong, with broken chains hanging from wrists and ankles, are potent and, again, credibly written out of an eyewitness' recollection.

5:38–41:

> When they came to the house of the ruler of the synagogue, he saw a tumult, and people weeping and wailing loudly. And when he had entered, he said to them, "Why do you make a tumult and weep? The child is not dead but sleeping." And they laughed at him. But he put them all outside, and took the child's father and mother and those who were with him, and went in where

the child was. Taking her by the hand he said to her, "Talitha koum"; which means, "Little girl, I say to you, arise."

The name of the *archisynagōgos* (Jairus), the sounds of wailing, the laughter, and the Aramaic words all contribute to a strong sense of an eyewitness account.

6:39–40:

> Then he commanded them all to sit down by companies upon the green grass. So they sat down in groups (prasiai prasiai, "garden beds"), by hundreds and by fifties.

This is an almost photographic image of people seated in ordered groups, their colorful gowns giving the appearance of garden beds set in green grass.

The words from these passages in Mark's Gospel leap from the page. Most likely they spring from the memory of someone who was struck by the scene or the drama of the moment or the impact of the sounds. If such details were constant throughout we could explain them as literary invention. Their occasional appearance, however, speaks against that explanation. A storyteller who was an eyewitness is the most likely reason for the appearance of these striking details.

(ii) Prominent among the vivid details in Mark's gospel are Jesus' emotional responses in various situations. These are some examples.

1:40–43:

> And a leper came to him beseeching him, and kneeling said to him.... Moved with pity he... touched him.... And he sternly charged him, and sent him away at once.

3:1, 2, 5:

> Again he entered the synagogue, and a man was there who had a withered hand. And they watched him, to see whether he would heal him on the Sabbath, so that they might accuse him.... And he looked around at them with anger grieved at their hardness of heart.

6:34:

> As he went ashore he saw a great throng, and he had compassion on them, because they were like sheep without a shepherd.

10:13–14:

And they were bringing children to him, that he might touch them; and the disciples rebuked them. But when Jesus saw it he was indignant, and said to them, "Let the children come to me, do not hinder them; for to such belongs the kingdom of God."

14:33–34:

And he took with him Peter and James and John, and began to be greatly distressed and troubled. And he said to them, "My soul is very sorrowful, even to death."

Are these observations the result of Mark's imagination or of his recollection of Peter's words? If the former, we would expect a more systematic development of these emotions. The writer's passing mention of them points rather in the direction of his recall of Peter's own reactions to Jesus in these situations.

On five occasions Mark observes that Jesus "looked right around" as in a circle (*periblepomai*):

3:5	in the synagogue when they watched if he would heal on the Sabbath
3:34	in the house in Capernaum, with mother and brothers outside
5:32	looked to see who touched him
10:23	to the disciples when he said how hard it was for the wealthy to enter the kingdom of God
11:11	on his arrival in the temple

Each of these was a dramatic occasion and Jesus' manner of "looking right around" left its imprint in Peter's memory. Matthew does not use this word and Luke does so only once (6:10).

(iii) On twenty-one occasions Mark uses a third person plural pronoun ("they") without an explicit antecedent, usually in passages that describe the movements of Jesus and his disciples, followed by a singular verb or pronoun referring to Jesus alone. Richard Bauckham calls this "the plural-to-singular narrative device."[29]

For example:

---

29. Bauckham, *Jesus and the Eyewitnesses*, 156–81. Bauckham acknowledges the influence of Turner, "Markan Usage," 225–40.

5:1–2:

> They came to the other side of the sea, to the country of the Gerasenes. And when he had stepped out of the boat.

8:22

> They came to Bethsaida. Some people brought a blind man to him.

14:32:

> They went to a place called Gethsemane; and he said to his disciples . . .

When we compare Mark with Matthew and Luke we find that these dependent authors frequently remove references to the disciples ("they") and narrate the incident as if between Jesus and the other person(s) (to be healed or addressed).

Matthew and Luke stand removed from the events but Mark remains close to the events. Richard Bauckham points out how easy it is to render the "they" as "we" reflecting Peter's presence as an eyewitness. Mark, however, who was not an eyewitness naturally (and honestly) expresses the eyewitness Peter's "we" as a non-witness narrator's "they."

Consider, for example, how easily Mark's text retroverts to Peter's eyewitness testimony.

1:29–31:

> And immediately he left the synagogue and entered the house of Simon and Andrew, with James and John. . . . Simon's [my] mother-in-law lay sick with fever, and immediately they [we] told him of her. And he came and took her by the hand.

This hypothesis resists ultimate confirmation. Nevertheless, it remains an interesting possibility, especially when added to the other indications of Peter's influence on this Gospel, noted above.

C. Geography and History in Mark

The "Jerusalem" chapters (Mark 11–16) are closely knit with many details of time and place. Many point out that the same is not true of the earlier part of the Gospel. However, upon closer examination we find that Mark tends to identify a *location* for the event he narrates.[30]

---

30. Some have faulted Mark's geography (5:1; 6:45; 7:31; 10:1). For response see Eddy and Boyd, *Jesus Legend*, 447–52.

1:21	*Capernaum*
1:35	throughout *all Galilee*
2:1	*Capernaum*
3:7	withdrew to *the sea*
4:1	beside *the sea*
4:35	the *other side*
5:21	the *other side*
6:1	his *hometown* [Nazareth]
6:6b	among *the villages*
6:7	He began to send them out two by two (among the villages?)
[6:14–29 In *Tiberias* King Herod hears about the disciples' mission]	
6:30	by boat *a desolate place* [on eastern side of the lake]
6:45	the *other side*
6:53	*Gennesaret*
7:24	the region of *Tyre and Sidon*
7:31	the region of *Tyre*...through *Sidon* to *the Sea of Galilee*, in the region of *the Decapolis*
8:22	*Bethsaida*
8:27	the villages of *Caesarea Philippi*
9:2-	a high *mountain*
9:14	(down from the *mountain*) to the disciples
9:30	they passed through *Galilee*
9:33	they came to *Capernaum*
10:1	the region of *Judea* and *beyond Jordan*
10:32	On the road going up to *Jerusalem*
10:46	they came to *Jericho*
11:1	they drew near to *Jerusalem*, to *Bethphage* and *Bethany*, at the *Mount of Olives*
11:11	He entered *Jerusalem*
11:20	they passed by in the morning
11:27	they came again to *Jerusalem*
12:41	he sat down opposite *the treasury*
13:1	he came out of the *Temple*
13:3	he sat on the *Mount of Olives*
14:3	*Bethany* in the house of Simon the leper
14:13	he sent two disciples, "Go into the *city*"
14:17	he came with the disciples to *a large upper room*
14:26	they went out to *the Mount of Olives*
14:32	they went to...*Gethsemane*
14:53	they led him to *the high priest*
15:1	they delivered him over to *Pilate*
15:16	inside *the palace*
15:22	a place called *Golgotha*
15:40	women looking on from a distance
15:46	Joseph took him down laid him in a *tomb*
16:2	Mary Magdalene, Mary mother of James and Salome... went to *the tomb*

Two features of Mark's geographical references should be noted. The first is that almost all events and incidents that Mark records, including chapters 1–10, are tied down to *a named* location. Mark's Gospel, including the early chapters, is by no means an undifferentiated narrative. History and geography come together. The named locations are a feature of the entire manuscript and are consistent with the known geography, topography, and history of the region.

Although the references in Jerusalem are more detailed, consistent with the author being a Jerusalemite and a witness to some of the events there, we are surprised at the extent of geographic details in Galilee and the north and east, where Mark was not one of the original disciples.

What is the function of the geographical references? It is to assure the reader of the veracity of the events. The named location may have been a prompt for Peter to narrate what happened there.

The second feature is that Jesus' movements are consistent with what we know of the political reality in Galilee under the rule of Herod Antipas, whose capital was Tiberias. For example, Jesus chose the other side of the lake as the rendezvous for the missionaries: "a desolate place . . . on the other side" (Mark 6:30, 45). After the Feeding of the Multitude Jesus departed from Galilee and traveled to the north and to the east of Galilee (7:24–9:13). Only at the end does he travel secretly through Galilee (Mark 9:30, 33).

Jesus and Jerusalem

Why does Mark record only one visit to Jerusalem? In this, Matthew and Luke follow their template, Mark (apart from the visits prior to the baptism). By contrast, John records multiple visits to the holy city.

The explanation is to be found in Mark's focus on the crucifixion of Jesus as the culmination and climax of the message of the Gospel. For Mark, nothing must divert attention from the cross of Christ, hence the single visit to Jerusalem.

However, Mark is not unaware of the passage of time. His account of the storm on the lake (4:37) presupposes winter, and his reference to "green grass" (6:39) presupposes the spring (that is, the spring of the year before the fateful Passover).

Conclusion

By common agreement Mark's Gospel is deeply theological, bringing many challenges to those considering becoming a disciple. Many, however, criticize Mark for his lack connection with the historical, cultural, and religious connections, especially to Galilee. Papias and others, however, make clear that Mark was not a disciple of Jesus, but of Peter.

That said, however, the fact is that there are many details in Mark's Gospel that support the influence of Peter the eyewitness on the author—the vivid descriptive details about events, references to Jesus' emotions, as well as to geographical and topographical items that establish the places where he engaged with his disciples and others.

Mark's focus on Jerusalem and the crucifixion tends to pass over the many journeys to Jerusalem that Jesus would have made to the holy city, as we find in John's Gospel. Here Mark's theology rules his sense of chronology. At the same time, however, references to a storm (winter) and to "green" (spring) grass give some hints about the change in the seasons.

seventeen

Matthew's "M" Source

The material found only in Matthew, which is referred to as "M" and which consists of approximately 320 verses, is longer than "Q" (250 verses) but shorter than "L" (580 verses).

The Content of "M"

It is not easy to identify a structure in this source. Nevertheless, "M" contains the following:

Matthew	Subject
1–2	Genealogy and Birth Narratives
3:14–15	John the Baptist's hesitation
5–8	Three fifths of the Sermon on the Mount
10:5–8	The Mission Charge
11:28–30	Jesus' Great Invitation
12:5–7; 11–12a	Teaching on the Sabbath
13:24–52	Parables
14:28–33	Peter walking on the Water
14:22–25	The Canaanitish Woman
16:17–19	The Promise to Peter
17:24–27	Coin in the Fish's Mouth
18:10, 12–14	Parable of the Lost Sheep
18:15–20	Discipline within the church
18:21–35	On Forgiveness: Unmerciful Servant
19:10–12	Celibacy and the Kingdom
19:28	The Twelve Thrones
20:1–16	Parable of Laborers in Vineyard
21:10–16	Jesus in Jerusalem
21:28–32	Parable of the Two Sons

22:1‑14	Parables of Wedding Feast and Wedding Garment
23:1–39	Woes on Scribes and Pharisees
24:10–12, 30	Sign of the Son of Man in Heaven
25:1–13	Parable of the Ten Virgins
25:14–30	Parable of the Talents
25:31–46	Parable of the Sheep and the Goats
25:52–54	Twelve Legions of Angels
27:3–8	The Death of Judas
27:19–25	Pilate's Wife and Hand Washing
27:51b–53	Resurrection of the Saints
27:62–66	The Watch at the Tomb
28:2–4	The Earthquake
28:9–10	Appearance to the Women
28:11–15	The Bribing of the Guard
28:16–20	In Galilee: The Great Commission

While "M" defies the attempt to discern a structure, it does follow the Galilee-to-Jerusalem sequence of the verbal *kerygma*, "Q," and the Gospel of Mark.

Of course, it is possible that Matthew's use of Mark directed the shape of the "M" source (as set out above). It is equally possible, however, that Matthew's "M" independently followed the given Jesus-narrative, that began with John's baptism of Jesus and ended with his resurrection in Jerusalem and the Great Commission in Galilee. That narrative as it stands quotes a significant part of the Sermon on the Mount, as well as a number of Jesus' parables and key incidents.

The Key Features of "M"

What are the key features of "M"? Paradoxically, this source has a Jewish "tone" and a pro-law stance ("Think not that I came to destroy the law or the prophets," Matt 5:17; "Whosoever, therefore, shall break one of these least commandments, and shall teach men so, shall be called least in the kingdom of heaven," Matt 5:19) while at the same time being stridently anti-Pharisee (Matt 23:1–39). According to "M," Jesus saw the law as a burdensome "yoke" and invited the people to come to him and instead to take his kindly yoke upon them, the yoke of personal discipleship (Matt 11:28–30).

Consistent with its focus on Jesus and his invitation to come to him is the absolute emphasis on *grace* in the Parable of the Laborers in the Vineyard (Matt 20:1–16). Through the generosity of the owner, the one who worked only for the eleventh hour was paid the same wage as those who had worked for the whole day. Rabbis' parables with a similar story line rewarded the eleventh hour worker because he *achieved as much* in his hour as those who labored all day. These parables elevate the "works of the law" whereas Jesus' parable teaches the kindness and mercy of God.

Likewise, Jesus taught that the house that withstood the storm was founded on his *teaching* (Matt 7:26). The rabbis taught that the tree that withstood the storm was rooted in *good works*.

A second feature of the "M" source is its strong ecclesiology. "M" singles out Simon Bar-Jonah as the one to whom the Father revealed Jesus' true identity and destiny, and upon whom as the foundation "rock" Jesus would build his eternally secure church (Matt 18:17-19). Furthermore, Jesus promised Simon Bar-Jonah the "keys of the kingdom of heaven."

This is astonishing. Peter had departed permanently from the holy city by the year 50 and, in any case, James the brother of the Lord had been the leader of the church from c. 42 until his martyrdom in 62. "M" recognizes the unique role of Peter in the churches of Israel in 33-42, and the role he was playing internationally subsequently. The name "James," brother of the Lord, appears only once (obliquely) in "M" (Matt 27:56).

At the same time "M" gave strong directions about local church discipline (Matt 18:15-20). If a brother sins against you, first approach him, and if that fails take two or three witnesses who can testify to the gathered church to expel the offending member. The decision of the church will be binding (Matt 18:18-20).

A third feature of the "M" source is its emphasis on mission. First, Jesus directed his disciples to go to the "lost sheep of the house of Israel" with strict instructions *not* to go to "any way of the Gentiles" or into any "city of the Samaritans" (Matt 10:5-8, 9-13, 16b, 23, 24-25, 40-42). Then, at the very end of "M" when the risen Jesus was in Galilee with the eleven he directed them to "go . . . make disciples of *all* the nations" (Matt 28:16-19).

Jesus' reference to "the end of the age" (Matt 28:20) sets the context of the parables about universal judgement, a strong characteristic of "M."

The Parable of the Tares	13:24-30, 36-40
The Parable of Drag Net	13:47-52
The Parables of the Marriage Feast	20:1-14
The Parable of the Ten Virgins	25:1-13
The Parable of the Talents	25:14-30
The Parable of the Sheep and the Goats	25:31-46

The emphasis of "M" on the universal judgment is consistent with the universal commission.

Does Matthew Preserve the Integrity of "M"

There is, however, a problem in isolating "M" (as there is also with "L") from its "parent" Gospel. How do we know that "M" as identified above was an independent entity? Given that there was such a body of tradition that goes by that name, what assurance can we have that Matthew has not redacted or reshaped "M" in line with the Gospel writer's own agenda? In that case, "M" would be irretrievably lost.

Our problem is that there is no way of knowing since the only version of "M" is the text that is already embedded in the Gospel of Matthew.

The situation of Matthew's use of Mark is different. We have both texts that we can set side-by-side and quickly see to what extent Matthew has redacted or changed Mark. We will consider that question in a later chapter.

What if after careful comparison Matthew proves to be a cautious user of Mark? As we will see in that later chapter, that is indeed the case (chapter 19). Matthew does indeed redact Mark, but in no way is it to "improve" or inflate Mark's version of Jesus. This gives us reason to hope that Matthew was likewise careful in his over-writing of the "M" source.

The Dating of "M"

The reference to "offering your gift on the altar" (Matt 5:23) points to "M" being earlier than the destruction of the temple in 70, and probably quite some time before that critical event. At the same time, however, it is not possible to find many earlier traces within "M." Paul's First Letter to the Thessalonians, written c. 50, appears to cite "M" (1 Thess 4:15–17; Matt 25:30–32) and his reference to "yoke" in Gal 5:1 (written c. 48) may echo the "yoke" oracle in Matt 11:28. These earlier connections, however, are less than certain.

There are a number of "M" echoes in the Letter of James (chapter 6). These predate 62, the year of James's martyrdom, and may go back as early as the 30s, yet beyond that we cannot be sure as the writing of the letter is debated.

A better guide to dating is the comment of James and the elders to Paul and Luke in Jerusalem in c. 57 that the Jerusalem Church consisted of "thousands . . . among the Jews of those who have believed . . . all *zealous for the law*" (Acts 21:20). This is confirmed in 62 by Josephus's comment that those who were "strict in observance of the law" were scandalized by the high priest Ananus's stoning of James (*Jewish Antiquities* 20.201). These "strict" observers of the law were probably Pharisees.

These texts portray a law-focused Jerusalem Church led by James that enjoyed the favor of the wider community in the holy city, influenced as it was by the Pharisees.

The Provenance of "M"

"M" points to a community of Jewish Christian believers who upheld the intent of the law but, equally, were dedicated to Jesus who fulfilled the law. Their attitudes to the Pharisees were ambivalent. They shared the Pharisees' loyalty to the nation, but rejected their opposition to Jesus. What then of the Pharisees who were believers (Acts 15:5), who seem to have mounted missions against Paul? In my view, they did not influence the developing Gospel source known as "M."

The document "M" seems to have found a home in Jerusalem and perhaps also in the Jewish churches of Judea (Gal 2:22; 1 Thess 2:14).

The Language of "M"

As discussed earlier, the language of "M" is Greek. So far as we can see, "M" was written in Greek from the beginning, whenever that was. As with the other synoptic sources we are not able to back translate "M" into Aramaic.

Mystery

Candor is needed. There is a strong case that "M" existed as an independent tradition that Matthew incorporated into his Gospel. Based on the clues, we have suggested that "M" was assembled in the period between 50–65. While such a view is cogent and consistent, it is not certain. But what if the "M" source had been assembled earlier, which is not unlikely? In any case, "M" was written in Greek not Aramaic, supporting the likelihood that from the beginning Greek was the preferred language of Jesus and the early Christians.

So once again we have to admit that we cannot answer these questions with certainty, and that considerable mystery surrounds the creation and preservation of a text that would later be incorporated into the Gospel of Matthew. That said, however, there are no grounds for suspicion that Matthew the author has behaved duplicitously. As we will see in a later chapter, this writer gives the impression of honesty and goodwill.

Besides this, it is good to recognize that "certainty" is not a word that can be applied to the study of history, especially of an era that is distant from us. There is a spectrum of verdicts that are appropriate, from faintly possible to highly probable. This, however, is not a counsel of despair. In the practice of the law, as in the practice of history, the notion of certainty is elusive. Making decisions on the basis of likelihood and probability is the nature of day-to-day life, as well as of history writing and in due legal process.

Conclusion

We find the synoptic source "M" by removing Mark and "Q" from the Gospel according to Matthew. "M" is longer than "Q" but its structure is not so readily identified. Nevertheless, like the primary text Mark, "M" locates the ministry of John the Baptist near the beginning (after the genealogy and the birth-boyhood narrative) and ends with the Easter events in Jerusalem. "M" contains a large part of the Sermon on the Mount, and parables and miracles, as in Mark. While "M" is committed to the law it nevertheless sees Jesus as the fulfiller of the law, who offers the easy "yoke" of following him.

"M" has a strong ecclesiology marked by the surprising elevation of Simon Bar-Jonah where we may have expected a reference to the martyred James who led the Jerusalem Church for twenty years (42–62). There is a strong emphasis on world mission in "M," which is buttressed by strong parables on universal judgment.

"M" is a Greek text that may have been formulated between 50–65 in Jerusalem and perhaps also in the churches of Judea. It appears that "M" was written in Greek from the beginning. It does not seem to have been a translation of an Aramaic original. As with other text-sources it appears that "M" was formulated as a basis for teaching gatherings of Christians in Jerusalem and the churches in Judea.

eighteen

Luke's "L" Source

LUKE'S GOSPEL IS LIKE an elaborate omelette. We can detect the ingredients but we are unable to unscramble them to ascertain how it was put together.

The Composition of Luke's Gospel

We note, first, that this Gospel follows the same broad sequence of Mark, which in turn followed the same sequence as the orally proclaimed gospel, as in the sermons of Peter and Paul.[1] That is to say, it begins with John's baptism of Jesus, followed by his ministry in Galilee, followed by the journey to Jerusalem, and concluded by the events of the first Easter in Jerusalem.

Luke omits altogether Mark's account of the travels of Jesus in Tyre, Sidon, and the Decapolis.[2] In effect, Luke replaces these travels to the north and the east with his extensive narration of Jesus' direct journey from Galilee to Jerusalem (see below).

The Extremities of Luke's Gospel

Found only in Luke is his narrative of Jesus' boyhood and his ministry in the synagogue in Nazareth.[3] This appears to have been directly written by

---

1. Acts 10:34–43; 13:16–41.
2. Mark 7:1–9:29.
3. Luke 1:5—3:38; 4:14–30.

Luke, perhaps based on his research while in Judea 57–59 while Paul was in prison in Caesarea.

Equally distinctive is Luke's Gospel at its other extremity in his narrative of Jesus' trial, crucifixion, and resurrection appearances in Jerusalem.[4] It is likely that Luke also wrote these events directly based on his own research while based in Judea 57–59.

Jesus in Galilee and Jerusalem

Broadly speaking, Luke follows Mark's account of Jesus' ministry in Galilee, from its beginnings to the moment when Jesus "set his face" to go to Jerusalem.[5] There are also several incidents in Galilee that are unique to Luke:

Jesus' call to his first disciples	5:1–11
The "woes"	6:24–26
The healing of the widow's son	7:11–17
The narratives about women	7:36–8:3
The perplexity of Herod Antipas	9:7–9

Luke has also employed the "Q" source in his Galilee narrative:

The Beatitudes	6:20–23
The call to love enemies	6:27–36
The call to "judge not"	6:37–42
The healing of the centurion's servant	7:1–10
Jesus' verdict on John the Baptist	7:18–35

Again in the broad, Luke follows Mark's account from the time Jesus arrived in Jerusalem until his burial there. Within that narrative, however, Luke inserts his own material, again most likely based on his research.[6]

---

4. Luke 23:1–43; 24:13–53.
5. Luke 4:31–9:50.
6.. Luke 21:34–38; 22:14–23; 22:31–46; 34; 23:1–43.

Jesus' Journey to Jerusalem

The longest and arguably the most important sequence in the Gospel of Luke is the narrative of Jesus' journey to Jerusalem. Mark also makes much of Jesus' journey to Jerusalem, referring to it three times.[7] But Luke's account is even more pointed and expansive. It sets out Luke's teaching on discipleship during that journey as a template for the believer's pilgrimage from Galilee to the kingdom of God (symbolized by his departure from Galilee up to his arrival in Jerusalem).

9:51	When the days drew near for him to be taken up he set his face to go to *Jerusalem*.
13:22	He went on his way through towns and villages, teaching and journeying toward *Jerusalem*.
14:25	Now great crowds accompanied him.
17:11	On the way to *Jerusalem* he was passing along between Samaria and Galilee.
18:15	Now they were bringing even infants to him that he might touch them.
18:31	And taking the twelve, he said to them, "See, we are going up to *Jerusalem*."
18:35	As he drew near to Jericho.
19:1	He entered Jericho and was passing through.
19:28	And when he had said these things, he went on ahead, going up to *Jerusalem*.
19:41	And when he drew near and saw *the city*, he wept over it.
19:45	And he entered *the temple*.

The greater part of this Galilee-to-Jerusalem journey is composed of material that is found only in Luke, most notably the great "narrative" parables of Jesus like the Good Samaritan and the Prodigal Son. Interspersed with this "L" material are teachings of Jesus from the "Q" source.

The Origin of "L"

Once again, we are in the realm of conjecture about the place of origin of this text. One possible clue is to note that it, or its separate parts, came into Luke's possession, "delivered" to him by "eyewitnesses" who had become "ministers of the word" (Luke 1:1–4). Where might that have

---

7. Mark 8:31; 9:30–32; 10:32–34.

been? Based on our knowledge of Luke's movements the two most likely possibilities are Israel (57–59) and Rome (60–62). Of the two, the case for Israel is stronger because Luke had an extended opportunity to meet long-time local Christians, visit important sites, and receive texts that had been used for ministry purposes. By this reasoning Luke probably gained possession of the material that we call "L" during his two-year sojourn in Israel.

Observation

It is not possible to discover Luke's literary processes in the weaving together of the sources at his disposal. We confront a finished work, which is one of considerable literary and spiritual power.

Conclusion

We can identify the constituent sources in Luke's Gospel: Mark, "Q," "L," and the author's own narratives. However, there is no way of knowing why he treated his sources as he did. Why did Luke omit or select, abbreviate or alter his sources? The answer is that we do not know and, further, that there is no way of knowing. All we can say is that the author had an audience to address in terms of their pastoral situation and that he shaped his sources to that end. Our investigation of Luke's use of Mark and other sources, however, reveals an author of skill and integrity.

nineteen

Luke's and Matthew's Use of Mark

Since Luke and Matthew both used Mark's text in their narratives we are able to check their accuracy in their employment of the earlier Gospel. However, there is no way of knowing if Luke or Matthew misused their constituent texts "L" and "M." Yet if they were careful in their use of Mark (where we can check them) it would encourage confidence in their use of "L" and "M" (where we have no way of checking them).

This is important because it gives us insight into the integrity of Matthew and Luke.

Luke's Use of Mark

I have selected seven key passages about Jesus that appear in Mark and then set out the parallel texts in Luke.

1. Mark 1:11

> And when he came up out of the water, immediately he saw the heavens being torn open and the Spirit descending on him like a dove. And a voice came from heaven, "You are *my beloved Son*; with you I am well pleased."

> Luke 3:21–22

> Now when all the people were baptized, and when Jesus also had been baptized and was praying, the heavens were opened, and the Holy Spirit descended on him in bodily form, like a dove; and a voice came from heaven, "You are *my beloved Son*; with you I am well pleased."

Comment

Luke portrays Jesus baptized with others and praying. However, Luke neither raises nor lowers Mark's Christology. The Holy Spirit descended on Jesus accompanied by the voice from heaven addressing him as "my beloved Son."

2. Mark 1:24

"What have you to do with us, Jesus of Nazareth? Have you come to destroy us? I know who you are—*the Holy One of God.*"

Luke 4:34

"Ha! What have you to do with us, Jesus of Nazareth? Have you come to destroy us? I know who you are—*the Holy One of God.*"

Comment

Luke follows Mark closely.

3. Mark 4:36–41

He said to them, "Why are you so afraid? Have you still no faith?" And they were filled with great fear and said to one another, "Who then is this, that even the wind and the sea obey him?"

Luke 8:25

He said to them, "Where is your faith?" And they were afraid, and they marveled, saying to one another, "Who then is this, that he commands even winds and water, and they obey him?"

Comment

Luke follows Mark closely, though not exactly. Mark's high Christology is neither elevated nor lowered.

4. Mark 8:29

And he asked them, "But who do you say that I am?" Peter answered him, "You are *the Christ.*"

Luke 9:20

Then he said to them, "But who do you say that I am?" And Peter answered, "*The Christ of God.*"

Comment

Luke follows Mark closely, but not exactly. He maintains Mark's high Christology.

5. Mark 9:7

> And a cloud overshadowed them, and a voice came out of the cloud, "This is my beloved Son; listen to him."

Luke 9:35

> And a voice came out of the cloud, saying, "This is my Son, my Chosen One; listen to him!"

Comment
Luke follows Mark closely, but not exactly.

6. Mark 12:6

> He had still one other, a *beloved son*. Finally he sent him to them, saying, "They will *respect* my son.

Luke 20:13

> Then the owner of the vineyard said, "What shall I do? I will send my beloved son; perhaps they will respect him."

Comment
Luke follows Mark closely, but not exactly.

7. Mark 15:39

> And when the centurion, who stood facing him, saw that in this way he breathed his last, he said, "Truly this man was the Son of God!"

Luke 23:47

> Now when the centurion saw what had taken place, he praised God, saying, "Certainly this man was innocent!"

Comment
It is not clear why Luke diminishes Mark's high Christology. Perhaps Luke overwrites Mark to establish that Christ and the Christian movement were politically benign.

Summary
Luke's use of Mark encourages confidence in his skill and integrity. He writes his Gospel for a different audience, yet he neither inflates nor deflates Mark's view of Jesus. This encourages us that he had also used the "L" source faithfully.

Matthew's Use of Mark

Is Matthew true to Mark's references to Jesus? Does he exalt or diminish the Jesus he finds. Only careful comparison will give the answers. So, let us examine thirteen passages in Mark to see the changes that Matthew makes.

1. Mark 1:1–3

> The beginning of the gospel of *Jesus Christ*, the Son of God. As it is written in Isaiah the prophet, "Behold, I send my messenger before your face who will prepare your way, the voice of one crying in the wilderness: 'Prepare the way of *the Lord*, make his paths straight.'"

> Matthew 1:21–23

> She will bear a son, and you shall call his name Jesus, for he will save his people from their sins. All this took place to fulfill what the Lord had spoken by the prophet: "Behold the virgin shall conceive and bear a son, and they shall call his name *Immanuel* (which means God with us)."

> Matthew 3:1–3

> In those days John the Baptist came preaching in the wilderness of Judea, "Repent, for the kingdom of heaven is at hand. For this is he who was spoken of by the prophet Isaiah when he said, 'The voice of one crying in the wilderness: Prepare the way of *the Lord*; make his paths straight.'"

Comment

Matthew does not reproduce Mark's opening statement (vv. 1–3) that Jesus Christ is "the Son of God" and "the Lord." Rather, Matthew establishes from the genealogy that Jesus is "the Christ" who is the one prophesied by Isaiah, "Immanuel (God with us)," who will "save his people from their sins."

Mark quotes the prophecies of Malachi (3:1) and Isaiah (40:3) to demonstrate that John the Baptist was God's messenger before *Jesus'* face to prepare *his* way, that is, of "Jesus Christ the Son of God." Matthew omits Malachi (3:1) but follows Mark in quoting Isaiah (40:3) as foreshadowing John the Baptist who preached in *the wilderness* (of Judea): "Prepare the way of *the Lord*; make his paths straight."

Matthew neither exalted nor diminished the figure of Jesus he found in Mark's Gospel. Rather, Mark and Matthew were writing for different audiences. Mark crafted the introduction to his Gospel to demonstrate that Jesus and not the Roman Caesar is the true "Son of God." His Gospel's climax is the centurion's recognition that the man the Romans crucified was "truly ... the Son of God" (Mark 15:39).

By contrast Matthew wrote to demonstrate to *Jews* that Jesus is "the Christ" who fulfills biblical prophecy including that he was "Immanuel ... God with us." It is clear that Matthew is addressing the Jews (in Galilee and Judea?) who were opposing the belief that Jesus was the long-awaited Messiah.

2. Mark 1:14

> Now after John was arrested, Jesus came into Galilee, proclaiming the gospel of God, and saying, "The time is fulfilled, and the kingdom of God is at hand; repent and believe in the gospel."

Matthew 3:1–3

> In those days John the Baptist came preaching in the wilderness of Judea, "Repent, for the kingdom of heaven is at hand." For this is he who was spoken of by the prophet Isaiah when he said, "The voice of one crying in the wilderness: Prepare the way of the Lord; make his paths straight."

Matthew 4:17

> From that time Jesus began to preach, saying, "Repent, for the kingdom of heaven is at hand."

Comment

Matthew places John the Baptist on the same level as Jesus; both preached the eschatological message pointing to imminent in-breaking of the kingdom of God/Heaven.

It's not that Matthew was exalting John and thereby diminishing Jesus. Rather, it was because the people were so in awe of John that his testimony to Jesus was so valuable.

Both Mark and Josephus (who wrote a few decades after Matthew) point to the veneration of John the Baptist among the Jewish people:

| Mark 11:32—"for they all held that John really was a prophet." | Josephus wrote, "[John] was a good man ... and exhorted the Jews to lead righteous lives.... The verdict of the Jews was that the destruction of the army of Herod the tetrarch was God's vindication of John." (*Jewish Antiquities* 18.119). |

3. Mark 1:27

And they were all amazed, so that they questioned among themselves, saying, "What is this? A new teaching with authority! He commands even the unclean spirits, and they obey him."

Comment
Matthew does not repeat this incident.

4. Mark 2:9–10

"Which is easier, to say to the paralytic, 'Your sins are forgiven,' or to say, 'Rise, take up your bed and walk? But that you may know that the Son of Man has authority on earth to forgive sins'—he said to the paralytic, 'I say to you, rise, pick up your bed, and go home.'"

Comment
Matthew does not repeat this incident

5. Mark 4:41

He said to them, "Why are you so afraid? Have you still no faith?" And they were filled with great fear and said to one another, "Who then is this, that even the wind and the sea obey him?"

Matthew 8:27

And the men marveled, saying, "What sort of man is this, that even winds and sea obey him?"

Comment
The disciples' question recorded in Mark ascribes deity to Jesus, whereas their question in Matthew's version "what sort of man?" implies merely a special kind of humanity.

6. Mark 6:50

But immediately he spoke to them and said, "Take heart; it is I (*egō eimi*). Do not be afraid."

Matthew 17:7

But Jesus came and touched them, saying, "Rise, and have no fear."

Comment

Mark's account explains the miracle as due to Jesus' deity ("I am"/ *egō eimi*). Matthew, however, has removed this from his account.

7. Mark 8:29

> And he asked them, "But who do you say that I am?" Peter answered him, "You are the Christ."

Matthew 16:16

> Simon Peter replied, "You are *the Christ, the Son of the living God.*"

Comment

Matthew's addition "the Son of the living God" removes any doubt that Jesus was merely a messianic figure; he is "the Son of the living God" (also 14:33).

8. Mark 9:7

> And a cloud overshadowed them, and a voice came out of the cloud, "This is my beloved Son; listen to him."

Matthew 17:5

> A bright cloud overshadowed them, and a voice from the cloud said, "This is my beloved Son, listen to him."

Comment

Matthew accurately replicates Mark's account: the voice from the cloud declared Jesus to be "my beloved Son" with the injunction, "listen to him."

9. Mark 10:45

> For even the Son of Man came not to be served but to serve, and to give his life as a ransom for many.

Comment

Matthew omits this reference. Matthew's omission of the ransom passage is consistent with Matthew's relatively minimalist attitude to Jesus' death as an act of atonement.

10. Mark 12:6

> He had still one other, a beloved son. Finally he sent him to them, saying, "They will respect my son."

> Matthew 21:37

Finally he sent his son to them saying, "They will respect my son."

Comment

Matthew omits the qualifying "beloved," which however he includes in 3:27.

11. Mark 12:37

> David himself calls him Lord. So how is he his son?

> Matthew 22:45

> "If then David calls him Lord, how is he his son?"

Comment

Matthew follows Mark in recognizing Jesus, the son of David, as David's Lord.

12. Mark 14:62

> And Jesus said, "I am, and you will see the Son of Man seated at the right hand of Power, and coming with the clouds of heaven."

> Matthew 26:64

> Jesus said to him, "You have said so. But I tell you, from now on you will see the Son of Man seated at the right hand of Power and coming on the clouds of heaven."

Comment

Matthew replicates Mark's text, with few alterations.

13. Mark 15:39

> And when the centurion, who stood facing him, saw that in this way he breathed his last, he said, "Truly this man was *the Son of God*"!

> Matthew 27:54

> When the centurion and those who were with him, keeping watch over Jesus, saw the earthquake and what took place, they were filled with awe and said, "Truly this was *the Son of God!*"

Comment

Matthew follows Mark in quoting the words of the centurion that Jesus was the Son of God. Matthew, however, attributed this statement to the centurion "and those who were with him" based on the occurrence of the earthquake, whereas for Mark it was the manner of Jesus' death.

Summary

Mark portrays Jesus Christ in elevated terms as the Son of God. But to whom does he address his Gospel? For several reasons it is widely held that Mark has a gentile readership in mind, including those of the Roman world that venerated the Roman Caesar. Reasons for this include Mark's prominent use of "Son of God," one of the titles for the Caesar (Mark 1:1; 13:32; 15:39).

Jesus, as recorded in Mark, made it clear that God and not the Caesar was to be worshipped (Mark 12:17). As well, the Latinisms[1] in Mark support the view that Rome was the provenance of a Gospel widely attributed to Mark the disciple of Peter, both of whom were in Rome from the middle-to-late 50s and early 60s. The Gospel of Mark is conscious that its message is for the "whole world," for "all nations" (Mark 13:10; 14:9); Rome was the center of the world.

By contrast, Matthew was directed to Jews who were believers but who were located in a hostile situation in Galilee, Jerusalem, and in the churches in Judea. This hostility was due to the influence of the Pharisees. Matthew faithfully endorses Mark's portrayal of Jesus as the Son of God and the Messiah. He was, however, strongly demonstrating that Jesus was the Christ, in fulfillment of the genealogy and of the various proof texts scattered throughout the Gospel.

Matthew's Jewish readership may be the explanation for the distinctive testimony of John the Baptist, whom the Jews honored. John preached the same message as Jesus ("the kingdom of heaven is at hand") and like Jesus, was followed by tax collectors and sinners (Matt 21:32).

In short, Matthew does not exalt Jesus beyond Mark's already high Christology. On the other hand, his many references to Jesus as "the Son" and the citation of numerous prophetic proof texts indicate that Matthew has his own ways of portraying Jesus in strong theological terms.[2]

---

1. See chapter 16.
2. See next chapter, "The Making of Matthew."

Conclusion

When examined, Luke and Matthew make careful use of Mark's statements about Jesus. In general they neither raise nor lower Mark's strong Christology. However, Matthew does elevate John the Baptist but it appears only as a means of elevating Jesus.

Their careful use of Mark encourages us that Luke and Matthew would have made responsible and prudent use of their constituent sources "L" and "M," which we are not able to check.

twenty

The Making of Matthew

THE VIEW TAKEN IN this book is that Mark completed his Gospel in Rome some time between c. 55–64 and published it soon afterward. The believers in Rome then disseminated copies of Mark's scroll to various parts of the empire. There is no way of knowing if a copy was deliberately sent to Matthew or whether it came to him by chance, although the former is the more likely.

Matthew wrote in Greek, the language of the Gentiles, and was aware of gentile practices ("do not heap up empty phrases as the *Gentiles* do—6:7; "the *Gentiles* seek after all these things"—6:32). Nevertheless, the setting of Matthew was overwhelmingly *Jewish*. See the discussion below on the Provenance of Matthew.

Who Was Matthew?

The title, "The Gospel according to Matthew," with the other three familiar "superscriptions" goes back to the first quarter of the second century. In c. 110 Papias, bishop of Hierapolis in western Asia Minor, a man who had contacts with earlier Christian leaders, refers specifically to "Matthew."

The uniform evidence from the second century is that Matthew was the author of the first Gospel.

The only "Matthew" known to us was one of the original twelve disciples. In Matthew's Gospel he is called "Matthew the tax collector" (10:3; 9:9) whereas Mark called him by another name, "Levi, son of Alphaeus sitting at the tax booth" (Mark 2:14). Luke referred to him simply as "a tax collector named Levi" (Luke 5:27). Matthew and Levi, both tax collectors, were one and the same person. It is assumed that he had two names. In Galilee, the tax collectors were employed by the local tetrarch, Herod Antipas, whose capital was Tiberias, a few miles to the south of Capernaum, Matthew's home.

The two main items of information about Matthew are, first that when Jesus confronted him at his customs booth with the command, "follow me" he did so immediately, and second that he invited many fellow tax collectors and other "sinners" to a meal to meet Jesus (Mark 2:13-15). As a tax collector, Matthew was a social outcast (unwelcome in the synagogues), but he was also wealthy enough to entertain a large gathering.

Very little is known about Matthew in the post-Easter period. His name is listed among the twelve apostles (Acts 1:13) but it does not appear again.

The Gospel's many references to Galilee (see below) suggest that Matthew ultimately returned to his home region. If so, Matthew would have been under the spiritual authority of James, brother of the Lord, and the leading "pillar" of the Jerusalem Church 42-47, and its sole leader 48-62. The spiritual rule of James extended beyond Jerusalem to the three regions of Israel, Judea, Galilee, and Samaria. It is even possible that the authority of James reached as far as Antioch in Syria in the north, beyond the traditional boundaries of the holy land.[1]

Sometime in the middle-to-late 60s Matthew acquired the manuscript of Mark's Gospel, but also the sources "Q" and "M," but we do not know how, or from whom. His access to these precious texts suggests that he was an important Christian leader.

Study of Matthew's Gospel reveals that he wrote grammatically correct Greek and that he was a skillful narrator of the deeds and words of Jesus. The text of this Gospel tells us that the author was educated and familiar with the Greek text of the Old Testament to which he refers frequently.

---

1. We recall that James sent envoys from Jerusalem to Antioch to impose dietary rules on the whole church, expecting the exclusion of gentile believers included (Gal 2:11-14). See Bockmuehl, "Antioch and James the Just," 155-98.

Matthew's Structure

The five discourses each end with a formulaic conclusion[2] that suggest the author's structural planning. Beyond that, however, there are few clear markers to identify the structure for this Gospel, as reflected by a lack of agreement among scholars.

Nevertheless, there is an overall logic to the narrative, which begins with the revelation of Jesus' messianic identity, the flight to Egypt, and his baptism by John (chapters 1–4). Matthew then narrates Jesus' ministry of healing and teaching in Galilee (chapters 4–15), which is followed by his journey to Jerusalem (chapters 16–20). Matthew concludes his Gospel with the disputes in Jerusalem, the climax of which is his crucifixion and resurrection (chapters 21–28).

The five discourses within the broad narrative provide a structure to this Gospel, which broadly follows the geographic sequence of the Gospel of Mark.

1:1—2:23	Prologue
3:1—4:25	Early ministry in Galilee
5:1—7:29	*First Discourse*: Sermon on the Mount
8:1—9:38	Kingdom ministry in Galilee
10:1—11:1	*Second Discourse*: Mission instructions
11:2—12:50	Rising opposition
13:1–53	*Third Discourse*: Parables of the kingdom
13:54—17:27	Increasing opposition
18:1—19:2	*Fourth Discourse*: kingdom greatness
19:3–23:39	Coming to Jerusalem
24:1—26:2	*Fifth Discourse*: God's future
26:3—28:20	The Passion and Resurrection of Jesus

Kingdom Righteousness

Two key teachings of Jesus in the Gospel of Matthew are "the kingdom of heaven" and "righteousness."[3] The kingdom of heaven is an almost reverent periphrasis for Almighty God.

---

2. 7:28–29; 11:1; 13:53; 19:1–2; 26:1.
3. "Righteousness" is a keyword in the Sermon on the Mount (5:6, 10, 20; 6:1, 33).

Within this Gospel it is the Sermon on the Mount in particular that explains the meaning of these two terms.

A key text is Jesus' warning to existing and potential disciples:

> For I tell you, unless your *righteousness* exceeds that of the scribes and Pharisees, you will never enter *the kingdom of heaven*. (Matt 5:20)

In the passage that follows Jesus exposes the Pharisees' self-centered and self-justifying reading of the commandments and other texts. Thus, for example:

- They do not murder but they express anger
- They do not commit adultery but they lust
- They keep the divorce rules lightly to dispatch their wives
- They over-use oaths of promise that they do not fulfill
- They exploit a scriptural text to justify revenge
- They twist another scriptural text to justify hatred (Matt 5:21–48)

Jesus accuses them of misusing the Scriptures for their own ends, and for doing so hypocritically. This is the antipathy of the kingdom righteousness that Jesus was proclaiming.

When Jesus came to Galilee from his baptism by John he declared, "Repent, for the kingdom of heaven is at hand" (Matt 4:17). He proclaimed this message in the synagogues of Galilee and in the open. Great crowds attended his teaching, from Galilee, the Decapolis, and Jerusalem (Matt 4:23–25).

Matthew immediately conveys Jesus' teaching about "kingdom righteousness" (5:2–10):

> Blessed are
> Those poor in spirit theirs is *the kingdom of heaven*
> who mourn they shall be comforted
> meek they shall inherit the earth
> hungry for righteousness they shall be satisfied
> merciful they shall obtain mercy
> pure in heart they shall see God
> peacemakers they shall be called sons of God
> persecuted theirs is *the kingdom of heaven*

We note the *inclusio* formed by the "kingdom of heaven." The eight items are windows into hearts that have truly repented, and that is now "in" and "subject to" the kingdom of heaven.[4] This is Jesus' eight-sided glimpse of the truly *righteous*, not only in the future heavenly kingdom but also in the here and now.

Jesus' "Great Commission" to disciples instructed in "kingdom righteousness" was to make other disciples from all the nations who fulfilled this penitent, "heart-centered" way of life (Matt 28:16–20).

Matthew's Sources

Source criticism reveals that Matthew incorporates approximately 500 verses of Mark's text, following his narrative order, often using his exact words. We conclude that Matthew approved of and endorsed Mark's text, probably because it enjoyed the stamp of Peter's authority. Matthew had been a fellow-disciple with Peter, the leading disciple, and a colleague in the birth of the church in Jerusalem.

Matthew, however, had other sources available to him. Matthew has 1,070 verses of which 500 are from Mark, 250 are from "Q," and 320 from Matthew's Special Source "M." Focus on "M" as Matthew's Special Source would prove useful in identifying his distinct pastoral concerns.

Provenance of Matthew

Many students of Matthew opt for Syria as the place he wrote this Gospel.[5] There was a large Jewish community in the capital, Antioch, as well as a history of sending missionaries from the Syrian capital to the Gentiles (e.g., Acts 13–14). Ignatius, Bishop of Antioch in the early second century, was familiar with Matthew's Gospel.[6] To my knowledge, however, there is no evidence of the Pharisees in Antioch, a detail that speaks against that city as the provenance of the Gospel of Matthew. Matthew has so much engagement with the Pharisees (as "hypocrites"), that it demands a place of origin where their interaction with the Christian community was an issue.

4. Many of the elements echo Isa 61:1–3, as well as from many Psalms.

5. For discussion see Morris, *Gospel According to Matthew*, 11.

6. Ignatius, *Smyrneans* 1:1 appears to quote Matt 3:15 ("that all righteousness might be fulfilled by him"). However, Clement writing from Rome in the 90s also appears to make reference to Matthew; compare 1 Clem 13:2 with Matt 7:2.

There is, however, a plausible case for Galilee (i.e., Capernaum) as the place from which Matthew wrote his Gospel.

- Matthew has sixteen references to Galilee (Mark has twelve), for example:

    4:15   Galilee of the Gentiles" (surrounded by gentile city-states).[6]
    28:16 Jesus' Great Commission to the nations was given in Galilee.

- Matthew/Levi was (probably) a native of Galilee.[7]
- Matthew refers to both Jews and Gentiles, both found in Galilee:
    (a) "Hypocrites" (Pharisees): 10 references; Mark has 1.
    (b) "Gentiles": 6:7, 32 (also 24:32; 25:32).
- Matthew corrects Mark's incorrect reference to Herod Antipas as "king" (Mark 6:14), correctly calling him "tetrarch" (Matt 14:1).
- Matthew's references to the "kingdom of heaven" judaizes Mark's references to the "kingdom of God," implying intended Jewish readers.
- Matthew wrote in Greek and incorporated Greek written sources Mark, "Q," and "M." Greek was widely spoken in "Galilee of the Gentiles."

Certainty in identifying the provenance of this Gospel is not possible. Yet Galilee is a plausible option. Who were Matthew's intended readers? One possibility is that Matthew wrote his Gospel for the churches that were within James' mission, that is, Jewish-Christian churches that were part of the Jewish diaspora in the eastern Mediterranean (see chapter 6).

Matthew's Pastoral Setting

Based on the statistics noted above it means that the 320 "M" verses are critical in helping us work out Matthew's pastoral situation and his motivation in writing his Gospel.

Matthew twice uses the word "church" (16:18; 18:17) but it would not be correct to think that he was directing his Gospel in a narrow sense to these Galilean congregations. This author's concerns are broader than that. Matthew's Gospel reflected at least some of the issues faced by those churches, but he did not write *for* his community, narrowly speaking,

---

7. Mark 2:14; Matt 9:9; 10:3.

but *out* of his community to other groups about which he was pastorally concerned.[8]

1. The following verses reveal Matthew's appeal to *Jewish* readers:
   (a) The genealogy of Jesus "son of David, son of Abraham"—1:1–17.
   (b) Numerous Old Testament texts now fulfilled.

1:23 (Isa 7:14)	Immanuel, who will save his people from their sins
2:6 (Mic 5:2)	From Bethlehem a ruler and shepherd
2:15 (Hos 11:1)	"Out of Egypt I have called my son"
4:15 (Isa 9:2)	A great light in Galilee of the Gentile
11:10 (Mal 3:1)	John the Baptist who will prepare Jesus' "way"
21:5 (Zech 9:9)	"Your king . . . mounted on a donkey"

(c) Pointed references in Jesus' reported words.

5:1—7:29	The call for a greater righteousness than mere law-keeping
10:1–42	The mission to the "lost sheep of the house of Israel"
11:2–19	The greatness of John the Baptist
11:20–24	Warning to the unrepentant Galilean "cities"
11:28–30	Jesus' invitation to take his "yoke" (in place of the law)
15:1–39	The new and true purity
23:1–36	Jesus' excoriation of the Pharisees

Matthew's references throughout the entire Gospel indicate his concern for Jewish readers. He is critical of the hypocrisy of the Pharisees, of their persecution of Jesus' disciples, but also of the gross injustice by the temple authorities and the cowardice of the disciples. Nevertheless, he directs Jesus' teaching to them, especially in the Sermon on the Mount (5:1–7:29) and in his admonitions to the Pharisees (23:1–36).

2. Matthew foreshadows the entry of *the Gentiles* into the kingdom of Heaven.

2:1–9	The coming of and worship by the gentile Magi
4:12–17	Jesus comes to Capernaum in "Galilee of the Gentiles"
6:7; 6:32	He is aware of the Gentiles' "babbling" prayers and materialism
12:18 (Isa 42:1)	He quotes prophecy for the hope of the Gentiles
28:16–20	The risen Jesus sends the disciples to the nations

8. See Bauckham, "For Whom Were the Gospels Written?" 9–48.

Matthew weaves into his Gospel from first to last a deep concern for the Gentiles and their inclusion in the kingdom of heaven. Yet his concern for the Gentiles is not at the expense of the Lord's historic people. Matthew was concerned for both.

3. Matthew's powerful Christology is a golden thread that runs through this Gospel from first to last.

Son of David (the Christ, the King)		1:1–17; 11:1; 25:34
Supernaturally conceived "Immanuel" and savior		1:18–25
God's beloved Son		2:15; 3:17; 25:34; 4:3, 6 [8:29], 14:33, 16:16, 17:5, 27:43, 27:54
Fulfillment texts	Ruler and shepherd of Israel	2:6; Mic 5:2
	A great light	4:15; Isa 9:2
	God's "servant"	12:18; Isa 42:1
	"Your king"	21:5; Zech 9:9
	Seated at God's right hand	22:44; Ps 110:1

4. The surprising role of Peter in Matthew's Gospel.

Matthew, in common with the other three Gospels, makes numerous references to Peter. Matthew follows Mark in identifying Peter as the leading disciple and like Mark does not minimize his apostasy. More than any other Gospel, however, Matthew signals Peter's future greatness. When Peter recognizes Jesus as "the Christ, the Son of the living God," Jesus declares

> Blessed are you, Simon Bar-Jonah!
> For flesh and blood has not revealed this to you,
> but my Father who is in heaven.
> And I tell you, you are Peter, and on this rock I will build my church, and the gates of hell shall not
> prevail against it.
>
> I will give you the keys of the kingdom of heaven,
> and whatever you bind on earth shall be bound in
> heaven, and whatever you loose on earth shall be
> loosed in heaven.
>
> —Matt 16:17–19

These words, which are quoted from the "M" source,[9] are Matthew's way of intimating that, despite Peter's great fall, God had a significant future for him. Peter would repeat his confession of Jesus as the Christ many times in Jerusalem after the Feast of Pentecost[10] and thus become the foundation "rock" on which the Risen Lord would build his church. "Binding and loosing" probably refer to Peter exercising church discipline,[11] as in the case of Ananias and Sapphira.

What is striking here is that Matthew in his Gospel only mentions James the brother of the Lord once (obliquely—Matt 27:56). Peter remained in Israel for only a decade and a half after the first Easter and to our knowledge did not return. James, however, was a member of the Jerusalem Church from its inception in 33 and its sole leader c. 48–62.

Had Matthew been mirroring church life in Israel in the 60s and 70s he would have mentioned James and been silent about Peter. However, Matthew's many and highly significant references to Peter are evidence of his continuing international eminence, including his inspiration for the Gospel of Mark, on whose narrative Matthew depended.

5. The Importance of Matthew 27:51–56.

This passage follows immediately after the words signalling Jesus' death: "And Jesus cried out again with a loud voice and yielded up his spirit." Matthew then interjected the demonstrative particle, "And *behold* (Greek, *idou*)."[12] This was Matthew's expression of awe and wonder at the unthinkable, unspeakable event that had just happened. The Jewish leaders, through the hands of the Gentiles, have killed the long-promised, righteous Messiah.

From his first words and throughout his Gospel Jesus proclaimed the imminence of the kingdom of heaven, which paradoxically was inaugurated by a cruel and unjust death.

The passage that now follows reflects the awestruck reactions of God, the Roman centurion, and the women. Verses 51 and 52 narrate the five events that occurred immediately following the death of Jesus:

---

9. Hengel, *Saint Peter*, casts doubt on the integrity of this passage. For a defense of its genuineness see Meyer, *Aims of Jesus*, 186–97.

10. For example, Acts 2:36, "God has made him Lord and *Christ*, this Jesus whom you crucified'; also 3:18; 4:11–12; 5:31–32.

11. See Josephus, *Jewish War* 5.111, for reference to "binding and loosing" as referring to the Pharisees exercising synagogue discipline.

12. Matthew employs the particle *idou* ("Behold!") sixty times throughout the Gospel.

And	the curtain of the temple[7]	was torn in two, from top to bottom
And	the earth	was shaken
And	the rocks	were split
And	the tombs also	were opened
And	the bodies of the saints	were raised

Matthew achieves a powerful impact by these five staccato statements that are joined by "and" where the verbs are each in the aorist tense, passive voice indicating a series of *decisive* events executed *by God*. Everything that seemed permanent was affected by these dramatic actions. God has spoken.

Matthew's account of these divine actions captures the paradox. On the one hand, God signals his judgment upon the evils perpetrated on his Son, the Christ, while on the other, it articulates his recognition that Jesus "Immanuel" has "saved his people from their sins" (1:21). The resurrection of the saints reminds us of the connection between the death and the resurrection of Jesus as a single saving event.

Verse 54 now directs us to the reaction of the centurion and the soldiers keeping watch over the Crucified One. They witnessed the death of Jesus followed directly as it was by the earthquake. So shaken were they that they exclaimed, "*Truly* this was the Son of God," a messianic confession.

On two earlier occasions Jesus was asked if he were the Son of God, first by the high priest (26:61–62) and second by mockers at the crucifixion (27:40). But the centurion and the Roman guards are in no doubt. "Truly," these Gentiles emphatically declare, "this was the Son of God."

In verses 55–56 Matthew makes it clear that there were "many women . . . from Galilee" who were "looking on from a distance," among them Mary of Magdala, Mary mother of James and Joseph and the mother of the sons of Zebedee. Some of these women (perhaps all) were also present for the burial of Jesus (27:61) and for his resurrection (28:1). As they had ministered to Jesus in life so too they ministered to him in his burial and were the first privileged to witness his resurrection.

They stand in contrast to the male disciples. One betrayed him to death, another denied him, and all deserted him. It was these women who, in the absence of the disciples, carried forward the narrative about Jesus.

These verses coming immediately after the death of Jesus provide an awesome commentary on it. They represent a climax to Matthew's

Gospel. In the Gospel of Mark Jesus' greatness was seen in the multiplicity of miracles that attracted great crowds. In Matthew, however, while there is considerable emphasis on the Christ's miracle "deeds" it was his *teaching*, as in the five discourses, that was the mark of his uniqueness.

Conclusion

It is assumed that, whether by accident or intent, Mark's scroll came into Matthew's hands in the late 60s or early 70s. Matthew would have been glad to embody Mark's Gospel within his own, knowing that Peter was its source and authority.

The view taken here is that Matthew wrote his Gospel out of a pastoral setting in Galilee in the 70s. Matthew's use of non-Markan sources provides possible clues to his pastoral setting, but also his pastoral objectives. The prominence of both Jews and Gentiles within the Gospel suggests that Matthew wrote with both groups in mind.

For Matthew, Jesus is the long-awaited Christ who has come to proclaim the imminence of the kingdom of heaven, and who instructed his disciples for them to teach that message to the Gentiles when he was no longer with them. Despite his great discourses the temple authorities arrested him and effectively forced Pilate to crucify him. Ironically, his death provided the way of salvation for the very group who instigated his death.

twenty-one

The Making of Luke[1]

MYSTERIES ALSO ABOUND FOR the study of the Gospel of Luke. The third Gospel, like the others, is anonymous. So who the author? We are accustomed to speaking about the Gospel of *Luke*? Are we justified in doing that, especially since the name "Luke" only appears three times in the New Testament and never in any connection with a Gospel?

Scholars (rightly) link the third Gospel with the Acts of the Apostles.[2] Luke says that "eyewitnesses and ministers of the word" (Luke 1:2) supplied him with the raw material for both the Gospel and the Acts of the Apostles. When and where did this happen? When and where did "Luke" eventually come to write his "books," as he calls them (Acts 1:1)? What was the provenance of Luke's "books"?

Where do we begin in order to unravel these mysteries?

The Unity of Luke and Acts

Let me begin with the almost universally agreed fact that the one author wrote both books. The opening of the Acts of the Apostles makes it clear that it is a sequel to the Gospel: "In the *first* book, O excellent Theophilus, I have dealt with all that Jesus *began* to do and to teach." His second book, he implies, will narrate "all that Jesus *continued* to do and to teach" as the ascended Lord, *through the apostles.*

The length of each book (actually "scroll") is significant.

---

1. See Moessner, "How Luke Writes," 149–70.
2. It is difficult to understand why the Gospel of John was interposed between the Gospel of Luke and the Acts of the Apostles.

| Luke | 1,149 verses |
| Acts | 1,007 verses |

Due to weight factors it has been calculated that the practical maximum length of a scroll was 32 feet (9.75 metres), which happens to be close to the estimated length of both the Gospel of Luke and the Acts of the Apostles. It was logistical reality that forced Luke to write in two scrolls.

Luke's combined writings account for more than a quarter of the volume of the New Testament (about 27 percent) and make him its major contributor. Luke begins with the birth of John the Baptist in c. 6 BC and concludes with Paul's "two whole years" in Rome, c. AD 62, a span of almost seven decades. Throughout those seventy years Luke tells the story about Jesus and then the story of the spread of Christianity from Jerusalem to Rome. Without Luke-Acts we would not know the relationship between Jesus and the rise and extension of Christianity from Jerusalem to the gentile world.

The Identification of Luke

The clue to the identity of this anonymous writer is found in the so-called Muratorian Canon, which expressed the opinion of the Church of Rome in c. AD 170:

> The third book of the gospel, according to Luke, Luke that physician ... after the ascension of Christ, when Paul had taken him as companion of his journey, composed in his own name on the basis of report.

This statement is helpful in several ways. First, it specifically identifies the author of the Gospel as "Luke that physician" who is so-named by Paul, in a letter he wrote from Ephesus in c. 55 (Col 4:14).[3] That letter also identified Luke as a Gentile (Col 4:11). However, Luke's extensive

---

3. Contrary to widespread opinion that Paul wrote to the Colossians from Rome, it is more likely that he wrote Colossians, Philemon, and Ephesians (a circular letter) from Ephesus. Paul's chance meeting with a runaway slave in a prison in distant Rome is unimaginable as compared with this occurring in nearby Ephesus. There is a long tradition that Paul was temporarily imprisoned in Ephesus. We can envisage Paul asking Philemon about staying with him in Colossae while in Ephesus (three days journey away) but not from Rome (a hazardous journey of many months); see Phlm 22. Paul also refers to Luke (*Loukas*) in v. 24 (my "fellow worker").

knowledge of the Septuagint (Greek Old Testament, abbreviated as the LXX) suggests he may have been a God-fearer, a Jewish sympathizer and a regular visitor to the synagogue.

Second, the "we"/"us" passages in Acts indicate the occasions when the author was Paul's companion in his journeys.[4] Luke seems to have traveled with Paul from the time of his final journey to Judea (*c.* 57) through to his imprisonment in Rome (*c.* 62), a period of about five years.

Third, in his prologue to Luke-Acts the author implies that he was not an "eyewitness" to Jesus but "received" documentation from those who were. Thus, the Muratorian Canon is correct in stating that Luke "composed in his own name on the basis of a report."[5]

A further clue to Luke's identity is the likelihood that he was from Antioch in Syria. Early Christian writers Eusebius and Jerome said as much,[6] and the interest of the book of Acts in Syrian Antioch supports it.[7]

Luke and the Eyewitnesses

Following the death of Judas, Luke records the criterion for the election of an apostle:

> One of the men who have accompanied us during all the time that the Lord Jesus went in and out among us, beginning from the baptism of John until the day when he was taken up from us—one of these men must become with us a *witness* to his resurrection. (Acts 1:21–22)

---

4. Acts 16:10-16; 20:5—21:17; 27:1—28:16. The prologues of both Luke and Acts are also written in the first person, but in the singular form "me." These connect the prologues to the "we"/"us" narratives later in Acts. It is assumed that the Muratorian Canon was aware of the first person plural pronouns in Acts indicating the author's presence with Paul.

5. There are also several occasions when Paul refers to an eminent Christian leader in Macedonia but without naming him. The "we"/"us" texts (Acts 16:16–20:5) indicate that Luke appears to have been in Macedonia 50–57. In 56 Paul wrote to the Corinthians from Macedonia (Berea?) commending "the brother who is famous among all the [Macedonian] churches for his preaching of the gospel" (2 Cor 8:18). Later, in c. 63, Paul addressed a member of the church in Philippi as a "true companion" (Phil 2:2). It is possible that either or both of these unnamed eminent Christians was Luke.

6. Eusebius, *History of the Church* 3.4.6; and Jerome's preface to his Commentary on Matthew.

7. There are thirteen references in the Acts of the Apostles to Antioch in Syria.

The elected apostle must have been present with Jesus from John's baptism of him through to his ascension in Jerusalem. John's baptism of Jesus marked his "beginning" (Luke 3:23) and his ascension its end (Luke 9:51). This is the biographical span that both Peter and Paul narrate in their sermons in Acts 10:34–43 and 13:16–41, and that Mark follows exactly in his Gospel. This core sequence is also the centerpiece of the Gospels of Matthew, Luke, and John.

The reason given for this criterion is that an elected apostle was thereby qualified to be a *witness* (Greek, *martys*) to Jesus' resurrection, but also to the events that began with John's baptism of Jesus.

This means that the verbal message of the apostles was *biographical*, history-based, and true, and not merely theological, sentimental, or existential. It follows, therefore, that the *written* message in the Gospels was likewise *biographical*, history-based, and factual.

It is not possible to overestimate the importance to Luke of eyewitness testimony to the deeds and words of Jesus.

Luke plainly states that he was not a disciple of Jesus and therefore had no claims to being an eyewitness or an apostle. He does assert, however, that the sources ("narrative[s]") he used to write his Gospel and Acts had been "delivered" to him by those who "from the beginning were eyewitnesses and ministers of the word" (Luke 1:2).

The "eyewitnesses" of the *person* of Jesus became "ministers" of the *word* that they preached about him. This means that the contents of Luke-Acts were *apostolic* and *eyewitness*-based, even though its author was not an apostle, nor an eyewitness.

Luke's Sources

Thanks to the work of careful scholarship we are able to identify the sources that Luke used in writing his Gospel. These included Mark, "Q" (the text common to Luke and Matthew), and "L" (material found only in Luke). As we will see, however, Luke's procedure was more complicated than the simple weaving together of three existing texts.

Luke would also have used sources (oral and written) for the writing of Acts, but unlike the Gospel we have no objective way of identifying these.

One critical question is: when and where did Luke acquire the sources from which he wrote the Gospel. There are several possibilities, but we must understand that our knowledge is fragmentary and incomplete. There are mysteries! Some speculation is unavoidable.

Luke and Mark were together with Paul in Ephesus in c. 55.[8] Mark may have produced earlier drafts that would find completion in his Gospel a decade later in Rome. Perhaps Luke had access to these?

Another and more likely opportunity for Luke the writer was during his visit to Judea 57–59 during Paul's imprisonment in Caesarea (Acts 21:17—27:1). During those many months Luke had the opportunity to meet disciples from earlier times, visit sites like Golgotha and the burial tomb, and collect documentary sources.

It has been plausibly suggested that local Christian leaders had already created a teaching manual by combining the sources we refer to as "Q" and "L" into a document, which is referred to as "Proto-Luke" ("Q" + "L"). This is a hypothesis and not accepted by all scholars. However, if there was such a text it is significant that it is dominated by Jesus' journey from Galilee to Jerusalem,[9] which became the core narrative in this Gospel.

Proto-Luke

The Journey to Jerusalem

Luke narrates Jesus' journey from Galilee to Jerusalem followed by his disciples as a genuine event. At the same time, however, he portrays that journey as a spiritual pilgrimage that anticipates what it will mean to "follow" Jesus when he was no longer physically present. Throughout this journey Luke makes many references to Jerusalem as Jesus' destination.[10]

Jesus "set his face to go to Jerusalem" (9:51) knowing what awaited him there.

> At that very hour some Pharisees came and said to him, "Get away from here, for Herod wants to kill you." And he said to them, "Go and tell that fox, 'Behold, I cast out demons and perform cures today and tomorrow, and the third day I finish my course."

---

8. Col 4:10, 14.
9. Luke 9:51—18:14; 19:1–48.
10. Luke 9:53; 13:22; 17:11; 18:11, 35; 19:1–2, 11, 28, 41.

Nevertheless, I must go on my way today and tomorrow and the day following, for it cannot be that a prophet should perish away from *Jerusalem*.

O *Jerusalem, Jerusalem*, the city that kills the prophets and stones those who are sent to it!'" (Luke 13:31–33)

Jesus invited the disciples to follow him on that "journey" to Jerusalem for he knew that in the years after his passing the cost of discipleship would be great.

The Parables of Proto-Luke

Fourteen of Jesus' most prominent and independently recorded parables are part of this extended Galilee-to-Jerusalem journey.

7:40–43	The two debtors
10:29–37	The good Samaritan
11:5–9	The friend at midnight
12:13–20	The rich fool
13:6–9	The barren fig tree
14:7–11	The wedding feast
14:12–24	The great banquet
14:28–32	The rash builder and the reckless king
15:3–32	The lost sheep, the lost coin, the lost sons
16:1–9	The dishonest steward
16:9–31	The rich man and Lazarus
17:7–10	The farmer and his servant
18:1–8	The unjust judge
18:9–14	The Pharisee and the Tax Collector

These parables are not the pithy aphorisms we meet in Matthew and Mark but are in the nature of plot and character-based stories. They are among the most distinctive, widely known teachings of Jesus. Yet we do not know how or by whom they came to be preserved for Luke to "receive" them and to incorporate them in his Gospel. The hypothesis is plausible that they were incorporated early in a document used for ministry to the churches in Israel that later came into Luke's possession. But this is not certain, and like so many aspects of this Gospel, it remains a mystery.

Proto-Luke is independent of Mark. We do not know who created Proto-Luke, but it is reasonable to believe it had been tried and tested in the churches in Israel before it was "delivered" to Luke (Luke 1:2).

Other Sources

Another distinctive in Luke's Gospel is the two opening chapters that contain the "hymns" known as *Benedictus*, *Magnificat*, and *Nunc Dimittis* that are integral to the Infancy Narratives. Like Proto-Luke, these appear to have been originally free standing, but which Luke skillfully adapted and made the prolegomena to his Gospel.

Another unique but distinctive text is the Resurrection Day Emmaus Story. This, too, Luke has built into his overall narrative.

Eventually Paul was released from prison in Caesarea and sent off to Rome to appear before Nero Caesar. Luke and Aristarchus accompanied Paul. It is likely that Luke brought with him the textual treasures he acquired in Israel. It is assumed that Luke secured these scrolls in watertight containers and somehow managed to save them during the storm and shipwreck at Malta, bringing them safely to Rome.

Luke in Rome (60-62)

In Rome with Paul under open arrest c. AD 60-62 Luke would have had the opportunity to meet with both Peter and Mark, who were then located there (1 Pet 5:1, 13). It is reasonable to suggest that Luke used his time in Rome to write an earlier form of his Gospel that combined the sources he had acquired in Israel. Some years later (in the later 60s) we can imagine Luke incorporating parts of Mark's finished Gospel to bring his Gospel to completion. His second volume, the Acts of the Apostles, would then follow reasonably soon afterward, but we do not know when Luke wrote this or where.

The earliest attestation of Luke's Gospel is in Paul's First Letter to Timothy (written c. 64): "The Scripture says . . . 'The laborer deserves his wages'" (1 Tim 5:18). The exact words quoted are found only in Luke 10:7.[11] There are two important observations: first Paul regards Luke's

---

11. But see also Matt 10:10—"the laborer deserves his *food.*" The similarity of Luke 10:7 and Matt 10:10 may be explained either by the evangelists' common dependence on a "Q" source, or alternatively that Jesus gave this teaching with slight variation on

text as "Scripture," and second that it had been written some time prior to 64 when Paul wrote his First Letter to Timothy.

55–64	Peter and Mark in Rome, collaborating in writing the Gospel of Mark
60–62	Luke with Paul in Rome
64	Paul quotes from the Gospel of Luke as "Scripture" (1 Tim 5:18)

Luke the Writer

Both Luke's "books" betray careful planning. The length of each scroll would have been calculated so as not to exceed the tolerable length (and weight) for each. The contents of each scroll must have been a matter for careful reflection.

Luke the writer would have needed reasonable space, a decent desk or table, a chair, and adequate lighting. Manipulating a twenty-three foot long leather or papyrus scroll would have been difficult. Since there was no easy way to correct mistakes our writer must have been quite sure what he was writing, as he gradually opened up the scroll. Luke must have been confident, page-by-page, what he would write. His texts would be in solid blocks of writing using capitalized Greek, with no numbered verses and little punctuation. The whole Gospel and each constituent part was carefully planned to occupy a scroll of definite length.

Then there is the question of financing this major project. The expense was considerable, including the payment of rent, provision of food for the writer (and his assistants?), the cost of the scroll, stylus, and ink.[12] Local Christians in Rome may have helped, but it is likely that a particular patron or patrons were the sources of the considerable funds needed for this project. Luke dedicated his books to Theophilus who may have been the major patron.[13]

---

different occasions, or that Matthew copied from Luke or vice versa.

12. For helpful discussion on the costs of writing see Richards, *Paul and First-Century* (especially 165–69).

13. It is unclear whether Theophilus is a literal or symbolic name ("Friend of God"). Religious sounding names were commonplace.

Luke's Stately Prologue (Luke 1:1–4)[14]

Luke identifies no less than four "parties" in his prologue:

- The "many" who compiled a "narrative" about "the things accomplished" [by Jesus].
- The "eyewitnesses . . . ministers of the word" who delivered each "narrative" to Luke.
- Luke who has combined each "narrative" into his accurate, "orderly account."
- Theophilus, the dedicatee of Luke-Acts, a catechumen.

Luke claims to have "followed all things closely for some time past," that is to say, from the ministry of Jesus to the more recent spread of Christianity. At the same time he implies that he was not an eyewitness to the historical Jesus or to the immediate aftermath, the birth of the church. His first person pronominal reference to "me" in the prologue connect him directly to the "we"/"us" narratives for the years 57–62 (Acts 21–28).

In the prologue the author states his purpose in *writing* his "orderly account." It was to give Theophilus "certainty" concerning the things he had been taught about Jesus and the rise and spread of Christianity. It is implied that to this point Theophilus had been dependent on oral instruction and fragmentary texts.

Luke's Distinctive Elements

We do not know the circumstances under which Luke wrote his Gospel or have answers to the *where* and *when* questions. However, thanks to the prior existence of Mark and our capacity to contrast Luke with that Gospel we are able to identify some of key elements that are distinctive. In turn, these may cast light on Luke's pastoral objectives.

---

14. See Moessner, "How Luke Wrote," 164–67.

Luke-Acts Is a History

Luke clearly valued Mark since he follows his exact narrative Galilee-to-Jerusalem sequence, often following the wording of the earlier text, as we will discuss shortly.

The big change that Luke makes is his addition of the book of Acts, his second volume. Mark calls his text "the Gospel," a narrative focused on Jesus over a narrow time frame that challenges the reader to become a disciple of Jesus. Luke-Acts, however, is a seventy-year *history* that begins with the birth of John the Baptist (*c.* 6 BC) and ends with Paul's two-year imprisonment in Rome (AD 62).

Yet, as the prologue states, it is a history that was intended to reinforce Theophilus's faith. In other words, Luke was concerned that his Christian reader understood both the story of Jesus and the story of Christianity, and the significance of the connection between the two.

The Acts of the Apostles routinely portrays Roman officials sympathetically. Even Pontius Pilate emerges from Luke's narrative as the victim of the ruthless pressure of the temple authorities. The Roman officials Cornelius and Sergius Paulus became believers. While Felix the Procurator is exposed as corrupt, his successor Festus sent Paul off to Rome for trial. Julius the shipboard centurion proved to be a generous supervisor of Paul, his prisoner. It seems that Luke was encouraging his readership to have a positive attitude to the *Pax Romana*.

The Gospels of Matthew, Mark, and John were written for church-based reading. Luke-Acts, however, may have been written for private reading. A problem for this hypothesis is the issue of laborious copying of a twenty-three foot long scroll and the consequent cost of its production. The evidence of widespread use of Luke and Acts points to significant exposure of these texts, suggesting widespread church-based use, especially of the Gospel. The veneration of the Gospels in the early church and the obvious quality of this Gospel guaranteed its extensive currency. According to Earle Ellis, "the third Gospel was widely used as an authority in the Church by the middle of the second century."[15]

Luke's intention to accurately write "an orderly account" (Luke 1:3) signals that what is to follow is historical in character.[16] Luke is unique among the Gospel writers for tying his narrative into world history:

---

15. Ellis, *Gospel of Luke*, 39–40.

16. See Ellis, *Gospel of Luke*, 4–6, for a discussion of the criteria for history writing in Greco-Roman antiquity and the degree to which Luke fulfills those criteria. He

Luke 1:5	In the days of *Herod*, king of the Jews there was a priest named Zechariah.
Luke 2:1–2	In those days a decree went out from *Caesar Augustus* that all the world should be registered. This was the first registration when *Quirinius* was governor of Syria.[9]
Luke 3:1–2	In the fifteenth year of the reign of *Tiberius Caesar*, *Pontius Pilate* being governor of Judea, and *Herod* being tetrarch of Galilee, and his brother *Philip* tetrarch of the region of Ituraea and Trachonitis, and *Lysanias* tetrarch of Abilene, during the high priesthood of *Annas* and *Caiaphas*, the word of God came to *John* the son of Zechariah.

Four of these named persons in Luke 3:1–2 are part of his Gospel as it unfolds, namely, John the Baptist, Herod the tetrarch, the high priest Caiaphas, and Pontius Pilate the governor of Judea. The details of the government of Herod's kingdom after his death in 4 BC are complex, but Luke's understanding is accurate. It is clear that he intends his readers to understand that the events involving Jesus and the disciples occurred within mainstream history.

Luke's rooting of Jesus and the spread of Christianity into the soil of history continues into the Acts of the Apostles. He refers to Theudas,[17] King Herod Agrippa I, the great famine in the days of Claudius, Proconsuls Sergius Paulos and Gallio, Claudius' exile of Jews from Rome, James, brother of the Lord, the Egyptian prophet, governors (technically, "procurators") Felix (and consort Drusilla) and Festus, King Herod Agrippa II (and sister Bernice),[18] and Publius, First Man of Malta. Most of these persons appear in Josephus and Tacitus.

Luke's great narrative, Luke-Acts, ties the people and events regarding Jesus and the rise of Christianity into world history.

---

draws attention to the accuracy of the speeches in Acts and the apparent departure from chronology.

17. See Barnett, *Gospel Truth*, 64–66, for addressing the historical problems regarding Theudas.

18. Luke's reference to Publius, First Man of Malta, is credible: "First Man" was a known title for the governor of Malta, and Publius is a relatively common Roman name. See Bruce, *Acts of the Apostles*, 532–33.

Luke's Greek

In the ancient world, various commentators understood Luke's Gospel to be the most *Greek* of the four canonical Gospels.[19] Because Luke used Mark's text, we are able to observe his use of Mark's vocabulary.

Luke tidies Mark's colloquialisms. Where Mark has *krabattos* ("stretcher," Mark 2:11) Luke substitutes *klinidion* ("bed," Luke 5:24). For Mark's "little girl" (*korasion*, 5:41) Luke has a more elegant substitute (*pais*, 8:51). William Barclay observes, "Luke is instinctively more fastidious in his choice of words."[20] This implies that Luke was writing for a more sophisticated readership than Mark.

The Beginning and Ending of Luke-Acts

Luke's early chapters connect Jesus first to Adam, but also to God's promises to Abraham and for the son of David, the long-awaited Messiah. His writings are in continuity with and fulfillment of the former Testament. In the "hymns" *Benedictus, Magnificat,* and *Nunc Dimittis* we hear echoes of, for example, the *Prayer of Hannah* (1 Sam 2:1–10).

If the opening chapters of Luke-Acts are the extension and completion of the former Testament, then the open-ended final chapter tells us that the mission of God for the world is unfinished and continuing until the return of the Lord and the advent of the kingdom of God in its fullness.

A Kingdom for the Lost

It is striking how Luke's narrative of the journey to Jerusalem brings out the mercy of Jesus toward the needy and marginalized.

9:52	He sent messengers to the *Samaritans*
10:25–37	His parable about a merciful *Samaritan*
10:39	The *woman* Mary sat at Jesus' feet
12:33	Sell your possessions and give to *the needy*
14:2	He healed the man with *dropsy* (on the Sabbath)

---

19. See Barclay, *Gospels and Acts*, 202.
20. Barclay, *Gospel and Acts*, 203.

14:13, 21	Invite *the poor, the crippled, the lame, the blind*
14:23	Invite those from the highways and byways [*Gentiles*]
15:1–2	He received and ate with *tax collectors and sinners*
17:11–19	The *Samaritan* leper who alone thanked God
18:16–17	He welcomed *children*
18:9–14	His favourable parable about *the tax collector*
18:35–43	He healed the *blind beggar*
19:1–10	His salvation of Zacchaeus, the *tax collector*
23:43	His promise to the penitent *criminal*

Jesus declared that he came to seek and to save the lost (19:10). These included the moral outcasts (tax collectors and sinners), the economic outcasts (the poor, the needy), the (then) sexually inferior (women), the maturity inferior (children), the physically defective (the man with dropsy, the crippled, the lame, the blind), the hygienically and ritually contaminated (the lepers), and the ethnically contaminated (Samaritans, Gentiles).

It may be asked: who marginalized these people? Israel itself began as a "marginalized" tribe, slaves in Egypt. In rescuing them God called them to be "holy" as he their Lord was "holy." The problem was that in their attempt to distinguish themselves from other nations they so emphasized issues of holiness and purity that they forgot about the mercy of God that took them out of Egypt and gave them the land. In the time of Jesus it was the Pharisees and their scribes (leading teachers) who intensified the demand for "separation" from the nations, by means of washings, fasting, Sabbaths, festivals, and the like. The religious elitism and legalism of the Pharisees inevitably created an underclass of those on the fringes of the covenant people.

Pharisees and Tax Collectors

Luke refers many times to the tax collectors, as those who came in repentance to be baptized by John the Baptist (3:12), whom Jesus welcomed and with whom he shared meals (5:29, 30). Jesus called Levi, a tax collector in Capernaum, to join his band of disciples (5:27). Another whom Jesus called was Zacchaeus, chief tax collector in Jericho (19:2, 9).

The Pharisees, by contrast with the tax collectors, refused to be baptized by John (7:30). They were indignant that Jesus welcomed the tax collectors and ate with them (5:30; 7:34; 15:1–2).[21] At the same time, they were deeply critical of Jesus for blasphemously claiming to forgive sins (5:21), for failing to fast (5:33), and for healing on the Sabbath (6:7; 14:1, 3). Since the Pharisees' goal was to force Israel to comply with the laws of purity they would have regarded Jesus as a major obstacle to that goal. Jesus and his supporters broke those very laws and, it appeared, encouraged others to do the same.

For his part Jesus condemned the Pharisees for hypocrisy (11:39, 42; 12:1), for social pretentiousness, for lack of compassion toward the needy (11:43; 14:7, 12–14), for greed (16:14), for a self-justifying spirit that lacked humility before God (10:29), and for wilfully refusing the invitation of God (14:18–20).

Women

Luke highlighted the involvement of women with Jesus' mission, especially the "many" women who accompanied the twelve as Jesus preached the gospel of the kingdom in the cities and villages of Galilee (8:1–3). Among these were Mary of Magdala, Joanna wife of Chuza estate manager of Herod the tetrarch, and Susanna, women who "provided for [Jesus and the disciples] out of their means."

These women came with Jesus and the Twelve to Jerusalem. They witnessed the crucifixion, the removal of the body from the cross, and the hasty burial in Joseph's tomb. They came to the tomb to anoint the body, found the body gone, and reported the empty tomb to the skeptical disciples.[22] But Mary, sister of Martha, is to be distinguished from these other women. Only Mary "sat at his feet" listening to him. Thus, Luke singles out Mary as a *disciple* (or, apprentice) of Jesus.

For Jesus to recognize and affirm Mary as a *disciple* represented a social revolution in that conservative and patriarchal society.

Conclusion

Luke's is a much-loved Gospel, as it has been from early times. While we are confident about Luke's identity and that he wrote his Gospel out of identifiable sources "delivered" to him by "eyewitnesses and ministers

21. Luke 5:30; 7:34; 15:1–2.
22. Luke 23:49; 23:55—24:11.

of the word" (the original disciples of Jesus) we can only guess *when* he wrote his Gospel and *where*. In modern times we would know the details about so gifted a writer, but with Luke we are only left with questions.

This author's chief point of difference from Matthew, Mark, and John is that his Gospel was a calculated prequel to a second volume, the Acts of the Apostles. This second "book" immediately makes him a *historian*, something confirmed by the many anchors that tie the totality of Luke-Acts into world history.

Yet the prologue states that Luke wrote to provide "certainty" to the catechumen, Theophilus. Evidently Luke believed that the new convert needed to know not only the Jesus-story but also its sequel, the account of the spread of Christianity from Jerusalem to Rome.

The beginning of Luke-Acts is an extension of the Old Testament that demonstrates how the promises of God were now, at last, being brought to fruition. At the same time the open-ended ending of the book of Acts implies that the ministry of the gospel will continue until the reappearance of the Lord.

The core narrative of this Gospel is the journey to Jerusalem, which is dependent on the "L" and "Q" sources, but without anything drawn from Mark. Arrival in the holy city will give the people opportunity to welcome their king. But Jesus understands that there will be no welcome for him there, only rejection. Implicit in the "journey" for the disciples is the inevitability of their suffering, as they share in the travails of Jesus at the hands of the religious leaders.

Luke-Acts is a remarkable text. Its author is a great storyteller, a disciple of the greatest storyteller, Jesus. The parables that are unique to Luke are much loved throughout the world, an appreciation not limited to Christians.

At the same time Luke is a great pastor. His powerful narrative of the Galilee-to-Jerusalem journey continues to define the "way" for a disciple to live, especially in the physical absence of the Master.

This author writes with great compassion toward the outsider and the marginalized. This is why the tax collectors, prostitutes, women, and children figure so prominently. Luke was not an immediate follower of the compassionate Jesus but he writes with great concern for those "lost" from God and alienated and marginalized within that unequal society.

twenty-two

The Making of John

MATTHEW AND LUKE ARE based on Mark's narrative sequence and employ many of his actual words. Patient comparison of the texts is able to identify the sources underlying Matthew and Luke and provide some answers to questions about their respective origins. Nevertheless, many questions remain for which there are no answers. There are enough answers, however, to inspire confidence in the integrity of these three Gospels.

For the Fourth Gospel we have only some answers, but many more questions. Unlike the synoptics Matthew and Luke, where it is possible to identify the sources Mark, "Q," "L," and "M," no such access to the sources of this Gospel is forthcoming. Attempts to discover sources have been made, but there is no agreement. It can be said with confidence that the Fourth Gospel has resisted the hard work of scholars to find its original components.

Source criticism provides no pathway to understanding the making of the Gospel of John. It is a seamless robe.

Who Wrote the Fourth Gospel?

Evidence from the Gospels

What then of its authorship? Here we are on firmer ground. A voice that speaks at the end of the Fourth Gospel declared that the Beloved Disciple is the author (21:20, 24). The Beloved Disciple sat closest to Jesus at the

Last Supper, stood with women at the cross, ran with Peter to the tomb, and was the last person about whom Jesus spoke.[1]

There are three further pieces of evidence from the Gospels.

First, the Beloved Disciple must have been *one of the twelve* original disciples since only they were present at the Last Supper (Mark 14:17).

Second, it is likely that the Beloved Disciple was *one of the inner three* closest to Jesus (Peter, James, and John), who were privileged to witness the raising of Jairus's daughter, the transfiguration of Jesus, and to be those next to Jesus in Gethsemane.[2] It is overwhelmingly likely that it was one of these inner three who sat closest to Jesus at the Last Supper (John 13:23-24). It was not Peter, so it must have been James or John Zebedee.

Third, the Beloved Disciple who wrote the Gospel (21:24) was *one of the seven disciples* who went fishing in the Sea of Tiberias (21:2). We eliminate Simon Peter, Thomas, and Nathanael leaving two unnamed disciples and the two sons of Zebedee. Since James Zebedee was martyred c. 42 (Acts 12:2) we are left with John Zebedee and the two unnamed disciples.

It seems that from within the text of the Fourth Gospel the author has deliberately veiled his identity. However, consideration of evidence from the Gospel of Mark about the inner circle of three (Peter, James, and John) and the evidence from the Fourth Gospel of the closeness of the Beloved Disciple to Jesus (in particular at the Last Supper and at the cross) provides strong circumstantial evidence that he was the younger Zebedee, John.

Evidence from the Second Century

Irenaeus, a church leader from Roman Asia, implicitly identifies the Beloved Disciple as "John the disciple of the Lord":

> After them (Matthew, Mark, and Luke) John the disciple of the Lord, who also reclined on his breast issued a Gospel while he was living at Ephesus in Asia.[3]

---

1. John 13:23; 19:26; 20:2-6; 21:22.
2. Mark 5:37; 9:2; 14:33.
3. Irenaeus, *Against Heresies* 3.1.1, in Roberts and Donaldson, *Ante-Nicene Fathers*; see also Polycrates, writing c. 190 (Eusebius, *History of the Church* 3. 31.3.

The only "disciple of the Lord" (i.e., one of the twelve) named John was John Zebedee.

According to Irenaeus, John was still living in Roman Asia in the time of the Emperor Trajan (AD 98–117).[4] Irenaeus is an important authority because, as he tells us, as a youth he heard Polycarp, Bishop of Smyrna, who in turn had known the Apostle John personally.[5] The Muratorian Canon, dated to the late second century, refers to "the fourth of the gospels is that of John, [one] of the disciples."

John Zebedee in the Early Church

Prior to the resurrection James Zebedee was the second listed "apostle" after Peter (Mark 3:17),[6] but after the resurrection his brother John is listed second after Peter (Acts 1:13). John's name is bracketed with Peter's in the earliest years of the Christian church.[7] In c. 47 Paul named John as the third "pillar" of the Jerusalem Church, after James and Cephas (Gal 2:9). That was the last occasion the book of Acts or the letters of Paul mentions John Zebedee by name, although we assume that he was among the "apostles" who participated in the Council of Jerusalem in c. 49.[8]

When the Acts of the Apostles allows us to see inside the Jerusalem Church (in c. 57) there is a reference to James, brother of the Lord, and the "elders" but no reference to "apostles." The book of Acts means us to understand that the apostles departed from Jerusalem some time between c. 49 and c. 57.

We next hear of John as the author of the Revelation written c. 95 from exile on the Island of Patmos. Although John in Revelation does not refer to himself as "apostle" or "disciple" it is reasonable to believe that he is John Zebedee. The John of Revelation exercised apostolic-like leadership in the widely scattered churches in western Asia. John, the "holy theologian," as he was called, was buried in the majestic Church in Ephesus (modern Selçuk).

---

4. Irenaeus, *Against Heresies* 2.22,5; 3.3.4, in Roberts and Donaldson, *Ante-Nicene Fathers*

5. Irenaeus, *Against Heresies* 3.3.4, in Roberts and Donaldson, *Ante-Nicene Fathers*; Eusebius, *History of the Church* 5.20.4.

6. James Zebedee was beheaded c. 42 by the initiative of King Herod Agrippa I (Acts 12:1–2).

7. Acts 3:1, 3, 4, 11; 4:13, 19; 8:14.

8. Acts 15:2, 6, 22, 23.

An Alternative View[9]

Not all agree that the Beloved Disciple, author of the Fourth Gospel, was John Zebedee. Martin Hengel, for example, does not begin with the evidence from the Gospels but with the early second century source, Papias, bishop of Hierapolis. Hengel notes that Papias lists seven original disciples, including John. Then, however, Papias mentions "Aristion and John the Elder." Based on Papias, Hengel and others argue that there were two Johns: John Zebedee and John the Elder.

> And if anyone chanced to come who had actually been a follower of the elders, I would enquire as to the discourses of the elders, what Andrew or what Peter *said*, or what Philip, or what Thomas or James, or what *John* or Matthew or any other of the Lord's disciples; and the things which Aristion and *John* the elder, the disciples of the Lord *say*.[10]

Papias makes an important distinction between what the original seven disciples said and what Aristion and John the elder say. The latter who *heard* what the seven of the Lord's disciples said is what they now also say.[11]

Martin Hengel identifies Papias's "the elder John" with "the elder" who was the anonymous author of 2 and 3 John. It was this "elder," according to Hengel, and not the Apostle John, who was the author of the First Letter of John and the Fourth Gospel.[12]

Hengel does not believe John the Galilean fisherman could have written this significant Gospel. Rather, according to Hengel, the Beloved Disciple was an otherwise unknown follower of Jesus—but not one of the twelve—who belonged to the priestly aristocracy in Jerusalem, who later migrated to Roman Asia where he composed and edited what would become the Fourth Gospel.

---

9. Hengel, *Johannine Question*. Bauckham, *Jesus and the Eyewitnesses*, 412–37, also argues against authorship by John Zebedee, with a list of scholars who share that view (p. 412 n. 1).

10. Eusebius, *History of the Church* 3.39.3, 4, quoted by Hengel, *Johannine Question*, 17.

11. Eusebius, who is the source of the Papias fragment, goes on to say independently that there were two persons in Asia named John, and two tombs in Ephesus each said to be "John's."

12. See Shanks, *Papias and the New Testament*, 269–70, for the view that Eusebius invented the myth of John the Elder.

But, as we have noted above, the Beloved Disciple was one of the twelve, who sat closest to Jesus at the Last Supper. There was only one John among the twelve, a fact that automatically excludes Hengel's "John the elder."

Martin Hengel's views are based mainly on the ambiguous Papias data (embedded in Eusebius's text), which is confusing in its references to elders and disciples. Hengel speculates as to what kind of person the author *must* have been (an aristocratic Jerusalemite), and firmly presumes that the Galilean John Zebedee could not have written such a book as this.

The combined effect of the primary information in the Gospels of John and Mark, however, and its corroboration by Irenaeus, points conclusively to John Zebedee as the author. It is right to give priority to the information from the Gospels rather than to Papias.

When Was the Gospel of John Written?

It is difficult to establish the date John wrote his Gospel. John's reference to the kind of death by which Peter "was to glorify God" (21:19) implies that this Gospel post-dated Peter's death, which is believed to have occurred in 64-65.

A later boundary is thought to be defined by a piece of papyrus (P^{52}) that contains John 18:31-33, 37-38. Unfortunately the date of this sliver of text is debated. Some say it was written in the first quarter of the second century, others rather later. There is, however, an echo of this Gospel in the writings of Ignatius, the martyr bishop, in c. 110.[13] On that basis it is possible to set the 90s as a later extremity for the writing of the Gospel of John.

There are other reasons for dating John late in the first century.

First, the famous statement of Clement of Alexandria (*c.* 200) supports a late dating:

> But that John, last of all, conscious that the outward facts had been set forth in the Gospels, was urged on by his disciples, and, divinely moved by the Spirit composed a spiritual Gospel. (Eusebius, *History of the Church* 6.14.7)

---

13. Ignatius, *Philadelphians* 7 ("the Spirit . . . knoweth whence it comes and whither it goes").

Based on Clement's statement many think that John wrote after the other Gospels (therefore in the 90s or later) and that he knew their contents. Referring to John's as a "spiritual Gospel" implies that he was not concerned about "outward facts," a view that many scholars hold.[14]

But these views are open to challenge. John did not necessarily write after the other Gospels because, as we will show, there is no certain evidence that he depended on their contents. As well, a careful reading of John reveals extensive and detailed knowledge of "the outward facts" about the Israel of Jesus' day and of the earliest years of Christianity in Jerusalem.

Second, some reason that the Gospel of John reflects the situation following the rabbis' conference at Jamnia, dated in the late 80s. Of particular interest is Benediction 12 (the so-called *birkath ha-minim*), a liturgical anathema that effectively excluded Christian Jews from attending the synagogues.

> Let . . . the Nazarenes and the *minim* [heretics] perish as in a moment and be blotted out from the book of life.

It is argued that John's three references to "synagogue exclusion" (9:22; 12:42; 16:4), which are found only in his Gospel, point to the "Heretic Benediction" enacted at Jamnia, and therefore to a later date for the Gospel of John.

This theory gained popular currency by J. Louis Martyn's reconstruction, based on the synagogue-exclusion texts in John as best explained by the *birkath ha-minim* ruling of Jamnia.[15] Serious doubts have been raised about this explanation, however, and in the eyes of some it has been overturned.[16] There is no reason why synagogue-exclusion of the kind reflected in the *birkath ha-minim* might not have been practised in Jesus' own day, and continued into the immediate post-Easter era. Synagogue exclusion was occurring in and before the New Testament era by Pharisees, and at Qumran.[17] The Jamnian anathema upon *minim* and Nazarenes probably grew out of earlier exclusion practices.

---

14. For a comprehensive survey of modern scholarship on the historical character of the Gospel of John see Blomberg, "John and Jesus," 209–26.

15. Martyn, *History and Theology*, 37–62.

16. See Hare, *Theme of Jewish Persecution*, 48–56; Kimelman, "Birkath ha-Minim," 226–44; Katz, "Issues in the Separation," 69–74; Reinhartz, "Johannine Community," 111–38; Bernier, *Aposynagōgos*; Porter, *John, His Gospel, and Jesus*, 149–73.

17. Ellis, "Dating the New Testament," 22.

The proposal that the author wrote late in the century and from a distant place (such as Ephesus) flies in the face of what we might call "the memory factor." If we imagine a world without such prompts to recollection as photographs, newspapers, and archives, I suggest that it is difficult to call to mind vivid detail when living in another country and writing many years after the events.

Let us consider three kinds of detail—geographical, cultural, and political.

i. Geographical

This author effortlessly reveals an awareness of the ups and downs of the topography of the land.[18] He knows the names of villages and their distinguishing qualifiers (e.g., Bethany "beyond Jordan," 1:28; 10:40; Cana "in Galilee," 2:1; 4:46; Aenon "near Salim," 3:23). This author displays more knowledge about Israel than the synoptic writers, including that Tiberias and Capernaum were major settlements on Lake Galilee and that the lake was only about five miles wide;[19] that in Jerusalem by the sheep gate was a pool called Bethesda with "five porches" (5:2); that there was a town called Ephraim "in the wilderness" (11:54);[20] that the governor mounted his *bēma* formally to pass judgement on the accused at a place called *lithostrōtos* and in Hebrew "Gabbatha" (19:13); that they crucified the three men at a place called "the place of a skull (*kraniou topon*), which is called in Hebrew Golgotha" (19:17).

Many of these topographical and geographical details have been corroborated by archaeology.[21] So extensive are the references and so sure footed that a provenance local to these places is more plausible than a distant one.

ii. Cultural

There are numerous examples of this author's awareness of the religious culture of Palestinian Jews of this era. These include the use of stone vessels for purifying (2:6);[22] the refusal of Jews to share drinking vessels with Samaritans based on mutual enmity (4:9);[23] the geographical conjunction of Sychar, Joseph's field, Jacob's well, and Mt. Gerizim

---

18. e.g., John 2:13; 4:47, 49, 51.

19. John 6:17, 19, 23.

20. See Meyers and Strange, *Archaeology*, 160–61.

21. See e.g., Charlesworth, *Jesus within Judaism*, 120; von Wahlde, "Archaeology and John's Gospel," 523–86.

22. Charlesworth, "Dead Sea Scrolls," 68.

23. Meier, "Historical Jesus," 229.

(4:4–6, 20); the manna *haggada* (teaching) underlying the "bread of life" discourse (6:1–59);[24] the debate over circumcising on the Sabbath, where Jesus employs the rabbinic "lesser to greater" argument (7:22);[25] the Pharisees' contempt for "this people who do not know the law" (7:45–49); references to water and light at the Feast of Tabernacles, where these elements are central to the ceremonies (7:37–39; 8:12);[26] the credible conjunction of a place of shelter (Solomon's Porch) and winter (a cold season) that occurs at the Feast of Dedication (*Hanukkah*, 10:22); the (attempted) stoning of a blasphemer (10:29–31); the pilgrimage of rural folk to Jerusalem for purification ahead of the Passover (11:55; 12:12); the refusal of the Jewish leaders to enter Pilate's Praetorium for fear of becoming unclean on "the day of preparation for the feast of Passover" (18:28; 19:13–14); the "custom" of releasing a prisoner at the Passover (18:39); and the burial "customs" of the Jews according to which Jesus was interred (19:40).

Our argument here is that there is a closeness of the text to the soil from which it grew that makes a Palestinian provenance plausible and an Asian provenance implausible (see later).

iii. Political

As C. H. Dodd pointed out, John's trial narrative belongs authentically and distinctively to the pre-66 period, when the Roman governor ruled the province of Judea as surrogate of the distant Caesar in an uneasy partnership with the high priest.[27] This was to change forever *after* the Roman invasion in the years 66–70, when there would be no more temple and no more high priests.

We note that only the Gospel of John implies the extensive and long-term involvement of the Roman authorities with the temple hierarchy in regard to Jesus.[28] Whereas the Synoptics imply a last minute participation by Roman interests, it is otherwise in John. A Roman "cohort" led by a Roman colonel, along with temple police, arrested Jesus and put him in shackles (18:3,12). In this Gospel the enquiries by high priests Annas and Caiaphas are minimally narrated. All attention is directed toward the Roman Pilate's interrogation of Jesus in the Praetorium (18:28—19:16).

24. See Borgen, *LOGOS*, 21–46.

25. Cf. Mishnah *Shabbath* 18:3–19:2; *Nedarim* 3:11; see Hengel, *Johannine Question*, 111.

26. Mishnah *Sukkah* 4:9–5:4.

27. Dodd, *Historical Tradition*, 120.

28. Hengel, *Johannine Question*, 118.

This implies a Roman interest that probably originated following the Jewish failure to stone Jesus for blasphemy (10:30–31), and in particular when he might have been the focus of a popular uprising after the raising of Lazarus (11:45–48). The mounted entry to the city clinched the Jewish case that the Galilean was a self-proclaimed "king of the Jews" (12:19).

That case fell apart once Pilate actually put Jesus on trial. This Gospel accurately portrays the temple authorities' blackmail of Pilate as the "friend of Caesar" (19:12), while also showing his mockery of the Jews for their mindless indictment of someone who for him was at worst a harmless religious fanatic (19:1–6, 12).

There were many changes following the invasion of the Romans, 66–70, and their assault on the landscape.[29] The physical appearance of the land was now different. From that time Jerusalem lay in ruins, its temple destroyed, to be replaced in due course by a pagan shrine. The hillsides surrounding Jerusalem were denuded of vegetation for use in the siege of the city. According to Josephus, "Those who visited the city could not believe it had ever been inhabited" (*Jewish War* 7.3). Other cities and towns throughout Israel were also ruined.

Likewise, long-standing institutions and prominent groups were no more. No longer would the Romans govern Judea through intermediary "client" kings or by a high priest-led Sanhedrin. Roman rule now would be direct and unmediated in a "full" military province renamed "Colonia Prima Flavia Augusta Caesarensis."

Various factions that figured significantly before the war disappear afterward, for example Sadducees, Zealots, and Essenes. The synagogue became the center of Jewish life, with Pharisaism becoming in time "rabbinic" Judaism.

The point is that in relation to geography, culture, and politics the Gospel of John portrays an earlier and different time. While memory can recapture things as they were, with the passage of time it is increasingly difficult to do so, especially in an age before photography, daily newspapers, and accessible archives. This author only had his memory.

The dating question also relates to the question of John's use and reliance on the other three Gospels, and to that question we now turn.

29.. See Schürer, *History of the Jewish People*, 514–28.

The Sources of the Gospel of John

Despite extensive efforts, it is all but universally agreed that underlying sources for the Gospel of John cannot be identified. The text and tone of this Gospel is so uniform throughout that its constituent parts cannot be identified with the necessary confidence.

This makes the question of John's relationship with the synoptic Gospels especially important. During the main era of biblical criticism it was widely believed that John's was the last-written of the Gospels and literarily dependent on the Synoptics, especially the Gospel of Mark.

That confidence was shattered after the Second World War by a study written by Percival Gardner-Smith in 1938, but which lay relatively unnoticed until the post-war period. In 1985, John A. T. Robinson argued powerfully for "the priority of John."[30]

In the years since, few have argued for the extreme views of John's absolute dependence on the Synoptics, on the one hand, or his absolute independence on the other. Most are prepared to recognize the distinct independence of some passages (especially the Feeding of the Multitude), while contending that both traditions refer to numerous incidents that are somehow shared or interlocking.[31] This viewpoint has had the effect of rescuing this Gospel from the outright skepticism with which it was regarded before the impact of the studies of Gardner-Smith and Robinson.

In what follows, however, I propose to make a case for the absolute literary independence of the Gospel of John from the Synoptics.

Differing Geography-Based Narratives

The major difference between John and Mark is their respective geography-based narratives. Mark describes Jesus' ministry in Galilee, Gaulanitis, and principalities to the north (Tyre and Sidon) and the east (the Decapolis). Only at three quarters of the way through this Gospel does Jesus come at last (once) to Jerusalem, and only for a matter of days before the crucifixion.

By contrast, John records Jesus' minimal presence in Galilee:

---

30. Robinson, *Priority of John*.
31. Porter, *John, His Gospel*, 71–72.

1:43—2:12	Galilee, Cana
4:43–54	Cana
6:1—7:9	the other (eastern) side of the Sea of Galilee
21:1–23	at the Sea of Tiberias

Apart from Jesus' visit to Samaria (4:4) he was in Jerusalem for the remainder of John's narrative except for several occasions he needed to escape from danger in the holy city:

| 10:40–42 | Bethany beyond Jordan |
| 11:54–57 | Ephraim |

While Mark describes Jesus' arrival in Jerusalem at Passover for the beginning of his final days, John has a dramatically different schema. According to John's account Jesus arrived in Jerusalem for the Feast of Booths (in September–October) and apart from the two occasions he escaped for his safety (as above) he remained there until the Passover (in March–April), a period of about seven months.

The two accounts are markedly different. John makes no reference to Mark's version of Jesus' journeys to the north and the east of Galilee, and Mark gives no indication of Jesus' visits to Jerusalem for the feasts, especially for the final seven months between the Feast of Booths and the Passover.

John's geographical and events-based narratives are so different from the Synoptic Gospels that a theory of literary dependency by John on the Synoptics or the Synoptics on John seems unlikely as a theory of relationship.

Omission of Key Incidents

John omits key events that are prominent in Mark, Matthew, and Luke.

- The temptations
- Jesus' public "kingdom" proclamation in Galilee
- harvest parables
- exorcisms
- table fellowship with "sinners"
- Jesus' formal appointment of twelve disciples

- Peter's messianic confession at Caesarea Philippi
- The transfiguration of Jesus
- The institution of the Eucharist
- Jesus' Gethsemane prayer
- The Sanhedrin trial
- The Great Commission

These omissions are striking and contribute to the sense of difference between John and Synoptics.

The Clearing of the Temple

A prominent difference is John's location of the Clearing of the Sellers from the Temple near the beginning of his Gospel whereas in Mark it occurs during Jesus' final visit to the holy city. So is one or the other of the accounts incorrectly located or did Jesus clear the temple twice? The various options have their advocates.[32]

Whatever the truth is about John's location of the incident[33] Mark's placement of it at the time of Jesus' final arrival in Jerusalem is surely correct since it is the catalyst of the ensuing events of the arrest, trial, and execution of Jesus.

John's Unique Account of Jesus' Earlier Ministry

According to Mark, the arrest of John the Baptist marked the beginning of Jesus' ministry in Galilee (Mark 1:14). John, however, narrates a significant sequence of events prior to the arrest of John the Baptist.

---

32. For the argument that John has the location right, against Mark, see Robinson, *Priority of John*, 127–131. Carson, *Gospel According to John*, 177–78, contends that Jesus cleared the temple twice.

33. It seems likely that John has relocated the Incident and the logion to fit thematically with a series of other "replacement" items that occur near the beginning of his Gospel (2:1–11, wine replaces purificatory water; 2:12–22, new "temple" replaces old temple; 3:1–14, new birth replaces old birth; 4: 4–26, new worship replaces old worship).

1:29–51	Jesus recruits five disciples
2:1–11	The marriage in Cana
2:12	The visit to Capernaum
2:13–22	Jesus clears the Temple
2:23–3:21	The Nicodemus incident
3:22–4:3	The disciples baptising

This is an extensive sequence involving some months, which does not correspond with Mark's narrative, except for the Clearing of the Temple (which, in any case, Mark locates at the end).

Mark relates that Jesus' Galilean ministry began when John the Baptist was arrested. John, however, teaches that after Jesus' baptism he engaged in extensive ministry *before* the arrest of the Baptist. A theory of John's use of or even knowledge of Mark's text is problematic.

Common Incidents

There are, however, nine incidents that are common to Mark and John.

	Mark	John
The dove-like descent of the Spirit	1:10	1:32
The temple-clearing incident	11:15–19	2:13–22
Triumphal entry	11:1–10	12:12–19
Feeding of the 5,000	6:30–44	6:1–14
Anointing at Bethany	14:3–9	12:1–8
Arrest of Jesus	14:43–50	18:1–11
Peter's denials	14:66–72	18:15–18 18:25–27
Soldiers' mockery of Jesus	15:16–20	19:1–3
Burial of Jesus in Joseph's tomb	15:42–47	19:38–4219 19:38–42

Briefly we note the following.

- In seven passages (the feeding of the 5,000; the triumphal entry; the anointing at Bethany; the arrest of Jesus; Peter's denials; the soldiers' mockery; the burial of Jesus) Mark and John appear to be depending on a common source or two parallel independent sources.

- In two passages (the descent of the Spirit; the temple-clearing) the common elements are minimal.

Analysis of the respective texts is open to diverging interpretations. Overall, however, it is reasonable to conclude that there is little firm evidence that John or Mark depended on one another. In seven passages, however, Mark and John appear to be depending on common, interlocking sources and in two passages each seem to have been adapting independent, parallel sources. The case for John's literary dependence on John or vice versa Mark is not strong.

Credible Detail in the Gospel of John

John's narrative often supplies details not present in Mark (or Matthew and Luke).

1:28	The location where John baptized was *Bethany-beyond-Jordan* (also 10:40)
1:35	Two (at least) of those who followed Jesus had been disciples of *John the Baptist*
1:44	The city of origin of Philip, Andrew, and Simon was *Bethsaida* (also 12:21)
2:19	John connects Jesus' *act* of clearing the temple with his *word* about raising it
3:22	Jesus' disciples were *baptizing in parallel* with John's disciples
3:24	Whereas Mark indicates that Jesus began in public only after John was arrested (1:14), John shows that the ministries of the two ran in *parallel* with a considerable overlapping period (as noted above).
6:15	John's detail that the crowd sought to impose the *kingship* upon Jesus coheres with Mark's otherwise inexplicable detail of Jesus *forcing* his disciples to leave (Mark 6:45–46)
11:47	Caiaphas' decision to *remove Jesus* before the Triumphant Entry.[10] Accordingly, *Judas* appears to have consulted early with the temple authorities
18:13	*Annas* was Caiaphas' father-in-law (a detail not found elsewhere). Former high priest *Annas* was still a powerful figure (cf. 18:24, 28)

Each of John's details listed above has an intrinsically high claim to be accurate. If it were possible to account for these by appeal to John's special theological interests it would weaken their credibility. But nowhere can this be demonstrated. Clearly, this writer is well informed and has an eye for detail. Since none of these details appear in Mark it supports the argument that John was literarily independent, and arguably at least as early if not earlier than the Synoptics.

The Roman Arrest, Trial, and Crucifixion of Jesus[34]

Most detailed of all, and strikingly so, is John's account of the *Roman* involvement in the arrest and trial of Jesus.[35] It is useful to compare the accounts of the Gospels of Mark and John.

We note only three points of agreement (the Jews accuse Jesus to Pilate, Pilate offers Passover release, Soldiers mock and torture Jesus), but John's account is overwhelmingly comprehensive, from the arrest through to the trial, followed by the crucifixion.

Likewise, critical is John's specific terminology for the "band of soldiers" (18:3), their "captain" (18:12), "the governor's head quarters" (18:28), and the Jewish leaders' "accusation" against Jesus (18:29), namely that he claimed to be "king of the Jews" (a treasonable offense, 18:33). See further in the appendix.

How can we explain John's great interest in the Romans' engagement with Jesus of Nazareth? Do the few (three) points at which Mark and John agree represent what actually happened and that John's extra details are his invention to add color to the story?

Against that, we notice that John's technical details are consistent with Roman military, forensic, and execution practice, supporting the argument that John merely wanted to provide an accurate account of what happened. These details do not tend to serve his theological interests.

John's account is consistent with Roman administration of Judea as a military province. Serious uprising led by Judas the Galilean marked the beginning of the Roman annexation of Judea in AD 6. The Jews, especially the Galileans, were volatile, and capable of creating serious disturbance. At that very time of Jesus' trial Barabbas had been arrested for "murder in *the insurrection*" (Mark 15:7).

John's extensive knowledge of and reference to the critical Roman involvement with Jesus is an expression of the imperial concern for the suppression of insurgency within the provinces. There was only one "king of the Jews" and that was the Caesar.

While this Gospel reflects a Judean setting, we note that according to early authorities it was "issued" from Ephesus, capital of *Roman* Asia. Perhaps John includes so much information about the Roman trial to help make the Gospel relevant to the people of that province.

The bolt from the Johannine blue?

---

34. See Appendix: Roman Involvement in the Arrest, Trial, and Execution of Jesus.
35. See Bruce, "Trial of Jesus," 7–20.

Careful readers of the Gospels have been intrigued by a text common to Matthew and Luke that sound remarkably like statements in the Gospel of John. As long ago as 1876 Karl von Hase referred to text as the "meteor from the Johannine sky."

The two passages are similar in wording, and points to their origin in the "Q" source.

> All things have been committed to me by my Father.
> No one knows the Son except the Father,
> and no one knows the Father except the Son
> and those to whom the Son chooses to reveal him. (Matt 11:27)

> All things have been committed to me by my Father.
> No one knows who the Son is except the Father,
> and no one knows who the Father is except the Son
> and those to whom the Son chooses to reveal him. (Luke 10:22)

In this "Q" text we note:

- *The* Father and *the* Son are spoken of in absolute terms
- The Father has handed over *all things* to the Son
- The Son and the Father have a unique and exclusive *knowledge* of one another
- Only the Son *reveals* the Father to others

Is there a relationship between this "Q" text and passages like this in the Gospel of John:

> So Jesus said to them,
> "Truly, truly, I say to you, the Son can do nothing of
> his own accord, but only what he sees the Father
> doing. For whatever the Father does, that the Son
> does likewise. For the Father loves the Son and
> shows him all that he himself is doing." (John 5:19)

> "No one can come to me unless the Father who sent
> me draws him." (John 6:44)

> "Even though you do not believe me, believe the
> works, that you may know and understand that

the Father is in me and I am in the Father." (10:38)

In the above three texts from John, we note the following:

- The Father and the Son are spoken of in absolute terms
- The Father and the Son enjoy exclusive relationship and mutual understanding
- The Father and the Son pursue exactly the same objectives.

It is clear that the ideas are similar. But has John depended on "Q" or has "Q" depended on John?

The most likely answer is that neither tradition has depended literarily on the other, but that similar ideas were current in both. This would mean that the high Christology that is a characteristic of the Gospel of John was prominent also in a synoptic tradition.

This should not surprise us since we also find a high Christology in Matthew's special source, "M."[36]

The "Q" text[37] is not a "meteor" from John's theology that has somehow exploded into the Gospels of Matthew and Luke. Rather, "Q," the Gospel of John, and Matthew's "M" source shared a common high Christology. Jesus is uniquely the Son of the Father, obedient to do his will. This is what believers from the worlds of these authors believed.

The Absence of Parables in the Gospel of John

Parables, which are so much a part of the Synoptic Gospels, simply do not appear in John's book. This is further evidence of John's non-dependence on the texts of Mark, Matthew, or Luke.

Nevertheless, John quotes Jesus speaking figuratively, for example "the good shepherd" (10:1–5), "the grain of wheat" (12:24), and "the woman in labor" (16:16–22).

At the same time, however, there is some overlapping imagery between the synoptic parables and John's similitudes.[38]

---

36. Matt 1:17; 11:2; 16:17; 25:34; 28:19.

37. Luke 10:22/Matt 11:27.

38. For a list of Johannine parallels to synoptic sayings see Howard, *Fourth Gospel*, 306–7 (also 216–27).

John		Synoptics
4:35	The harvest	Luke 10:2/Matt 9:37–38
5:19	The apprenticed Son	Matt 11:27
8:32	The slave and the son	Luke 11:11–3/Matt 7:9–11
10:11	The shepherd	Matt 10:16
11:25	The riddle of life and death	Mark 8:36–37
13:15	The servant/master	Mark 10:45
15:1	The true vine	Mark 12:1–9

We must allow that Jesus, the master of imagery, spoke figuratively in ways that John notes, but in ways that do not occur within the synoptic tradition. What is striking, however, is the distinctive imagery of Jesus in the Gospel of John on the one hand, and the absence of synoptic parables on the other. Taken together, these contribute to the case for the verbal independence of the Gospel of John.

Summary

There are so many points of difference between John and the Synoptics and so few of agreement that it is difficult to escape the conclusion that John did not depend on or adapt material from the Synoptic Gospels.

The Provenance of the Gospel of John

Evidence from the second century points to Ephesus in Roman Asia as the place where the Gospel of John was "issued."[39] However, it was *written* in Israel, as its concentration of geographical, cultural and political information combine to establish. Westcott's observation still holds true:

> The writer of the fourth Gospel was an *eyewitness* of the events he describes ... not only a Jew, but *a Palestinian Jew* of the first century ... who had known *Jerusalem* before its fall.[40]

---

39. Irenaeus, *Against Heresies* 3.1.1, in Roberts and Donaldson, *Ante-Nicene Fathers*; see also Polycrates, writing c. 190 (Eusebius, *History of the Church* 3. 31.3).

40. Westcott, *Gospel According to St John*, xviii, x, x11.

John's Focus on Jerusalem

Mark's Gospel is constructed around a north-to-south axis. Jesus travels from Galilee to Jerusalem. In John, however, Jerusalem and Judea in the south are "his own country" where, as a prophet he is "not honored" (4:44-45). In John's account, Jesus comes *from* Judea *to* Galilee (1:43; 4:47).

True, he is "Jesus from Nazareth" (1:45) in Galilee, but so far as John is concerned he spends the greater part of his time in Jerusalem and Judea (2:13-4:2; 5:1-47; 7:10-20:31), where the "sin of the world" is revealed and where the redemptive drama is played out.

This focus on Jerusalem and Judea is reflected in John's topographical references:

- The deep pool at Bethesda (5:2)
- The Treasury (8:20)
- The Siloam Pool (9:7)
- Solomon's Porch (10:23)
- Bethany, two miles from Jerusalem (12:1)
- The olive grove near the "wadi" Kedron (18:1)
- Gabbatha (*Lithostrōtos*—19:13)
- Golgotha (19:17)

These detailed references are consistent with John's preoccupation with Jerusalem.

The original disciples of Jesus came with him from Galilee to Jerusalem where they remained. Galilee was no longer their home. For the next decades they were now firmly established in Jerusalem.

Jerusalem in Mark and John: Why the Disparity?

In Mark's narrative, Jesus goes to Jerusalem *only once* and for just a few days, although this brief visit represents a quarter of the Gospel. It is not difficult to work out Mark's motive for this disproportionate allocation of his text. For Mark, the crucifixion of Jesus *is* his message because it is God's means of liberating captives from supernatural evil. That is the crux of the Gospel of Mark.

In John's Gospel, however, Jesus was in Jerusalem *many* times, on each occasion at the time of a Feast.

John	Feast
2:13	Passover
5:1	Passover (?)
7:10	Booths
10:22	Dedication
11:55	Passover

What is John's motive in emphasizing Jesus' multiple visits to the holy city? It was to demonstrate that the Son of God fulfilled symbolism of those feasts and thereby abrogated them. In particular, he is the Passover Lamb who takes away the sin of the world (John 1:29).

Pastoral Immediacy

There is some evidence within the Gospel of John that Jerusalem AD 33–49 was indeed the place where this Gospel was first written.

First, one passage that reflects the post-Easter setting is Jesus' dialogue with Nicodemus. At a critical point in the dialogue John has Jesus say, "*We* speak of what *we* know and *we* bear witness of what *we* have seen but *you* (plural) do not receive *our* witness" (3:11). This is the post-Easter church addressing unbelieving Israel.

This contrasts pointedly with Jesus' earlier, "*I* say to you (singular)" in verses 3:3, 5, 11a, and the sharp "*I* say to you (plural), you (plural) must be born from above" (verse 7). In other words, John writes with a "double vision" in which he *simultaneously* reports the historic words of Jesus to this distinguished "ruler of the Jews" while also reporting the later "witness" of the apostolic community ("we") to "the Jews" ("you") and their failure to accept the church's "witness" to Jesus in Judea.

Second, the farewell discourses and prayer (chapters 13–17) on the eve of the crucifixion envisage a situation that will *soon* occur, beginning with the betrayal (13:18–30), the denial (13:37–38), and the oblique references to Jesus' death and resurrection (13:33, 36; 14:1–3, 5, 18, 28–31; 16:16–24).

Looking onward beyond his death and resurrection Jesus speaks of his going or departing that will be matched by the coming of the Paraclete to teach and remind of everything he told them (14:25–26; 15:26;

16:7–15). This "remembering" points to the disciples' Spirit-led reflections on Jesus' pre-Easter works and words as fulfillment of prophecy (2:17, 22; 12:16). The Paraclete will engage in a twofold "witness," first to the disciples, and then through them to the world.

One way of reading these prospective acts of the Paraclete is that they began to be fulfilled soon after his coming, that is, soon after the first Easter as the original disciples were engaged in their mission in the Land of Israel.

Third, that mission would attract severe persecution (15:20; 16:1), including synagogue-exclusion and death (16:2). Against this expected onslaught Jesus admonished his disciples to remain in him, the "true vine" who is the *true* Israel (15:4, 9). Jesus' absence will be replaced by the Paraclete's presence, but the persecution and hatred that was directed toward him by the Jews will continue to be directed toward them.

This would help explain the world-view of the Gospel of John that saw Jerusalem so negatively. Instead of acclamation in Samaria (4:42) and welcome in Galilee (4:45), the people of Jerusalem misread his signs (2:23–24) and the rulers in Jerusalem reject Jesus altogether and bring about his death. In this respect the rulers embody the darkness (1:5; 12:35) of the world (e.g., 8:23, 26; 15:18–19) that is subject to its murderous father and ruler (8:44; 12:31; 18:11).

Fourth, we are struck by John's thoroughgoing emphasis on Christ as the absolute fulfillment of Israel's past ("law was given through Moses . . . grace and truth through Jesus Christ"—1:17) as well as of her present religious life (as expressed in Judaism). Because Jesus is the "lamb of God" whose bones were unbroken in death (1:29; 19:33–37) John is implying that the Feast of Passover is now superseded and finished.

Because Jesus is the source of divine "water" (7:37–39) and is the "light of the world" (8:12) he fulfills the Feast of Booths, where the great ceremonial acts were centered on *water* and *light*. Like the Passover the Booths festival is now overtaken and discontinued by Jesus the Christ. The water for purification in the stone jars is not only replaced, it is destroyed (2:6).

According John, Jesus is the true light, the means to true worship, the true bread, and the true vine (1:9; 4:23; 6:32; 15:1), where the word "true" (*alēthinos*) implies his supersession of all previous understandings of "light," "worship," manna, and Israel (the "vine") herself.[41]

---

41. *Contra* Beutler, *Judaism and the Jews*, 154–57.

John in Jerusalem (33–c. 55)

For almost a decade after the first Easter John Zebedee was the second most senior apostle in Jerusalem (Acts 1:13; 3:1, 3, 4, 11; 4:13, 19; 8:14; cf. 12:2) and then (in c. 47) the third most senior "pillar." (Gal 2:7–9)

I believe that the Gospel of John reflects the mission of John in Jerusalem from 33 to the middle 50s.[42]

First, the many references from Acts (just noted) and Paul's recognition of John as the third "pillar" in the Jerusalem Church points to his ministry to Jews, especially in Jerusalem. This finds confirmation in the many examples of Jewish response to Jesus in this Gospel—positive, shallow, or hostile.[43]

Such is the detailed narrative about Nicodemus, Joseph of Arimathea, and the blind man that it is reasonable to assume that these men had become part of John's mission in the holy city.

Second, John's interest in the "Greeks" (that is, not Gentiles, but Greek-speaking *Jews*) is significant. Within John's narrative we meet Greeks who have come to Jerusalem for the feast, that is, Greek-speaking Jews from the Diaspora (12:20; cf. 7:35—"the Dispersion among the Greeks"). John's interest in these is also signalled by his references to "the scattered children of God" (11:52) and "the other sheep that are not of this fold" (10:16).

Flavius Josephus' famous passage about Jesus asserts that he "won over many of the Jews and many of the Greeks" (*Jewish Antiquities* 18.63). While this may refer to the actual ministry of Jesus of Nazareth, it may also point to the responses to early missionary work in Jerusalem by the apostles, including John as a leading figure.

Third, the unnamed disciple who was "known to the high priest," who knew the serving girl freely entered the "court" (18:15). This suggests that John himself, or a disciple close to him, was on familiar terms with the high priest, the layout of his mansion and his servants. If this were true before the death of Jesus it would have been true afterward. John alone mentions the name of the high priest's servant, Malchus, which may mean he was known to John as part of his mission.

Fourth, it is assumed that the Beloved Disciple had a house in Jerusalem to which he took the grieving mother of Jesus (19:27). It is further assumed that such a house belonged to an embryonic Christian

---

42. See further Robinson, *Priority of John*, 59–67.
43. John 2:23; 7:40–52; 8:30; 9:35–38; 10:21; 11:45, 48; 12:11–19, 42–45;

quarter in Jerusalem, in the Mount Sion area. According to Epiphanius (320–403) James the brother of the Lord and the two Zebedee brothers had a house in which they cared for the mother of Jesus.[44]

Fifth, it may be relevant that an Essene community was located close to the Mount Sion area. Josephus refers to the "gate of the Essenes" (*Jewish War* 5.145), which may have been archaeologically identified, although doubt remains. But it is an intriguing possibility that some of the Qumran sounding dualities (light and darkness; death and life; above and below) that feature in John may have been influenced from that quarter.

These circumstantial threads appear to support a two-decade long, John-led mission in Jerusalem, the fruit of which was the Gospel he wrote. Forced from Jerusalem by the rising tide of Jewish religious nationalism in the 50s John took his precious scroll to Ephesus where after some further editing he "issued" it. A member of the church of Ephesus adds his appreciative affidavit at the end of the text: "This is the disciple [the Beloved Disciple] who is bearing witness about these things, and who has *written* these things and we know that his testimony is true" (21:24).

Conclusion

It is not possible to identify underlying sources to the Gospel of John. There may have been such sources but it is not possible to convincingly isolate them. Furthermore, as we have argued throughout this chapter, there is no evidence that John was depending on or using a prior Gospel. In fact, it must be questioned whether John wrote after the other three. The weight of evidence points in another direction. John may have written his Gospel at about the same time as Mark.

In the course of his narrative John quietly provides information—geographical, topographical, architectural, cultural, and political—that no other Gospel yields.

The political situation revealed in this Gospel came to an end with the destruction of the temple and the greater part of the city in AD 70. After that time there was no high priest or temple hierarchy. Judea was amalgamated with other principalities into a single, governor-controlled Roman province. In other words, John's version of the sensitive

---

44. *Heresies* 78:13.

relationships between Roman Governor and the temple authorities as portrayed in this gospel simply did not exist after 70.

This points to an earlier rather than a later date for this Gospel. It is difficult to imagine John writing as accurately about the topography and buildings of Jerusalem and the political structure twenty years later in distant Ephesus. John's narrative is fresh, immediate, and confident, suggesting that it was written prior to the Roman invasion of Israel in AD 66.

The one possible temporal anchor is the Gospel's reference to the involuntary death of Peter in the mid-60s (John 13:36; 21:18–19). Accordingly, I suggest John wrote his Gospel some time between 65–70.

Excursus: Roman Involvement in the Arrest, Trial, and Execution of Jesus

We note the "Roman" elements in the narrative of John 18–19.

18:3 A "band" (*speira*[45]) of Roman soldiers arrest Jesus in the Kedron garden.

18:12 The *speira* was led by a Roman captain (*chiliarchos*).

18:13 The soldiers and Jewish attendants brought Jesus bound to high priest Annas.[46]

18:15 A disciple who followed was known to Caiaphas[47] and admitted to his house.

18:28 Jewish chief priests convey Jesus from Caiaphas' house to the *Praetorium*. They refuse to enter for fear of defilement at Passover time.

18:29 Pilate asks what is their "accusation" (*katēgoria*)[48] against this man.[49]

18:30 The Jews assert Jesus is an evildoer (*kakon poiōn*), without being more specific.[50]

18:31 The Jews observe that it was "not lawful" (*ouk exestin*) for them to execute anyone.[51]

18:33 Pilate "calls" (*ephōnēsen*) Jesus.[52] We infer that the chief priests' accusation was that Jesus claimed to be "king of the Jews" (*basileus tōn Ioudaiōn*).[53]

18:39 Pilate asks about the "Paschal Privilege" to release Jesus.

18:40 Barrabas was a political insurgent (*lēstēs*).[54]

19:1–3 Pilate hands Jesus to the soldiers for flogging.[55]

---

45. A *speira* was a tenth of a legion, which seems excessive for the task of arresting one man.

19:6	Pilate declares that he finds no "charge" (*aitia*) against Jesus.
19:10	Pilate refers to his "authority" (*exousia/imperium*) to execute Jesus.
19:12	Chief priests appeal to Pilate as "friend of Caesar" (*amicus Caesaris*).[56]
19:13	The *bēma* was located on the stone pavement (*lithothstrōtos*: in Aramaic: *Gabbatha*[57]).
19:20	The superscription (*titlon*) of Jesus' crime was written in Aramaic, Latin and Greek.[58] The location of *Golgotha*[59] was near the city walls.
19:23	There were four soldiers in the execution squad.
19:31	Jews seek the breaking of legs so bodies do not remain on Passover-Sabbath.[60] The next day was to be a special Sabbath.[61]
19:33	The soldier's spear thrust to ascertain death.
19:41	Joseph's family tomb was in a garden.

46. Annas was the patriarch of his dynasty and evidently a continuing dominant influence (Josephus, *Jewish Antiquities* 18.26; 20.197-198; Luke 3:2). See further, Smallwood, "High Priests," 14-34.

47. Josephus refers to Caiaphas (*Jewish Antiquities* 18.35, 95). See further Bond, *Caiaphas*.

48. The process was called *cognitio*: the judge establishing the charge he must adjudicate.

49. Josephus narrates a trial by Governor Florus some years later, which illuminates Pilate's trial process:

> Florus lodged at [Herod's] palace, and on the following day had a tribunal (*bēma*) placed in front of the building and took his seat; the chief priests, the nobles and the most eminent citizens then presented themselves before the tribunal. [These] implored a pardon for the individuals who had acted disrespectfully. (*Jewish War* 2.301-4)

50. The accusers, called *delatores*, were the temple authorities.

51. Only the Roman governor, who bore the Emperor's *imperium*, had the *ius gladii*. See Josephus, *Jewish War* 2.117. The Synoptics presuppose that the temple authorities had to hand Jesus over to the Romans for their trial procedures, but it is only John who explains this. See Sherwin-White, "Trial of Jesus," 108.

52. The technical term for charging a person.

53. Only the Roman Caesar appointed a "client king."

54. Josephus' frequent use of the word *lēstēs* suggests that it had political associations; a *lēstēs* was not a mere robber.

55. Torture of the victim (*addida ludibria*) routinely accompanied and preceded the act of crucifixion. See Hengel, *Crucifixion*, 25-30.

56 The term "friend of Caesar" (*amicus Caesaris*) was a technical term for someone who enjoyed the patronage of the emperor and who may have benefitted by an imperial appointment, e.g., to the lucrative position as a provincial governor. See generally,

None of these details appears in Mark's account of the Jewish and Roman trials or the Roman execution so that the question of their origin arises. Generally speaking, John's information is consistent with the practices of the Jews (e.g., avoidance of contamination by going indoors with Gentiles) and with the apparently continuing power of Annas, the former high priest.

More pointedly still, John displays easy familiarity with Roman military structure (a *speira* led by a *chiliarchos*): a Roman governor's authority (*exousia*) in the province, the Roman (not Jewish) authority for capital punishment, Roman trial processes (*katēgoria, aitia, bēma*), and Roman crucifixion practices (*titlon*, the leg-breaking and spear thrust).

John makes explicit what Mark and Matthew and Luke assume about the relationships between the Jewish sacral authorities and the Roman jurisdiction. Under Roman administration the high priest had no authority to execute Jesus; he must send him to the military governor. Jewish trial processes will not achieve the desired outcome. The case must be tried again in the only tribunal that will achieve this. It is John's account, not Mark's, that makes this clear. At the same time, John discloses that it was still the Jews' case; the Romans did not initiate it.

Furthermore, John alone supplies the reason the chief priests had their way in face of the opposition of the otherwise omnipotent Roman prefect. It was due to the "patronage"-factor, that Pilate held his office for one reason only: he was *philos tou Kaisaros* (19:12). Evidently, Pilate knew that the high priest had some hold over him in this.[57]

So has John contrived these details to create the impression of reality, or do they arise innocently and genuinely from the events as they happened? True, the details about Jesus' unbroken bones could be accounted for theologically (19:31), but this explanation is not applicable

---

Bruce, "Trial of Jesus" 16–18; Goodman, *Rome and Jerusalem*, 81–82, 232–33, 375–76. Tacitus wrote, "Whoever was close to Sejanus [Praetorian prefect] had a claim on the friendship with Caesar [Tiberius]" (Annals 6.8). Pontius Pilate probably held his office through Sejanus's patronage so that when Sejanus fell from imperial favour in 31 his "friend" Pilate became vulnerable to the threat that he was not a "friend of Caesar."

57. If the crucifixion occurred in 33 (not 30) then Pilate's patron Sejanus was no longer there, having been executed in 31. By 33, Tiberius had regained the reins of power and was attempting to rectify Sejanus's anti-Semitic policies around the empire, including in Judea under his protégé Pilate. After the fall of Sejanus, Tiberius instructed his governors to "speak comfortably to the members of our [Jewish] nation in the different cities . . . to disturb none of our established customs but even to regard them as a trust committed to their care" (Philo, *Embassy to Gaius* 160–61).

to the mass of other information as noted above and expanded in the footnotes.

We conclude that these details are gratuitous and authentic and contribute significantly to our sense of the historical integrity of the Fourth Gospel. There appears to be no good reason to disparage or doubt these details, not least since they significantly exceed those found in Mark and the synoptic parallels. Accordingly, it is difficult to escape the conclusion that John and Mark wrote their Gospels independently of one another.

twenty-three

Why Are There Four Gospels?

By the end of the second century there were as many as twelve known Gospels in circulation.[1]

Matthew, Mark, Luke, John

Marcion's version of Luke

Gospel of Thomas, Gospel of Peter, "Unknown Gospel," Gospel of Truth, Gospel of the Ebionites, Gospel of the Nazoreans, Gospel of the Hebrews

Throughout history, mainstream Christians have regarded the Gospels printed in our Bibles as the only valid sources of information about Jesus.

How do we distinguish between authentic and inauthentic Gospels?

Authentic Gospels

Our method of identifying authentic sources is based on straightforward historical procedures.

---

1. In addition to manuscripts of Matthew, Mark, Luke, and John there are surviving texts of the Gospel of Thomas (P. Oxy. 1), The Gospel of Peter (P. Oxy. 4009), an "Unknown Gospel" (P. Egerton 2), and Valentinus' Gospel of Truth. As well there are Patristic references to the Gospel of the Ebionites (Irenaeus, *Against Heresies* 1.26.2, in Roberts and Donaldson, *Ante-Nicene Fathers*; 3.21.1), the Gospel of the Nazoreans (Eusebius, *History of the Church* 4.22.8), and the Gospel of the Hebrews (Clement, *Miscellanies* 2.9.45).

Witness of the Earliest Post-Apostolic Writers

We are fortunate in having texts from writers who immediately follow the New Testament era. These writers quote from, allude to, or echo many New Testament texts.[2]

Clement (c. 95)	Didache (c. 90)	Ignatius (c. 110)
Matthew	Matthew	Matthew
Mark	Mark	Mark
Luke	Luke	Luke
		John[3]
Acts		
		Romans
1 Corinthians	1 Corinthians	1 Corinthians
Ephesians		
		Philippians
	1 Thessalonians	1 Thessalonians
	2 Thessalonians	
	1 Timothy	
Hebrews		
James		
	1 Peter	

Based on these early "citations" we make two observations.

The first is that the major texts of the New Testament, including the four Gospels, had been written and were in circulation and use by the end of the first century, but most probably earlier.[4]

Accordingly, the earliness of *these* Gospels qualifies them to be regarded as primary sources for Jesus the Messiah. This has always been the view of mainstream Christians and historians. The other so-called Gospels are not referred to—whether positively or negatively—in the early post-apostolic writings for a very simple reason: *they had not yet been written.*

---

2. See the Reference Index in Lake, *Apostolic Fathers*, 383–96.

3. Ignatius, *Philadelphians* 7:1 ("the Spirit . . . knoweth not whence it comes or whither it goes") appears to echo John 3:8.

4. Revelation was not written until the mid-90s, explaining why it is not quoted in the early post-apostolic writings.

Second, the post-apostolic writers' early endorsement of the letters of the New Testament indicates that they believed the same doctrines as the apostles did about Jesus, that is, he was Messiah. The early acceptance of the *teachings* of the letters of the New Testament about Christ logically meant that the post-apostolic writers also accepted the Gospels' *narratives* about Jesus as the Messiah. This is confirmed in a mini-creed that we find in Ignatius' writings.

> Jesus Christ . . . was of *the stock of David*,
> who was from Mary,
> who was truly born, [ate] and drank,
> was truly persecuted under Pontius Pilate,
> was truly crucified and died . . .
> who also was truly raised from the dead,
> His Father raising him.[5]

Ignatius' reference to "the stock of David" is clear evidence of his commitment to Jesus as *Messiah*. Ignatius followed the teaching of the apostles before him. Similarly firm views are found in Polycarp who wrote soon after Ignatius, and in Justin Martyr who came after Polycarp.

Specific Early References to the Gospels

Papias, bishop of Hierapolis (Pamukkale in modern Turkey), writing in the first decades of the second century (probably c. 110), quotes from one whom he calls John the Elder whose views went back well into the previous century. John the Elder explains the origins of Mark's and Matthew's Gospels.[6] Furthermore, by asserting that Mark "accurately" wrote Papias was making an oblique reference to Luke (see Luke 1:3 where in Greek he uses the word "accurately").

As well, by giving the name of six disciples in the order they appear in the Gospel of John, Papias seems to know that Gospel also.[7] We conclude that Papias referred directly to the origins of the Gospels of Mark and Matthew and indirectly to the Gospels of Luke and John. Papias's information confirms the point made above from the post-apostolic

---

5. *Epistle to the Tralians* 9:4, quoted in Kelly, *Early Christian Creeds*, 68.
6. Reported in Eusebius, *History of the Church* 3.39.3–16.
7. See Bauckham, *Jesus and the Eyewitnesses*, 417–20.

writings, that the four gospels were in circulation and use by the end of the first century at the latest.

Reading and Quoting the Gospels

The earliest post-New Testament reference to the written Gospel is found in the *Didache* at the end of the first century.[8] The next extant reference to "gospel" is by Justin Martyr (*c.* 150) who refers to "the memoirs composed by the [apostles], which are called *gospels*."[9] Justin describes how the church leaders read and applied the message of the Gospels to the assembled believers each Sunday in every city.

In his extensive writings, Justin frequently echoes texts from each of the four Gospels.[10] We reasonably assume, therefore, that by his reference to "gospels" Justin has in mind the Gospels from apostolic times.

The view of mainstream Christians as supported by scholarly research is convinced that the four Gospels in our Bibles are the closest historically to Jesus and represent the views of his earliest followers and are for these reasons authentic. This conviction is based on the accumulated consideration of early referencing in the post-apostolic writings, the specific identification of Gospels by name by John the Elder (quoted by Papias) and by the numerous fragments of early Gospel manuscripts.

The Fourfold Gospel (c. 150–180)

We recall from chapter 1 our reference to the challenge to mainstream Christians by Marcion's emasculated single Gospel (Luke) and the Gnostics' multiplication of Gospels in the first part of the second century. These forced the church leaders in the years following to confirm the authentic *fourfold* gospel.

In that chapter we referred to Irenaeus' "quadriform" Gospel, who asserted that there were neither more nor less than four Gospels. Irenaeus was dependent on Polycarp, Bishop of Smyrna, who in turn was mentored by the Apostle John in Roman Asia. Other pointers to the fourfold gospel were located in the four "superscriptions," and Tatian's

---

8. *Didache* 8:3; 11:4; 15:5; 15:7. The name of the author is unknown.

9. Justin, *First Apology*, 66–67.

10. For example, Matt 1:22 (*First Apology* 33), Mark 2:17 (*Dialogue with Trypho* 8), Luke 1:32 (*First Apology* 33), and John 3:5 (*First Apology* 61).

Diatessaron ("through the four") that combined the four Gospels into one harmonized version, and to the discovery of P[45] (from late second century). This papyrus contained the four Gospels and the Acts of the Apostles. It is likely that codices containing the four Gospels were created from the beginning of the second century; all the surviving fragments of the Gospels from the second century were codices (i.e., "books" not scrolls).

Irenaeus and Tatian faced different problems that were, respectively, the *number* of authentic gospels and *discrepancies* between the four true Gospels. Outwardly, their responses were different. Yet Irenaeus' *quadriform* Gospel and Tatian's *Diatessaron* both sought to defend the common conviction that Matthew, Mark, Luke, and John were the only authentic apostolic gospels.

We conclude that the four Gospels in our Bibles belong to the first century and that they are the only "gospels" that qualify for this early dating. The implications of this are considerable, chiefly that the four Gospels were in use in the churches within six decades of Jesus.

From the early decades of the second century, however, there were various attempts to change the message of those Gospels, whether by radically reducing their content (Marcion) or by adding extra texts (e.g., *Gospel of Thomas*). The insistence on the fourfold Gospel by Irenaeus, Tatian, the Muratorian Canon, and the Codex P[45], represents the continuing conviction by later second century mainstream leaders about the unique authority of Matthew, Mark, Luke, and John.

By their commitment to the four Gospels the leaders of the churches in the second century maintained the messianic faith of Jesus and of his immediate followers.

Why Are There Four Gospels?

We may be grateful for Irenaeus's insistence that there were four Gospels. However, modern readers find unconvincing his explanation that it was because of the *four* creatures of Revelation. This is a problem. So we ask, why are there four Gospels?

In many ways it would have been easier if there were but one Gospel. For example, it would have avoided "mysteries" like explaining the origin of the sources underlying the Synoptic Gospels, or why the Gospel of John is so different from the others.

Martin Hengel captures the issues of *four* Gospels:

> It is almost a miracle that the church preserved the four earliest Gospels that we have, so often differing in part, despite their striking discrepancies, indeed contradictions, and resisted any attempt at harmonization.[11]

So, why are there *four* Gospels? The answer is that these texts are historically closest to Jesus, and furthermore that they are such edifying and inspiring texts. All true, of course. But there is another suggestion.

Fourfold Mission in the Apostolic Age (33–80)

The Four Mission Groups

From the late 40s four overlapping mission groups emerged, led by Peter, James, John, and Paul.[12] These four men met in Jerusalem in c. 47 to agree upon future missionary work, especially along ethnic lines (Gal 2:7–10). Networks of mission churches were established in the eastern Mediterranean through the initiative of these four leaders and the labors of their colleagues. Through Paul's letters to his churches and Acts 13–20 it is his mission that we know most about.

The evidence for these missions is found in the letters of the New Testament, especially the encyclicals of James, Peter, and John. Paul's Letter to the Galatians was an encyclical, written to "the churches of Galatia" (Gal 1:2). It is possible that Paul's Letter to the Ephesians was also an encyclical.

(1) Paul's letters to churches in Galatia, Macedonia, Achaia, and Asia are tangible evidence of congregations established through his mission.

(2) James' encyclical to the "twelve tribes of the Diaspora" point to his spiritual leadership over scattered congregations of Jewish Christians (Jas 1:1).

---

11. Hengel, *Four Gospels*, 106.

12. This view broadly depends on the analysis of Ellis, *Making of the New Testament*, 32–36, 251–66, 307–14. Ellis draws attention to the comment of Clement of Alexandria to "the true tradition of the blessed teaching in direct line from Peter, John, and Paul, the holy apostles" (309).

(3) Peter's encyclical to Pontus, Galatia, Cappadocia, Asia, and Bithynia likewise indicates his leadership over a "brotherhood" distributed throughout the provinces of northern Asia Minor (1 Pet 1:1).

(4) John's encyclical "book of prophecy" to seven churches in Roman Asia assumes his authority over these widely scattered churches (Rev 1:4, 11; 2:1—3:22).[13]

At the same time, however, the base from which these leaders wrote their mission letters was the center of their mission authority. For James it was Jerusalem, for Peter Rome, for John Ephesus, and for Paul wherever he was at the time of writing—Antioch, Corinth, Ephesus, Berea, or Rome.[14]

The sphere of the mission leader's authority was both (1) his geographic home base, and (2) the jurisdiction represented by the region (or ethnicity in the case of James) to which the leader's letters were directed.

What then of the Gospels? These leaders (or their associates) produced mission literature for the churches in their respective missions. Initially, various letters were written and brought to the intended churches to meet current pastoral needs. Subsequently, a leader from each group compiled a Gospel narrating a "biography" of Christ with challenging words about following him.

Accordingly, one Gospel and one or more letters are associated with each of the four mission leaders.[15]

---

13. Apostolic authorship of the Apocalypse historically is a moot point. Nevertheless, earliest authorities are in no doubt that the author was John Zebedee (Justin Martyr, *Dialogue with Trypho* 81.4; Irenaeus, *Against Heresies* 4.30.4; 5.26.1, in Roberts and Donaldson, *Ante-Nicene Fathers*). Furthermore, the author's assumed unquestioned authority over these churches (Rev 1:3; 2:7, 11, 17; 3:6, 13, 22; 22:18–19) is consistent with apostolicity (and not with being a mere "prophet"). Differences in style from the Fourth Gospel can be partly accounted for by genre differences between a Gospel-biography and a "book of prophecy" written in a quasi-apocalyptic manner. John's implied portrayal of himself as the true prophet against the "false prophet" (Rev 16:13; 19:30; 20:10), and the calculatedly "prophetical" authority of the "book" (1:1–3; 22:6, 18–19) is explanation enough for the author's failure to claim apostolicity. The books dependence on hundreds of OT echoes and its quasi-apocalyptic style points to the author as a Palestinian Jew.

14. Whether it was *Antioch* (for Galatians?), *Corinth* (for 1 & 2 Thessalonians, Romans), *Ephesus* (for 1 Corinthians [and Ephesians, Colossian, Philemon?]), *Berea* (2 Corinthians?) or *Rome* (Philippians, 2 Timothy).

15. I agree with Bauckham, "For Whom Were the Gospels Written?" 9–48, that the Gospels were not primarily written for the narrow interests of the authors' domestic faith community. However, his view of the authors' implied *indefinite* readership in each case is too broad; the mission literature inevitably is conditioned by the needs

Mission leader	Mission literature
Peter	1 Peter, 2 Peter, Gospel of Mark
James	Letter of James, Gospel of Matthew
John	1 John, Revelation, Gospel of John
Paul	Paul's letters, Luke-Acts

The hypothesis stated above explains the widespread dissemination of Christian belief as well as the origin and purpose of the greater part of the NT. The fourfold character of mission in the apostolic age may have been retained in the memories of the churches in the decades following, influencing the insistence on the *fourfold* Gospel from the early years of the second century.

The theory of the four mission groups and their creation of pastoral literature is historically realistic. Furthermore, and very importantly, this hypothesis meshes exactly with the patristic insistence on the *fourfold* gospel. Irenaeus's basis for the fourfold gospel in the four creatures of the Apocalypse is curious. The four mission groups, however, led by James, John, Peter, and Paul helps us understand the insistence on four Gospels.

Conclusion

Marcion's single Gospel and the Gnostics' multiple Gospels forced mainstream Christian leaders to identify the Gospels that would have had the imprimatur of the apostles. Irenaeus was key to this. As the pupil of Polycarp, disciple of apostles, Irenaeus asserted the legitimacy of the fourfold Gospel of Matthew, Mark, Luke, and John. In this he had the support of the Superscriptions, the Muratorian Canon, the *Diatessaron*, and the presence of the four Gospels in the one codex from the second century.

Irenaeus's dependence on the four creatures of the Apocalypse is an inadequate basis for the "quadriform" Gospel, which prompts the question: why is the number *four* so important? The answer is twofold. First,

---

of the mission jurisdiction, both home-based and distant. Against Bauckham's arguments see, e.g., Sim, "Gospel for All Christians," 3–7; Mitchell, "Patristic Counter-Evidence," 36–79.

the fourfold Gospel had the endorsement by Irenaeus, whose mentor was Polycarp, associate of the apostles. Second, there are four Gospels because there were initially four mission groups, led by James, Peter, John, and Paul, each who wrote an encyclical. There were four Gospels because there were four apostolic mission groups.

By the end of the first century with the passing of the mission leaders the mission groups would have dissolved. The four Gospels then became and remained "the Gospels for all Christians."

twenty-four

Making the Gospels

1. THE LOGICAL STARTING point is to consider P^{46}, a codex (a book) dated to the end of the second century (or earlier) that contains the four Gospels (and the Acts of the Apostles). Moving backward from the end through to the beginning of the second century we note numerous references to the *fourfold* gospel (by Irenaeus, Tatian, and the Muratorian Canon).

There are also a number of partial or whole manuscripts of Matthew, Luke, and John, but not Mark. Sources late in the first century (Clement, the *Didache*) and early in the second century (Papias, Ignatius, Polycarp) point to the Gospels having been written by (approximately) the third quarter of the first century.

2. Based on references by Papias and Justin Martyr we date the Gospel of Mark to the mid-60s and locate its provenance to Rome. Analysis of speeches by Peter and Paul in the book of Acts identifies a *verbal* statement of the gospel message that became the skeletal basis for Mark's *written* Gospel.

3. Traditional source criticism demonstrates that Matthew and Luke based their narratives on the Gospel of Mark, which Matthew complemented by the sources "Q" and "M," and which Luke complemented by the sources "Q" and "L."

4. The differences between the "primary" Gospels of Mark and John are so extensive that I conclude them to have been written independently. Such is the depth and extent of historical, geographical, topographical, and cultural detail in the Gospel of John that its first and comprehensive draft version appears to have been written close to the soil in Palestine by the 50s. I believe it was "issued" later by John in Ephesus, capital of Roman Asia.

5. The letters of Paul, James, and (First) Peter were written to churches in the period between Jesus and the writing of the Gospels. These letters quote from or echo Mark, "Q," "L," and "M," the sources that will later undergird Matthew and Luke. It is likely that these (embryonic) sources were written in *Greek* from or close to the beginning of Christian history.

Jesus	Gospel Sources echoed in the *letters* of Paul, James, Peter	*Sources*—Mark, "Q," "L," and "M" as they appear in Matthew and Luke	*Completed Gospels*: Matthew, Mark, and Luke
Taught in Greek?	Written in Greek	Written in Greek	Written in Greek

6. Jesus chose his disciples to be "with" him (Mark 3:14) from the beginning of his ministry throughout its duration until his departure. He instructed them in private as well as in public for a defined purpose, to be witnesses to his words and works once he was no longer "with" them. Initially, this witness was oral, but soon these disciples created written versions that became the sources destined to become the texts of the Synoptic Gospels.

7. The narrative basis of each Gospel is *eyewitness* testimony. Mark was dependent on Peter; Matthew and John themselves were original eyewitnesses; the "narratives" Luke used for his Gospel were "delivered" to him by those who were "eyewitnesses and ministers of the word" (i.e., original disciples). Whether directly or indirectly each Gospel was based on eyewitness testimony. Paul was dependent on eyewitness testimony (1 Cor 15:3-7, 11).

8. It must be acknowledged that there are many things we do not understand about the *Making of the Gospels*.

- In which languages did Jesus teach: Aramaic, Hebrew, or Greek?
- How were Jesus' words remembered—by oral communication or by scribal copying, or both?
- Who created the verbal version of the gospel that Peter and Paul preached?
- When and where did Peter create the stories about Jesus that would be incorporated in the Gospel of Mark?

- Who formulated the early "traditions" that Paul "received" and that he "delivered" to the church in Corinth (and most likely also other churches)?
- Who began assembling the sources "Q," "L," and "M," and where?
- How can we explain the depth of cultural, geographic, and historical detail in so "theological" a Gospel as John's?

9. Despite our inability to answer these and other questions the fact remains that the Gospel of Mark was written within a generation of Jesus, a mere thirty years in which we observe busy missionary activity throughout the eastern Mediterranean, as witnessed by the letters of Paul, James, and Peter to networks of churches. The written Gospel evolved organically out of the verbal gospel that was proclaimed during those few years that was the instrument that created those churches.

10. Many, however, cannot believe that Jesus was actually a redeemer, but was in reality merely a prophet, a sage, a social reformer, or a political activist. They look to Paul and Mark as having reshaped Jesus into the mythical figure of a resurrected redeemer. Conspiracy theories flourish in part because of the many unanswered questions noted above.

11. Critical to our understanding of Jesus are the verbatim "traditions" embedded in First Corinthians, which almost certainly Paul "received" in Jerusalem when he returned to Jerusalem after the Damascus encounter (in c. 37). The Eucharistic "tradition" and the Easter "tradition" combine to teach that "Christ died *for* our sins" and was "raised on the third day," and that his people met to remember that his "body" and "blood" were given *for* them. These "traditions" would have been created in Jerusalem within three years of the first Easter and are reasonably reckoned to be true to the mind of Jesus himself. The earliest "traditions" are focused on the *redemptive* Jesus.

12. Paul boldly claimed that the "pillars" of the Jerusalem Church endorsed his teaching that "faith" not "works of the law" was the pathway to acceptance with God (Gal 2:2–6). His redemptive message based on Christ's death and resurrection was identical with that of the other apostles (1 Cor 15:11—"Whether then it was I or they, so we [apostles] preach and so you [Corinthians] believed"). Paul's message was "apostolic" and consistent with the teaching of the Gospels written soon afterward.

13. Those who blame Mark for reshaping Jesus depend upon a late dating of that Gospel and a conjectural setting that deconstructs its

essential and straightforward message that the Son of God was crucified to liberate captives oppressed by supernatural evil.

14. In summary, our argument is that there are numerous unanswered questions about the making of the Gospels, but these do not open the doors to theories claiming the Gospels are not what they appear to be because they portray a Jesus who was different from the rabbi from Nazareth.

15. Echoes within the letters of Paul, James, and Peter suggest that the Sermon on the Mount had from early times been shaped into an entity in its own right.

16. The writers of the Gospel inevitably reflected the values and issues of the community from which they wrote. At the same time, however, they wrote to address their sense of the needs of the churches to which they wrote.[1] The Gospels are "destination-centered."

17. We may liken the making of the Gospels to four gifted artists, each with brushes in hand seated behind their easels interpreting Jesus according to their impressions of him. Like good artists each writer captures insights into Jesus that are uniquely true to his character.

Mark portrays Jesus as the all-powerful Son of God paradoxically crucified to set free those who are captive to endemic spiritual and moral wickedness. Matthew presents him as the Messiah who teaches the way to the blessings of the kingdom of heaven. For Luke, Jesus is the gifted storyteller who encourages those who follow him on the road to "Jerusalem." John sees him through the eyes of the disciple whom Jesus loved, who witnessed his miracle signs, his crucifixion, and who conversed with his resurrected person by the side of the lake.

How grateful we are for four different but complementary portraits of the towering, transcendent figure of the Son of God.

18. John quotes Jesus as teaching that the Paraclete (the Holy Spirit) would stir the memories of the disciples to recapture the true Jesus (John 16:12–15). So profound are these four books that we are unable to explain their depth of insight apart from the divine inspiration of their authors.

---

1. See further Bauckham, "For Whom Were the Gospels Written?" 9–48; Klink, *Audience of the Gospels*.

Bibliography

Adamson, J. B. *The Epistle of James*. NICNT. Grand Rapids: Eerdmans, 1976.
Akenson, Donald H. *Saint Saul: A Skeleton Key to the Historical Jesus*. Oxford: Oxford University Press, 2000.
Ashley, Evelyn. "The Miracles of Jesus." In *The Content and Setting of the Gospel Tradition*, edited by Mark Harding and Alanna Nobbs, 395–417. Grand Rapids: Eerdmans, 2010.
Bailey, Kenneth. "Informal Controlled Oral Tradition and the Synoptic Gospels." *Asia Journal of Theology* 5 (1991) 34–54.
Baird, William. *History of New Testament Research: From C. H. Dodd to Hans Dieter Betz*. Vol. 3. Minneapolis: Fortress, 2013.
Bammel, Ernst. "Ex Illa itque die consilium fecerunt." In *The Trial of Jesus*, edited by E. Bammel, 11–40. London: SCM, 1970.
———. "The Titulus." In *Jesus and the Politics of his Day*, edited by E. Bammel and C. F. D. Moule, 353–65. Cambridge: Cambridge University Press, 1984.
Barclay, William. *The Gospels and Acts*. Vol. 1. London: SCM, 1976.
Barnett, Paul W. *The Birth of Christianity: The First Twenty Years*. Grand Rapids: Eerdmans, 2005.
———. *Gospel Truth*. Nottingham: IVP, 2012.
———. *The Importance of Peter in Early Christianity*. Milton Keynes, UK: Paternoster, 2016.
———. *Paul in Syria*. Milton Keynes, UK: Paternoster, 2014.
Barrett, C. K. "Paul's Opponents in II Corinthians." *New Testament Studies* 17 (1971) 233–54.
Bauckham, Richard. "For Whom Were the Gospels Written?" In *The Gospels for all Christians*, edited by Richard Bauckham, 9–48. Grand Rapids: Eerdmans, 1998.
———. *God Crucified*. Grand Rapids: Eerdmans, 1999.
———. *Jesus and the Eyewitnesses*. Grand Rapids: Eerdmans, 2006.
Bernier, Richard. *Aposynagōgos and the Historical Jesus in John: Rethinking the Historicity of the Johannine Expulsion Passages*. Leiden: E. J. Brill, 2013.
Best, E. *1 Peter*. NCB. London: Oliphants, 1971.
Beutler, J. *Judaism and the Jews in the Gospel of John*. Studia Biblica 30. Rome: Editrice Pontificio Instituto Biblico, 2006.
Bird, Michael F. *The Gospel of the Lord*. Grand Rapids: Eerdmans, 2014.
Blomberg, Craig L. "John and Jesus." In *The Face of New Testament Studies*, edited by S. McKnight and G. R. Osborne, 209–26. Grand Rapids: Baker Academic, 2004.

Bock, Darrell L. *The Missing Gospels: Unearthing the Truth Behind Alternative Christianities*. Nashville: Thomas Nelson, 2006.

Bockmuehl, Marcus. "Antioch and James the Just." In *James the Just and Christian Origins*, edited by B. Chilton and C. A. Evans, 155–98. Leiden: E. J. Brill, 1999.

———. *The Remembered Peter in Ancient Reception and Modern Debate*. WUNT 262. Tübingen: Mohr Siebeck, 2010.

———. *Simon Peter in Scripture and Memory*. Grand Rapids: Baker Academic, 2012.

Bockmuehl, Marcus, and Donald A. Hagner, eds. *The Written Gospel*. Cambridge: Cambridge University Press, 2007.

Bond, Helen K. *Caiaphas: Friend of Rome or Judge of Jesus?* Louisville, KY: Westminster John Knox Press, 2004.

Borgen, Peter. *LOGOS Was the True Light and other Essays on the Gospel of John*. Trondheim: Tapir Publishers, 1983.

Boyd, Gregory A. *Cynic, Sage or Son of God*. Wheaton, IL: Bridgepoint, 1995.

Brandon, S. G. F. *Jesus and the Zealots*. Manchester: Manchester University Press, 1967.

Bruce, F. F. *The Acts of the Apostles: Greek Text with Introduction and Commentary*. Grand Rapids: Eerdmans, 1990.

———. "The Trial of Jesus in the Fourth Gospel." In *Gospel Perspectives: Studies in the History and the Tradition of the Four Gospels*, edited by R. T. France and D. Wenham, 7–20. Vol. 1. Sheffield: JSOT Press, 1980.

Bultmann, Rudolph. *The History of the Synoptic Tradition*. Oxford: Blackwell, 1921.

Burridge, Richard A. *What Are the Gospels? A Comparison with Graeco-Roman Biography*. 2nd ed. Grand Rapids: Eerdmans, 2004.

Buth, Randall, and R. Steven Notley, eds. *The Language Environment of First Century Judaea: Jerusalem Studies in the Synoptic Gospels*. Vol. 2. Leiden: E. J. Brill, 2014.

Carson, D. A. *The Gospel According to John*. Grand Rapids: Eerdmans, 1991.

Cartlidge, David, and David Dungan. *Documents for the Study of the Gospels*. Philadelphia: Fortress, 1980.

Casey, Maurice. *An Aramaic Approach to Q: Sources for the Gospels of Matthew and Luke*. NSNTSMS 122. Cambridge: Cambridge University Press, 2002.

———. *From Jewish Prophet to Gentile God: the Origin and Development of New Testament*. Louisville: Westminster John Knox, 1991.

———. "In Which Language Did Jesus Teach?" *Expository Times* 108/11 (1997) 326–28.

Charlesworth, James. "The Dead Sea Scrolls and the Gospel according to John." In *Exploring the Gospel of John*, edited by R. A. Culpepper and C. Clifton Black, 65–98. Louisville, KY: Westminster John Knox, 1996.

———. *Jesus within Judaism*. London: SPCK, 1988.

Chilton, Bruce. "The Whip of Ropes in John 2:15." In *Jesus in Context: Temple, Purity and Restoration*, edited by C. A. Evans and B. Chilton, 450–60. Leiden: Brill, 1997.

Crossan, John Dominic. *The Historical Jesus: The Life of a Mediterranean Jewish Peasant*. San Francisco: HarperSanFrancisco, 1992.

———. *Jesus: A Revolutionary Biography*. San Francisco: HarperSanFrancisco, 1994.

Cullmann, Oscar. *Peter: Disciple, Apostle, Martyr*. Philadelphia: Westminster, 1958.

Dodd, C. H. *The Apostolic Preaching and Its Development*. London: Hodder and Stoughton, 1936.

———. *Historical Tradition in the Fourth Gospel*. Cambridge: Cambridge University Press, 1963.

Dunn, James D. G. *Beginning from Jerusalem*. Grand Rapids: Eerdmans, 2009.
———. *Jesus Remembered*. Grand Rapids: Eerdmans, 2003.
Eddy, Paul Rhodes, and Gregory A. Boyd. *The Jesus Legend: A Case for the Historical Reliability of the Synoptic Jesus Traditon*. Grand Rapids: Baker Academic, 2007.
Ehrman, B. *Jesus: Apocalyptic Prophet of the New Millennium*. New York: Oxford University Press, 2002.
Ellis, E. Earle. "Dating the New Testament." *New Testament Studies* 26 (1980) 487–502.
———. *The Gospel of Luke*. New Century Bible. London: Nelson, 1966.
———. *The Making of the New Testament Documents*. Leiden: Brill, 2002.
———. "New Directions in Form Criticism." In *Prophecy and Hermeneutic in Early Christianity*, by E. Earle Ellis, 237–53. Grand Rapids: Eerdmans, 1978.
———. "Paul and His Opponents." In *Christianity, Judaism and Other Greco-Roman Cults: Studies for Morton Smith at Sixty*, edited by Jacob Neusner, 264–98. Leiden: Brill, 1975.
Eusebius. *Ecclesiastical History*. Translated Kirsopp Lake. Vol. 1. Loeb Classical Library. Cambridge: Harvard University Press, 1992.
Feldman, L. *Jew and Gentile in the Ancient World*. Princeton: Princeton University Press, 1996.
Fiensy, David A. "Jesus' Socioeconomic Background." In *Hillel and Jesus: Comparative Studies of Two Major Religious Leaders*, edited by James H. Charlesworth and Loren L. Johns, 224–55. Minneapolis: Fortress, 1997.
Fitzmyer, J. A. "The Priority of Mark and the 'Q' Source in Luke." In *To Advance the Gospel: New Testament Studies*, by Joseph A. Fitzmyer, 3–39. Grand Rapids: Eerdmans, 1998.
Freyne, Sean. *Galilee, Jesus and the Gospels: Literary Approaches and Historical Investigations*. Philadelphia: Fortress, 1988.
Gathercole, Simon. *The Gospel of Thomas*. Leiden: Brill, 2012.
———. *The Preexistent Son: Recovering the Christologies of Matthew, Mark, and Luke*. Grand Rapids: Eerdmans, 2006.
Gerhardsson, Birger. *The Gospel Tradition*. Lund: Gleerup, 1986.
———. *The Origin of the Gospel Traditions*. London: SCM, 1977.
———. *The Reliability of the Gospel Tradition*. Peabody, MA: Hendrickson, 2001.
Gleaves, G. Scott. *Did Jesus Speak Greek? The Emerging Evidence of Greek Dominance in First-Century Palestine*. Eugene, OR: Pickwick, 2015.
Goodacre, Mark "A Monopoly on Markan Priority? Fallacies at the heart of Q." *Society of Biblical Literature Seminar Papers 2000*, 562–83. Atlanta: SBL, 2000.
Goodman, Martin. *Rome and Jerusalem: The Clash of Civilizations*. London: Allen Lane, 2007.
Guelich, R. A. "The Gospel Genre." In *Das Evangelium und die Evangelien*, edited by P. Stuhlmacher, 181–210. WUNT 29. Tübingen: Mohr, 1983.
Gundry, R. H. "Further *Verba* on the *Verba Christi* in First Peter." *Biblica* 55 (1974) 211–32.
———. *Mark: A Commentary on His Apology for the Cross*. Grand Rapids: Eerdmans, 1993.
———. "'Verba Christi' in 1 Peter: Their Implications Concerning the Authorship of 1 Peter and the Authorship of the Gospel Tradition." *New Testament Studies* 13 (1966/67) 336–59.

Hafemann, S. J. "Paul and His Interpreters." In *Dictionary of Paul and His Letters*, edited by G. F. Hawthorne et al., 666–71. Downers Grove, IL: InterVarsity, 1993.

Hare, D. R. A. *The Theme of Jewish Persecution of Christians in the Gospel of St. Matthew*. Cambridge: Cambridge University Press, 1967.

Harris, Murray J. *The Second Epistle to the Corinthians*. NIGTC. Grand Rapids: Eerdmans, 2005.

Head, P. M., and P. J. Williams. "Q Review." *Tyndale Bulletin* 54.1 (2003) 131–44.

Hengel, Martin. *Acts and the History of Earliest Christianity*. London: SCM, 1979.

———. *Crucifixion*. London: SCM, 1977.

———. "Eye-Witness Memory and the Writing of the Gospels: Form Criticism, Community Tradition, and the Authority of the Authors." In *The Written Gospel*, edited by Marcus Bockmuehl and Donald A. Hagner, 70–96. Cambridge: Cambridge University Press, 2007.

———. *The Four Gospels and the One Gospel of Jesus Christ*. London: SCM, 2000.

———. *Hellenism and Judaism*. Philadelphia: Fortress, 1974.

———. *The Johannine Question*. London: SCM, 1989.

———. *The Pre-Christian Paul*. London: SCM, 1991.

———. *Saint Peter: The Underestimated Apostle*. Grand Rapids: Eerdmans, 2010.

———. *Studies in the Gospel of Mark*. London: SCM, 1976.

Horbury, William. "'Gospel' in Herodian Judaea." In *The Written Gospel*, edited by Marcus Bockmuehl and Donald Hagner, 7–30. Cambridge: Cambridge University Press, 2005.

Horsley, G. H. R. *New Documents Illustrating Early Christianity*. The Ancient History Document Research Centre, Macquarie University. Grand Rapids: Eerdmans, 1981.

Howard, W. F. *The Fourth Gospel in Recent Criticism and Interpretation*. London: Epworth, 1955.

Hultgren, A. J. *The Rise of Normative Christianity*. Minneapolis: Fortress, 1994.

Hurtado, Larry W. *The Earliest Christian Artifacts*. Grand Rapids: Eerdmans, 2006.

———. *One God One Lord*. Philadelphia: Fortress, 1988.

Hurtado, Larry W., and Paul Owen, eds. *"Who Is This Son of Man?": The Latest Scholarship on a Puzzling Expression of the Historical Jesus*. London: T. & T. Clark, 2010.

Ingolfsland, D. "Kloppenborg's Stratification of Q and Its Significance for Historical Jesus Studies." *Journal of the Evangelical Theological Society* 46/2 (June 2003) 227–31.

Jeremias, Joachim. *New Testament Theology*. New York: Scribner, 1971.

Johns, Loren L. *Hillel and Jesus: Comparisons of Two Major Religious Leaders*. Minneapolis: Fortress, 1997.

Josephus. *The Jewish War*. Translated H. St J. Thackeray. Loeb Classical Library. Cambridge: Harvard University Press, 1997.

Katz, T. "Issues in the Separation of Judaism and Christianity after 70 CE: A Reconsideration." *Journal of Biblical Literature* 103 (1984) 69–74.

Keener, Craig S. "Assumptions in Historical-Jesus Research: Using Ancient Biographies and Disciples' Traditioning as Control." *Journal for the Study of the Historical Jesus* 9.1 (2011) 26–58.

———. *The Historical Jesus of the Gospels*. Grand Rapids: Eerdmans, 2009.

Kelly, J. N. D. *Early Christian Creeds*. London: Longmans, 1963.

Kimelman, R. "The Birkath ha-Minim and the Lack of Evidence for an Anti-Christian Prayer in Late Antiquity." In *Jewish and Christian Self-Definition*. Vol. 2, *Aspects of Judaism in the Greco Roman Period*, edited by E. P. Sanders, A. L. Baumgarten, and A. Mendelssohn, 226–44. Philadelphia: Fortress, 1981.

Klink, Edward W., III, ed. *The Audience of the Gospels: The Origin and Function of the Gospels in Early Christianity*. LNTS 353. London: T. & T. Clark International, 2010.

Kloppenborg, J. *The Formation of Q*. Harrisburg, PA: Trinity Press International, 1987.

———. "The 'Messianic' Implications of the Q Material." *Journal of Biblical Literature* 118/2 (1999) 255–89.

Kloppenborg Verbin, J. *Excavating Q: The History and Setting of the Sayings Gospel*. Minneapolis: Fortress, 2000.

Lake, Kirsopp, ed. and trans. *The Apostolic Fathers*. Vol. 2. Loeb Classical Library. London: W. Heinemann, 1976.

Lane, W. *The Gospel according to Mark*. Grand Rapids: Eerdmans, 1974,

Last, Richard "The Social Relationships of the Gospel Writers: New Insights from Inscriptions Commending Greek Historiographers." *Journal for the Study of the New Testament* 37 (2015) 235–52.

Lieberman, S. *Hellenism in Jewish Palestine*. New York: Jewish Theological Society, 1962.

Lukaszewski, Albert L. "Issues Concerning the Aramaic Behind the Son of Man: A Critical Review of Scholarship." In *"Who Is the Son of Man?" The Latest Scholarship on a Puzzling Expression of the Historical Jesus*, edited by Larry W. Hurtado and Paul L. Owen, 1–27. London: T. & T. Clark, 2011.

Mack, Burton L. *The Lost Gospel: The Book of Q and Christian Origins*. San Francisco: HarperSanFrancisco: 1993.

———. *A Myth of Innocence*. Philadelphia: Fortress, 1988.

Manson, T. W. *The Sayings of Jesus*. London: SCM, 1948.

Martyn, J. L. *History and Theology in the Fourth Gospel*. Nashville: Abingdon, 1979.

McNicol, A. J., et al., eds. *Beyond the Q Impasse: Luke's Use of Matthew*. Valley Forge, PA: Trinity Press International, 1996.

Meier, John P. "The Historical Jesus and the Historical Samaritans." *Biblica* 81.2 (2000) 220–39.

Meyer, B. F. *The Aims of Jesus*. London: SCM, 1979.

Meyers, Eric M., and James F. Strange. *Archaeology, the Rabbis and Early Christianity*. London: SCM, 1981.

Millard, A. *Reading and Writing in the Time of Jesus*. Sheffield: Sheffield Academic, 2000.

Mitchell, M. M. "Patristic Counter-Evidence to the Claim that the Gospels Were Written for All Christians." *New Testament Studies* 51/1 (2005) 36–79.

Moessner, David P. "How Luke Writes." In *The Written Gospel*, edited by Marcus Bockmuehl and Donald A. Hagner, 149–70. Cambridge: Cambridge University Press, 2007.

Morris, Leon. *The Gospel According to Matthew*. Grand Rapids: Eerdmans, 1992.

Painter, John. *Just James*. Columbia: University of South Carolina, 1998.

Peppard, Michael. *The Son of God in the Roman World: Divine Sonship in Its Social and Political Context*. Oxford: Oxford University Press, 2011.

Perrin, Nicholas. *Thomas, The Other Gospel*. London: SPCK, 2007.

Philostratus. *Apollonius of Tyana*. Translated Christopher Jones. Loeb Classical Library. Cambridge: Harvard University Press, 2005.

Porter, Stanley E. *The Criteria for Authenticity in Historical Jesus Research.* Sheffield: Sheffield Academic Press, 2000.

———. "Did Jesus Ever Teach in Greek?" *Tyndale Bulletin* 44 (1993) 199–235.

———. "Jesus and the Use of Greek: A Response to Maurice Casey." *Bulletin of Biblical Research* 10.1 (2000) 71–87.

———. *John, His Gospel, and Jesus: In Pursuit of the Johannine Voice.* Grand Rapids: Eerdmans, 2015.

———. "The Use of Greek in First-Century Palestine: A Diachronic and Synchronic Examination." *Journal for the Study of Greco-Roman Christianity and Judaism* 12 (2016) 203–28.

———. *When Paul Met Jesus: How an Idea Got Lost in History.* New York: Cambridge University Press, 2016.

Price, R. M. *Deconstructing Jesus.* Amherst, NY: Prometheus, 2000.

Price, S. R. F. *Rituals and Power: The Roman Imperial Cult in Asia Minor.* Cambridge: Cambridge University Press, 1984.

Reinhartz, A. "The Johannine Community and Its Jewish Neighbours: A Reappraisal." In *"What Is John?" Literary and Social Readings of the Fourth Gospel Society of Biblical Literature,* edited by F. F. Segovia, 111–38. SS 7. Atlanta: Scholars Press, 1998.

Richards, E. Randolph. *Paul and First-Century Letter Writing: Secretaries, Composition and Collection.* Downers Grove, IL: IVP, 2004.

Roberts, A., and J. Donaldson, eds. *The Ante-Nicene Fathers: The Writings of the Fathers Down to A.D. 325.* Vol. 1. Grand Rapids: Eerdmans, n.d.

Robinson, J. A. T. *The Priority of John.* London: SCM, 1985.

———. *Redating the New Testament.* London: SCM, 1976.

Robinson, J. M., P. Hoffman, and J. S. Kloppenborg, eds. *The Critical Edition of Q.* Leuven: Peeters, 2000.

Sanders, E. P. *Jesus and Judaism.* London: SCM Press, 1984.

Schürer, E. *The History of the Jewish People in the Age of Jesus Christ.* Edinburgh: T. & T. Clark, 1973.

Selwyn, E. G. *The First Epistle of Peter.* New York: Macmillan, 1961.

Shanks, Monte A. *Papias and the New Testament.* Eugene, OR: Pickwick, 2013.

Sherwin-White, A. N. "The Trial of Jesus." In *Historicity and Chronology in the New Testament,* edited by D. E. Nineham et al., 101–18. London: SPCK, 1965.

Sim, D. C. "The Gospel for All Christians? A Response to Richard Bauckham." *Journal for the Study of the New Testament* 24/2 (2001) 3–7.

Smallwood, E. Mary. "High Priests and Politics in Roman Palestine." *Journal of Theological Studies* 13 (1962) 14–34.

Smith, Justin Marc. *Why Bíos? On the Relationship Between Gospel Genre and Implied Audience.* The Library of New Testament Studies 518. London: T. & T. Clark, 2015.

Tacitus. *Annals.* Translated J. Jackson. Loeb Classical Library. Cambridge: Harvard University Press, 1989.

———. *Histories.* Translated C. H. Moore. Loeb Classical Library. Cambridge: Harvard University Press, 1989.

Talmon, S. "Oral and Written Tradition in Judaism." In *Jesus and the Oral Tradition,* edited by H. Wansbrough, 157–15. JSNT Supplement 64 Sheffield: Sheffield University Press, 1991.

Thompson, Alan J. *Luke: Exegetical Guide to the Greek New Testament*. Nashville: B&H Academic, 2016.
Turner, C. H. "Markan Usage: Notes Critical and Exegetical, on the Second Gospel V. The Movements of Jesus and His Disciples and the Crowd." *Journal of Theological Studies* 26 (1925) 225–40.
Vegge, Ivar *2 Corinthians—A Letter about Reconciliation: A Psychagogical, Epistolographical and Rhetorical Analysis*. WUNT 2/239. Tübingen: Mohr Siebeck, 2008.
Vermes, Geza. *Jesus the Jew: A Historian's Reading of the Gospels*. London: Collins, 1973.
von Wahlde, Urban C. "Archaeology and John's Gospel." In *Jesus and Archaeology*, edited by James H. Charlesworth, 523–86. Grand Rapids: Eerdmans, 2006.
Watson, Francis. *Gospel Writing: A Canonical Perspective*. Grand Rapids: Eerdmans, 2013.
———. *Paul, Judaism and the Gentiles*. SNTSMS 56. Cambridge: Cambridge University Press, 1986.
Welborn, L. L. *An End to Enmity: Paul and the "Wrongdoer" in Second Corinthians*. Berlin: de Gruyter, 2011.
Wenham, D. *Paul: Follower of Jesus or Founder of Christianity?* Grand Rapids: Eerdmans, 1995.
Westcott, B. F. *The Gospel According to St John*. London: John Murray, 1903.
Witherington, Ben, III. "Christianity in the Making: Oral Mystery or Eyewitness History?" In *Memories of Jesus*, edited by Robert B. Stewart and Gary R. Habermas, 197–226. Nashville: B&H Publishing, 2010.
———. *The Jesus Quest: The Third Search for the Jew of Nazareth*. 2nd ed. Downers Grove, IL: IVP, 1997.
Wrede, William. *The Origin of the New Testament*. London: Harper & Brothers, 1909.
———. *Paul*. Boston: American Unitarian Association, 1908.
Wright, N. T. "Dating the New Testament." *New Testament Studies* 26 (1980) 487–502.
———. *Judas and the Gospel of Jesus*. London: SPCK, 2006.
———. "Resurrection in Q?" In *Christology, Controversy and Community*, edited by D. R. H. Horrell and C. M. Tuckett, 78–89. Leiden: Brill, 2000.
———. *The Resurrection of the Son of God*. London: SPCK, 2003.

Author Index

Akenson, Donald H., 105n4
Ashley, Evelyn, xvn12

Bailey, Kenneth, 93, 93n20, 97
Baird, William, 108n13
Barclay, William, 193, 193n19, 193n20
Barnett, Paul W., 20n4, 64, 64n7, 64n8, 71n5, 80n1, 192n17
Barrett, C. K., 65, 65n10, 66
Bauckham, Richard, xiv, 6n8, 93n19, 102, 102n10, 129, 129n6, 130n8, 146, 146n29, 147, 177n8, 200n9, 226n7, 230n15, 236n1
Bernier, Richard, 202n16
Best, E., 71n8
Beutler, J., 217n41
Bird, Michael F., 14n6, 27n14
Blomberg, Craig L., 202n14
Bock, Darrell L., xiiin1
Bockmuehl, Marcus, xixn14, 91n14, 172n1
Borgen, Peter, 204n24
Boyd, Gregory A., 116n1, 116n4, 143n28, 147n30
Brandon, Samuel, xiii, xiiin4
Bruce, F. F., xiin1, 192n18, 211n35, 222n56
Bultmann, Rudolph, 96, 96n2, 97
Burridge, Richard A., 11n3, 121n7
Buth, Randall, 90n7

Carson, D. A., 208n32
Cartlidge, David, xiv, xivn10

Casey, Maurice, xiv, xivn7, 114n43, 114n44
Charlesworth, James, 203n21, 203n22
Crossan, John Dominic, 116–17, 116n1, 116n2, 116n3, 116n4, 117n5, 118, 140, 141
Cullmann, Oscar, 29n17

Dodd, C. H., 134, 134n17, 204, 204n27
Donaldson, J., 127n4, 198n3, 199n4, 199n5, 214n39, 224n1
Dungan, David, xiv, xivn10
Dunn, James D. G., 64n9, 93, 93n20, 96, 96n4, 97–98

Eddy, Paul Rhodes, 116n4, 143n28, 147n30
Ehrman, Bart, 108, 108n13
Ellis, E. Earle, 61, 74n10, 93n19, 191, 191n15, 191n16, 202n17, 229n12

Feldman, L., 66n11
Fiensy, David A., 92n17
Fitzmyer, J. A., 105n5
Frazer, James, xiii
Freyne, Sean, 92n17

Gathercole, Simon, xiin1, 44n7
Gerhardsson, Birger, 14–15, 15n10, 93n19, 96, 96n3, 97
Gleaves, G. Scott, 89n3
Goodacre, Mark, 104n1

AUTHOR INDEX

Goodman, Martin, 222n56
Guelich, R. A., 134, 134n18
Gundry, Robert H., 71n8, 72, 72n9, 140n25, 142, 143, 143n27

Hafemann, S. J., 61
Hare, D. R. A., 202n16
Harris, Murray J., 64n9
Hartin, P. J., 53
Head, P. M., 114n43
Hengel, Martin, xiv, xivn8, 29, 29n17, 42, 42n10, 90, 90n9, 90n10, 92n16, 102, 102n10, 106n6, 117n8, 126n1, 129, 129n7, 132, 132n15, 179n9, 200, 200n9, 200n10, 201, 204n25, 204n28, 221n55, 229, 229n11
Horbury, William, 120n3, 120n4, 120n5
Horsley, G. H. R., 89n4
Howard, W. F., 213n38
Hultgren, A. J., 111n25
Hurtado, Larry W., xiv, 1n1, xivn9

Ingolfsland, D., 108n12

Jeremias, Joachim, 90n6

Katz, T., 202n16
Keener, Craig S., 92n17, 93n19
Kelly, J. N. D., 226n5
Kimelman, R., 202n16
Klink, Edward W., III, 236n1
Kloppenborg, John, 105n3, 105n4, 107, 107n9, 108n11, 109n15
Kloppenborg Verbin, J., 107, 107n10, 108, 108n12, 109, 111

Lake, Kirsopp, 225n2
Lane, W., 120n5, 142
Lieberman, S., 14, 14n9
Lukaszewski, Albert L., 89n3

Mack, Burton L., xiii, xiiin5, 116–17, 116n1, 117n6, 117n7, 118

Manson, T. W., 34n3, 53n13, 106n8, 107
Martin, Ralph, 53
Martyn, J. Louis, 202, 202n15
McNicol, A. J., 106n7
Meadors, Edward, 108, 109
Meier, John P., 203n23
Meyer, B. F., 13n5, 179n9
Meyers, Eric M., 90, 90n7, 203n20
Millard, A., 14n7, 14n8, 89n5, 90n6, 91n13, 92n18
Mitchell, M. M., 231n15
Moessner, David P., 182n1, 190n14
Morris, Leon, 175n5

Notley, R. Steven, 90n7

Painter, John, 53, 53n12
Peppard, Michael, 137n23
Perrin, Nicholas, xiiin1
Porter, Stanley E., 31n1, 89n3, 90n7, 90n8, 92n15, 114n44, 202n16, 206n31
Price, Robert, xiii, xiiin6
Price, S. R. F., 137n23

Reinhartz, A., 202n16
Richards, E. Randolph, 189n12
Riesenfeld, Harald, 96
Roberts, A., 127n4, 198n3, 199n4, 199n5, 214n39, 224n1
Robinson, John A. T., 50n4, 206, 206n30, 208n32, 218n42

Sanders, E. P., xiii, xiiin3
Schürer, E., 205n29
Schürmann, Hans, 93n19
Selwyn, E. G., 71n7
Shanks, Monte A., 200n12
Sim, D. C., 231n15
Smith, Justin Marc, 121, 121n7
Strange, James F., 90, 90n7, 203n20

Thompson, Alan J., 99n7
Turner, C. H., 146n29

Vegge, Ivar, 64n9
Vermes, Geza, xiii, xiiin2, xvn11

von Hase, Karl, 212
von Wahlde, Urban C., 203n21

Watson, Francis, 65n10, 104n1
Welborn, L. L., 64n9
Wenham, D., 40n6, 40n7, 40n8
Westcott, B. F., 214, 214n40
Williams, P. J., 114n43

Witherington, Ben, III, 92n17, 97n5, 98, 98n6, 108n14, 116n1
Wrede, William, xiii, xvii, 43, 43n1, 43n2, 47, 49, 140, 141
Wright, N. T., xiin1, 104, 104n2, 108, 108n14, 112n38, 112n54

Scripture Index

Old Testament

Genesis
2:24	36n4

Exodus
34:29–35	65

Leviticus
19:18	34

Deuteronomy
6:5	34
21:23	23, 24, 25
25:1–3	64n7

2 Samuel
4:10 LXX	120n2
7:14	111
18:22, 25 LXX	120n2

Psalms
2:7	111
16:10	24
110:1	22–23, 24, 25, 178
117:27 LXX	111
118:22	24

Proverbs
3:34	75

Isaiah
3:13, 26	24
4:27, 30	24
7:14	177
9:2	177, 178
29:18	109
35:5–6	109
40:3	164
40:9 LXX	120
42:1	177, 178
42:19	109
52:13	23n11, 24, 25
61:1–3	109, 175n4

Daniel
7:13–14	141

Hosea
11:1	177

Joel
2:17	24
2:28–32	24

Micah
5:2	177, 178

Zechariah
9:9	177, 178

Malachi

3:1	164, 177

Pseudepigrapha (Old Testament)

1 Enoch, 62:12–16	110n21
2 Apoc. Bar., 29:1–8	110n21
Enoch, 48:2–10	111n23

Dead Sea Scrolls

1QSa, 2:11–21	110n21
4Qflor	111
Qumran fragment, 4Q521 (7–14)	109

Ancient Jewish Writers

Josephus
Against Apion, 1.50

	95

Jewish Antiquities

18.119	165
18.26	221n46
18.35, 95	221n47
18.63	218
19:346	50n2
20.11	94–95
20.197–198	221n46
20.200	51n5
20.201	113, 155
20.211	135n19, 137n21

Jewish War	94, 95
1.3	94n22
1.6	94n21
2.117	221n51
2.220, 223	63n6
2.301–4	221n49
7.3	205
Philo, *Embassy to Gaius*, 160–161	222n57

Rabbinic Works

Benediction 12 (*birkath ha-minim*)	202
Mishnah	10, 11, 21, 97
Nedarim, 3:11	204n25
Shabbath, 18:3–19:2	204n25
Sukkah, 4:9–5:4	204n26

∞

New Testament

Matthew	xviii, xix, 4, 5, 6, 8, 16, 22, 27, 29, 34, 53, 76, 79, 80, 85, 105, 108, 109, 113, 117, 122, 130n8, 161, 164–69, 171–81, 185, 187, 191, 197, 207, 212, 225, 226, 228, 231, 234, 236
1	6
1:1—2:23	173
1:1–17	177, 178
1–2	151
1–4	173
1:16	41
1:17	213n36
1:18–25	178
1:21	180
1:21–23	164
1:22	227n10
1:23	177
2:1–9	177
2:6	177, 178
2:15	177, 178
3 and 5	6
3:1–3	164, 165
3:1—4:25	173
3:7–10	112n36
3:11–12	110n16
3:14–15	151
3:15	53, 175n6

SCRIPTURE INDEX

Matthew (continued)

3:17	178
3:27	168
4:3, 6	178
4:12–17	177
4–15	173
4:15	176, 177, 178
4:17	165, 174
4:23–25	174
4:24	92
4:25	92
5:1—7:29	173, 177
5:2–10	174
5:3	54
5:5	55
5:6, 10, 20	53, 173n3
5:7	55
5:8	56
5–8	151
5:10	72, 83
5:10, 12	54
5:11	72, 83
5:16	72, 83
5:17	152
5:19	55, 152
5:20	174
5:21–48	174
5:22	54, 56
5:33–37	53
5:34–35	57
5:36	72, 83
5:39	39, 81
5:44	38, 39, 72, 81, 83
5:48	53
6:1, 33	53, 173n3
6:7	171, 177
6:7, 32	176
6:20	57
6:24	56
6:32	171, 177
7:1	56
7:2	175n6
7:7	54
7:9–11	214
7:11	54
7:17	55
7:21	55
7:24	54
7:26	153
7:28–29	173n2
8:1—9:38	173
8:5–13	89
8:11–12	112n35
8:20	112n32
8:27	166
8:29	178
9:9	171, 176n7
9:37–38	214
10:1—11:1	173
10:1–42	177
10:3	171, 176n7
10:5–8	151
10:5–8, 9–13, 16b, 23, 24–25, 40–42	153
10:10	37, 80
10:16	214
10:25	13
10:38	111n26
11:1	173n2, 178
11:2	213n36
11:2—12:50	173
11:2–19	177
11:4–6	109
11:5	112n33
11:10	177
11–12a	151
11:20–24	110n18, 177
11:25–27	44n4, 111n22
11:27	212, 213n37, 214
11:28	59, 80, 154
11:28–30	12, 33–34, 151, 152, 177
11:29	41, 45, 46
12:5–7	151
12:18	177, 178
12:28	110
12:32	113
12:40	112
13 and 14	6
13:1–53	173
13:24–30, 36–40	153
13:24–52	151
13:47–52	153
13:53	173n2
13:54—17:27	173
14:1	176

SCRIPTURE INDEX

14:22–25	151	23:37–39	111n24, 111n28
14:28–33	151	24:1—26:2	173
14:33	167, 178	24:3, 27, 37, 39	53
15:1–39	177	24:10–12, 30	152
16:16	167, 178	24:32	176
16:17	213n36	24:33	35, 80
16:17–19	151, 178	25:1–13	152, 153
16:18	53, 176	25:14–20	111n30
16–20	173	25:14–30	152, 153
17:2	41	25:30–31	35, 80
17:5	167, 178	25:30–32	154
17:7	166	25:31–46	152, 153
17:24–27	151	25:32	176
18:1—19:2	173	25:34	178, 213n36
18:10, 12–14	151	25:52–54	152
18:15	57	26	6
18:15–20	151, 153	26:1	173n2
18:17	53, 176	26:3—28:20	173
18:17–19	153	26:61–62	180
18:18–20	153	26:64	168
18:21–35	151	26:67	73
19:1–2	173n2	27:3–8	152
19:3—23:39	173	27:19–25	152
19:10–12	151	27:40	180
19:21	53	27:43	178
19:23	57	27:51–56	179
19:28	110n19, 112n37, 151	27:51b-53	152
		27:54	168, 178, 180
20:1–14	153	27:55–56	180
20:1–16	151, 152	27:56	153, 179
20:25	73	27:61	180
20:28	73	27:62–66	152
21	6	28:1	180
21:5	177, 178	28:2–4	152
21–28	173	28:9–10	152
21:28–32	151	28:11–15	152
21:32	169	28:16	176
21:37	168	28:16–19	153
22:1–10	110n20	28:16–20	152, 175, 177
22:44	22n6, 178	28:19	213n36
22:45	168	28:20	153
22:114	152	51 and 52	179
23	6		
23:1–36	177	Mark	xiii, xviii, xix, 4, 5, 6, 10, xixn14, 15–16, 21, 22, 27, 28, 29, 30, 33, 58, 70, 71, 77, 79, 81,
23:1–39	152		
23:6	110n17		
23:12	56		
23:37	112n31		

SCRIPTURE INDEX

Mark (*continued*)
    89, 93, 102, 105, 108, 116, 117, 122, 123–25, 126–50, 130n8, 152, 161–70, 186, 187, 191, 193, 197, 206, 207, 208, 209–10, 215, 223, 225, 226, 228, 231, 233, 234, 235, 236

1:1	122, 169
1:1–3	164
1:1–11	134
1:10	209
1:11	161
1:12—10:52	134
1:14	165, 208
1:16–20	12
1:21	134, 148
1:21–32	134–35
1:21–34	27
1:24	162
1:27	166
1:29	13, 134
1:29–31	147
1:32	135
1:32–33	144
1:35	27, 135, 148
1:40–43	145
2:1	148
2:1—3:6	27
2:9–10	166
2:11	193
2:13—3:6	10n2, 21n5
2:13–15	172
2:14	171, 176n7
2:17	227n10
3:1, 2, 5	145
3:5	146
3:6	143
3:7	148
3:14	10, 26, 234
3:14 pars	41
3:16–17	124n8
3:17	199
3:22–27	138–39
3:34	146
4:1	135, 148
4:1—5:1	135
4:1–34	27
4:10–11	13
4:21	143
4:28	143
4:33–34	13
4:35	135, 148
4:35–5:43	27
4:35–38	144
4:36–41	162
4:37	149
4:41	166
5:1	135, 147n30
5:1–2	147
5:1–20	137
5:2–5	144
5:9, 15	143
5:21	148
5:32	146
5:33	143
5:37	198n2
5:38–41	144–45
5:41	130, 193
6:1	148
6:6b	148
6:7	148
6:10	146
6:14	176
6:14–29	148
6:27	143
6:30	148
6:30, 45	149
6:30–44	209
6:30–53	135
6:31	135
6:34	145
6:37	143
6:39	149
6:39–40	145
6:45	135, 147n30, 148
6:45–46	210
6:50	166
6:53	135, 148
7:1—9:29	157n2
7:1–13	10n2
7:1–23	21n5
7:4	143
7:11	130
7:15	39, 81

SCRIPTURE INDEX 253

7:17	13	11–16	147
7:19	39, 81, 136	11:20	148
7:24	148	11:27	148
7:24—9:13	149	11:32	165
7:26	89	12:1–9	214
7:31	147n30, 148	12:4	143
7:34	130	12:6	163, 167
8:22	147, 148	12:13	143
8:27	135, 148	12:17	39, 81, 136, 138, 169
8:27—9:2	135	12:31	34, 54, 80
8:27–30 pars	41	12:36	22, 22n6
8:28	18	12:37	168
8:29	162, 167	12:41	148
8:31	xvn13, 159n7	13	27n14, 124
8:36–37	214	13:1	148
9:2	41, 135, 148, 198n2	13:1–2	124
		13:1–37	27
9:7	163, 167	13:3	148
9:14	148	13:10	122, 138, 143, 169
9:28	13	13:14	27–28, 129, 136
9:30	148	13:32	169
9:30, 33	149	14:1—16:6	27
9:30–31	xvn13	14:3	148
9:30–32	159n7	14:3–9	209
9:33	148	14:9	122, 124, 138, 143, 169
9:42	136	14:10–11, 42	38n5
9:42–50	27	14:13	148
9:50	39, 81	14–15	27n14
10:1	147n30, 148	14:17	148, 198
10:8	36	14:26	148
10–10	149	14:32	147, 148
10:11	36	14:33	198n2
10:11–12	80	14:33–34	146
10:13–14	146	14:36	41
10:23	146	14:43–50	209
10:32	148	14:53	148
10:32–34	xvn13, 159n7	14:61–62	111n23
10:42	73, 137n22	14:62	168
10:42–45	141	14:65	73
10:45	xvi, 73, 141, 167, 214	14:66–72	209
		15:1	148
10:46	148	15:1, 10	38n5
11:1	148	15:2–5	89
11:1–10	209	15:7	211
11:1—16:8	134	15:15	38n5, 143
11:9	111n29	15:16	143, 148
11:11	146, 148		
11:15–19	209		

SCRIPTURE INDEX

Mark (*continued*)

15:16–20	209
15:21	111n27
15:22	148
15:34	130
15:39	137, 139, 143, 163, 165, 168, 169
15:40	148
15:42–47	209
15:46	148
16:2	148

Luke	xviii, xix, 4, 5, 6, 8, 16, 22, 29, 79, 80, 85, 100, 102, 105, 108, 109, 113, 117, 122, 130n8, 157–60, 161–63, 182–96, 197, 207, 212, 225, 228, 234, 236
1, 2, 3, 4	6
1:1	27, 93
1:1–2	99
1:1–4	12, 159, 190
1:2	133n16, 182, 185, 188
1:3	191, 226
1:4	26
1:5	192
1:5—3:38	157n3
1:32	41n9, 227n10
1:68–70	41n9
1:69	41n9
2:1–2	192
2:42	41n9
3, 4, 5, 6, 7, 9, 17, 22	6
3:1–2	10n1, 192
3:2	221n46
3:8	112n36
3:12	194
3:16–17	110n16
3:21–22	161
3:23	41n9, 185
4:14–30	157n3
4:31—9:50	158n5
4:34	162
5:1–11	158

5:21	195
5:24	193
5:27	171, 194
5:29, 30	194
5:30	195, 195n21
5:33	195
6:7	195
6:17	92
6:20	54
6:20–23	158
6:22	54, 72, 83
6:24–25	57
6:24–26	158
6:25	56
6:27	39, 72, 81
6:27–36	158
6:28a	38, 81
6:29	38, 81
6:32–34	72, 83
6:37	55
6:44	55
6:46	55
7:1–10	158
7:11–17	158
7:18–35	158
7:22	109, 112n33
7:30	194
7:34	195, 195n21
7:36—8:3	158
7:40–43	187
8:1–3	13, 195
8:25	162
8:51	193
9:7–9	158
9:20	162
9:35	163
9:51	159, 185, 186
9:51—18:14	186n9
9:52	193
9:53	186n10
9:58	112n32
10:2	214
10:7	37, 80, 188, 189n11
10:13–15	110n18
10:21	13
10:21–22	111n22
10:22	212, 213n37

10:25–37	193	16:14	195
10:27–28	54	17:3	57
10:28	34	17:7–10	187
10:29	195	17:11	159, 186n10
10:29–37	187	17:11–19	194
10:36	46	18:1–8	187
10:36–37	45	18:9–14	187, 194
10:39	12, 193	18:11, 35	186n10
10:58	41n9	18:15	159
11:3	106	18:16–17	194
11:5–9	187	18:31	159
11:9	54	18:35	159
11:11	214	18:35–43	194
11:13	54	19:1	159
11:20	110	19:1–2, 11, 28, 41	186n10
11:31–32	112	19:1–10	194
11:39, 42	195	19:1–48	186n9
11:43	110n17, 195	19:2, 9	194
12:1	195	19:10	45, 46, 194
12:10	113	19:12–27	111n30
12:13–20	187	19:41	159
12:33	193	19:45	159
12:39	35, 80	20:13	163
13:6–9	187	20:43	22n6
13:22	159, 186n10	21:34–36	36, 80
13:28–29	112n35	21:34–38	158n6
13:31–33	187	22:14–23	158n6
13:34	112n31	22:19–20	37–38, 80
13:34–35	111n24, 111n28	22:28–30	110n19
14:1, 3	195	22:30	112n37
14:2	193	22:31–46	158n6
14:7, 12–14	195	23:1–43	158n4, 158n6
14:7–11	187	23:43	194
14:11	56	23:47	163
14:12–24	187	23:49	195n22
14:13, 21	194	23:55—24:11	195n22
14:18–20	195	24:13–53	158n4
14:23	194	24:21	73
14:25	159	34	158n6
14:27	111n26		
14:28–32	187	John	xv, xviii, xix, 4, 5, 6, 8, 10n1, 15–16, 22, 48, 76, 77, 99–100, 122, 182n2, 185, 191, 197–223, 225, 226, 228, 231, 233, 234, 235, 236
15:1–2	194, 195, 195n21		
15:2	46		
15:3–32	187		
15:24	110n20		
16:1–9	187		
16:9–31	187		
16:13	56		

John (*continued*)

1:1–3, 14	44n6	4:44–45	215
1:5	217	4:45	217
1:9	217	4:46	203
1:14	210	4:47	215
1:17	217	4:47, 49, 51	203n18
1:28	203, 210	5:1	216
1:29	216, 217	5:1–47	215
1:29–51	209	5:2	203, 215
1:32	209	5:19	212, 214
1:35	210	6:1—7:9	207
1:43	215	6:1–14	209
1:43—2:12	207	6:1–59	204
1:44	210	6:15	210
1:45	215	6:17, 19, 23	203n19
2:1	203	6:32	217
2:1–11	208n33, 209	6:44	212
2:6	203, 217	7–10	11n4
2:12	209	7:10	216
2:12–22	208n33	7:10—20:31	215
2:13	203n18, 216	7:15	18
2:13—4:2	215	7:22	204
2:13–22	209	7:35	218
2:17, 22	217	7:37–39	204, 217
2:19	210	7:39	17n12
2:21	48	7:40–52	218n43
2:22	17n12	7:45–49	204
2:23	218n43	8:12	204, 217
2:23—3:21	209	8:20	215
2:23–24	217	8:23, 26	217
3:1–14	208n33	8:30	218n43
3:3, 5, 11a	216	8:32	214
3:5	227n10	8:44	217
3:7	216	9:7	215
3:8	225n3	9:22	202
3:11	216	9:35–38	218n43
3:22	210	10:1–5	213
3:22—4:3	209	10:11	214
3:23	203	10:16	218
3:24	210	10:21	218n43
4:4	207	10:22	204, 216
4:4–6, 20	204	10:23	215
4:4–26	208n33	10:29–31	204
4:9	203	10:30–31	205
4:23	217	10:38	212–13
4:35	214	10:40	203
4:42	217	10:40–42	207
4:43–54	207	11:25	214
		11:45, 48	218n43

SCRIPTURE INDEX

11:45–48	205	18:1–11	209
11:47	210	18:3	211, 220
11:52	218	18:3, 12	204
11:54	203	18:11	217
11:54–57	207	18:12	211, 220
11:55	204, 216	18:13	210, 220
12:1	215	18:15	218, 220
12:1–8	209	18:15–18	209
12:11–19, 42–45	218n43	18–19	6, 220
12:12	204	18:24, 28	210
12:12–19	209	18:25–27	209
12:16	17n12, 217	18:28	204, 211, 220
12:19	205	18:28—19:16	204
12:20	218	18:29	211, 220
12:20–22	91	18:30	220
12:21	210	18:31	220
12:24	213	18:31–33, 37–38	201
12:31	217	18:33	211, 220
12:35	217	18:39	204, 220
12:42	202	18:40	220
13:15	214	19:1–3	209, 220
13:16	48n10	19:1–6, 12	205
13–17	216	19:6	221
13:18–30	216	19:10	221
13:23	198n1	19:12	205, 221, 222
13:23–24	198	19:13	203, 215, 221
13:33, 36	216	19:13–14	204
13:36	220	19:17	111n27, 203, 215
13:37–38	216	19:20	221
14:1–3, 5, 18, 28–31	216	19:23	221
14:25–26	216	19:26	198n1
15:1	214, 217	19:27	218
15:4, 9	217	19:31	221, 222
15:18–19	217	19:33	221
15:20	217	19:33–37	217
15:26	216	19:34–35	99, 100
15:27	100	19:38–42	209
16:1	217	19:40	204
16:2	217	19:41	221
16:4	202	20:2–6	198n1
16:7–15	217	20:30	100
16:12–14	17n12	20:30–31	11
16:12–15	236	21:1–23	207
16:16–22	213	21:2	198
16:16–24	216	21:15–17	73, 74
18	6	21:18	128
18:1	215	21:18–19	70, 220
		21:19	128, 201

SCRIPTURE INDEX

John (*continued*)

21:20	100
21:20, 24	197
21:22	198n1
21:24	100, 198, 219

Acts	xx, 11, 21, 28, 63, 69, 76, 77, 84, 87, 122, 182–83, 182n2, 188, 191, 192n16, 199, 225, 233
1:1	182
1:13	172, 218
1:21–22	18, 26, 98, 99, 133n16, 184
2–10	20, 24, 26
2:10	69
2:16–21	24
2:17	24
2:25–28	24
2:27	24n13
2:32	99n8
2:34	22n6, 24, 25
2:36	179n10
2:42	20n2
3:1, 3, 4, 11	48n9, 199n7, 218
3:13	23n11
3:13, 26	25
3:15	99n8
3:18	179n10
3:26	23n11
4:2, 18	20n2
4:11	24
4:11–12	179n10
4:13, 19	48n9, 218
4:27	25
4:27, 30	23n11
5:20	24
5:21, 25, 28, 42	20n2
5:28	20n3
5:30	23n9, 23n10, 25
5:30–32	99n8
5:31	23n7
5:31–32	179n10
8:1	19
8:14	48n9, 199n7, 218
8:14–25	52n8
9:1–9	31n1
9:5	44
9:19–22	44
9:27–28	31
9:30—12:25	80n1
9:31–32	15, 15n11, 28n16, 51
10	133
10 and 13	134
10:1—11:18	52n8
10:14–16, 28	61n2
10:34–43	11, 21, 133, 134, 157n1, 185
10:39	23n9, 23n10, 24, 25
10:39–43	99n8
11:3	61
11:19–26	67
11:26	67
11:29–30	31
12:1–2	199n6
12:2	198, 218
12:12, 17	130n9
12:17	19n1, 50n1, 81
12:20–23	50n2
13	133
13:1	68
13:5	122, 131n10
13–14	175
13:16, 26, 43, 48	27
13:16–41	133, 157n1, 185
13:16–43	11
13–20	80, 229
13:29	23n10
13:30–31	99n8
13:35	24n13
15:1	113n39
15:1–2	63
15:2, 6, 22, 23	199n8
15:5	66n12, 155
15:6	101n9
15:8	32
15:10	34
15:19–21	50n4
15:23	113n40
15:23, 41	63
15:35–41	131n11

16:10–16	184n4	15:3	41, 45
16:16—20:5	184n5	15:7	46
16:23	63	15:8	41
16:37	71	15:18	42
16:41	63	15:20	70n4
18:2	69n2	15:20–21	70
18:22	32	16	70n4, 83–84
19:16	73	16:3–16	69
20:5—21:17	184n4		
20:28	75	1 Corinthians	30, 32, 36, 44, 46–47, 49, 93, 225, 230n14, 235
21:1—28:16	184n4		
21:20	52, 155		
21:20–21	66n12	1:9	44n3
21:21	113	1:23	119
21–28	190	3:16	48n11
		4:11	73
Romans	22, 32, 38, 44, 51, 76, 77, 84, 225, 230n14	5:5	41
		6:16	36
		7:10–11	36
1:3	41, 41n9	7:11	80
1:3, 4, 9	44n3	9:1	31n1, 40
4:1–6	51n6	9:5	41, 52n10
5:10	44n3	9:14	37, 80
8:3, 32	44n4	10:33—11:1	45
8:3, 39	44n3	11:23–24	xvi
8:15	20, 41, 89	11:23–25	25–26, 41, 47, 80, 89
8:34	23n7		
9:5	41	11:23–26	37
12	38	11:26	38
12 and 13	74	12:2	48n11
12:2	41	15:3	41
12:3	74	15:3–6, 11	xvi–xvii
12:6	74	15:3–7	26, 47, 89, 101
12:7	74	15:3–7, 11	234
12:13	74	15:4	41
12:14	38	15:5	23n12
12–14	40	15:5–7	41
12:14	81	15:11	47, 101, 235
12:17	38, 81	15:25	22n6
12:18	39, 81	15:28	44n3
12:20	39, 81	15:34	xvii
13:7	39, 81, 136	16:22	20, 23n8, 89
13:12	74		
14	39	2 Corinthians	44, 64–66, 64n9–65n9
14:13	136		
14:14	39, 81, 136	1:1	65
14:20	39, 81	1:19	44n3

SCRIPTURE INDEX

2 Corinthians (continued)

1:20	20, 89
2:17	64, 65, 91n11
3:7–18	65
3:18	41
4:2	65
4:5	48n10, 65
5:16	31n1, 40
6:3	65
8:9	41, 41n9, 44n5
8:18	184n5
10:1	41, 45
10:14	65
11:1–4	40
11:4	65
11:5	65, 66
11:5, 13	65
11:5–6	91n11
11:22	65
11:23	65
11:23, 4	65
11:24	64n7
12:2–3	64
12:7	64, 73
12:11	65

Galatians — 40, 44, 51, 63, 230n14

1:2	229
1:6–9	113n41
1:7	62
1:16	44n3
1:18	25, 37, 101
1:18–19	29n18, 31, 49
1:19	41
1:21–23	51n7
1:22–24	63
2:1	68
2:1, 3	62
2:1, 9	31
2:1, 11	101n9
2:2–6	235
2:3	47, 64
2:7–8	15n11, 28n16, 41, 51
2:7–9	218
2:7–10	229
2:9	48, 50, 50n1, 52, 64
2:9, 12	50n4
2:11	50, 68
2:11–13	68
2:11–14	52, 63, 113n39, 172n1
2:11–16	52n9
2:14	65n10
2:16	51n6
2:20	44n3
2:22	155
3:1	33, 41
3:6	51n6
3:6–14	62n4
3:7–14	62n5
3:13	23n10
3:16	41
4:4	41
4:4, 6	44n3
4:4–5	41
4:4–6	41n9
4:6	20, 41, 89
4:10	62n3
4:21–31	62n5
5:1	33, 80, 154
5:2	62n3
5:10	62
5:14	34, 80
6:2	34
6:12–13	113n41
6:16	62n4
6:17	33, 41

Ephesians — 183n3, 225, 229, 230n14

Philippians — 225, 230n14

2:2	184n5
2:5–6	46
2:6–7	44n5
2:8	41
2:9–11	44

Colossians — 183n3, 230n14

4:10	32n2, 122, 131n12
4:10, 14	186n8

4:11	183
4:14	183
1 Thessalonians	44, 77, 84, 225, 230n14
1:10	44n3
2:14	155
2:14–15	41
4:15–17	35, 80, 154
5:2	35
5:3	36, 80
5:6	76
5:6, 23	76
5:6, 25	77
5:23	76
5:24	76
2 Thessalonians	34, 225, 230n14
1 Timothy	188, 225
4:13	7n10
5:18	188
6:13	41
2 Timothy	230n14
4:11	131n14
Titus	
2:14	73, 141
Philemon	183n3, 230n14
22	183n3
22:24	183n3
24	32n2
Hebrews	22, 58, 225
1:2–3	44n6
1:3	23n7
1:13	22n6
10:13	22n6
James	50, 53, 58, 59, 71, 76, 77, 81–82, 84, 154, 225, 231, 234
1:1	229
1:2	54
1:4	53
1:5	54
1:12	54
1:17	54
1:20	53, 54
1:21	58
1:22	54
2:1	58n14, 82
2:5	54
2:8	54
2:10	55
2:13	55
2:14	55
2:14–16	51
2:14–26	51n6
3:12	55
3:13	55
3:18	53
4:4	56
4:6	75
4:7–10	75
4:8	56
4:9	56, 75
4:10	56
4:11	56
5:1	57
5:2	57
5:6–11	75
5:7	53
5:7–9	58n14
5:12	53, 57
5:18	82
5:19–20	57
1 Peter	xixn14, 58, 72–73, 74–76, 77, 82, 83, 85, 124, 138, 225, 231, 234
1:1	70, 123, 230
1:18–19	73, 141
1:20	44n6
2:12	72, 83
2:17	137n24, 138
2:19	72, 83
2:20	73
2:24	23n10
3:9	72, 83

SCRIPTURE INDEX

1 Peter (*continued*)	
3:14	72, 83
3:22	23n7
4:7	74
4:9	74
4:10	74
4:11	74
4:12	71, 82, 82n3
4:14	72, 83
4:17	119
5:1	70
5:1, 12–13	123
5:1, 13	188
5:1–2	74
5:2	73, 75
5:3	73
5:5	75
5:5–9	75
5:6	75
5:8	76
5:8, 10	77
5:9	75, 82n3, 124, 137n24
5:9, 13	143
5:10	76
5:12	71
5:12–13	71, 124
5:13	70, 71, 129, 131n13
15:20	70
2 Peter	128, 231
1:13–14	128
3:1	128
1 John	200, 231
2 John	200
3 John	200
Revelation	199, 231
1:1–3	230n13
1:3	230n13
1:4	119n1
1:4, 11	230
2:1—3:22	230
2:7, 11, 17	230n13
3:6, 13, 22	230n13
5:1	23n7
14:6	119
14:8	71n6
16:13	230n13
16:19	71n6
17:5	71n6
18:10	71n6
19:30	230n13
20:10	230n13
22:6, 18–19	230n13
22:18–19	230n13

∾

Apocrypha (New Testament)

1 Clement	
5:1–5	124n9
13:2	175n6

Gospel of Judas	xii, xiin1
Gospel of Peter, P. Oxy. 4009	224n1
Gospel of Philip	xii
Gospel of Thomas	xiin1
P. Oxy. 1	224n1
Valentinus, *Gospel of Truth*	2, 94

∾

Gospel Sources

L source   xv, xix, 15–16, 17, 22, 27, 28, 36, 37, 40, 42, 45, 46, 53n13, 54, 66, 81, 85, 88, 154, 157–60, 185, 233, 234, 235

M source	xv, xix, 15–16, 17, 22, 27, 28, 34, 35, 37, 40, 42, 45, 46, 53n13, 55, 56, 57, 58, 59, 66, 72, 76, 79, 80, 81, 82, 83, 85, 88, 151–56, 175, 213, 233, 234, 235	Ignatius	
		Epistle to the Tralians, 9:4	226n5
		Philadelphians	
		7	201n13
		7:1	225n3
		Smyrneans, 1:1	175n6
		Irenaeus	
Q source	xv, xix, 15–16, 17, 22, 27, 28, 37, 38, 39, 40, 42, 53n13, 54, 55, 56, 57, 58, 59, 66, 67, 72, 76, 77, 79, 80, 81, 82, 83, 85, 88, 104–15, 104n1, 105n4, 152, 156, 158, 185, 189n11, 196, 212, 213, 233, 234, 235	*Against Heresies*	4
		1.26.2	224n1
		3.1.1	4n5, 127n4, 198n3, 214n39
		3.11.6	4n3
		3.11.8	4n4
		3.3.4	4n2, 199n4, 199n5
		4.30.4	230n13
		5.26.1	230n13
		Against the Heresies, III.1.1	48n8
		Against Heresies, V.33.4	127n2
		quadriform Gospel	228

Early Christian Writings

		Justin Martyr	
		Dialogue with Trypho	
Clement, *Miscellanies*, 2.9.45		8	227n10
	224n1	81.4	230n13
Codex Sinaiticus	2	106	127n3
Didache		106.3	124n8
8:3	227n8	*First Apology*	7
11:4	227n8	33	227n10
15:5	227n8	61	227n10
15:7	227n8	65–67	7n9
Epiphanius,		66–67	227n9
Against Heresies, 78:13	219n44	Muratorian Canon	
Euesbius,			5, 8, 183, 184, 184n4, 231
History of the Church, 3.39	124n8		
Eusebius		Papyrus 1	6
History of the Church		Papyrus 4	6
3.31.3	198n3, 214n39	Papyrus 45	xx, 1–8, 126, 228
3.39.3, 4	200n10	Papyrus 46	2, 233
3.39.3–16	6n7, 226n6	Papyrus 47	2
3.39.15	127n2	Papyrus 52	6, 201
3.4.6	184n6	Papyrus 64	6
4.22.8	224n1	Papyrus 66	6
4.29.6	4n6	Papyrus 67	6
5.20.4	199n5	Papyrus 75	6
6.14.7	201	Papyrus 77	6

Papyrus 90	6
Papyrus 103	6
Papyrus 104	6
Tatian, *The Diatessaron*	4, 228, 231
"Unknown Gospel,"	
P. Egerton 2	224n1

Greco Roman Writings

Philostratus, *Life of Apollonius*, 5.33	61n2
Suetonius	
Claudius, 5.4	69n1
Life of Tiberius	87
Tacitus	
Annals of Imperial Rome	
6.8	222n56
15.44	82n2, 124n9
xv.14	128n5
Histories, 5.5	61n2

www.ingramcontent.com/pod-product-compliance
Lightning Source LLC
Chambersburg PA
CBHW022001220426
43663CB00007B/917